Maria Webb

The Penns & Peningtons of the seventeenth century in their

domestic and religious life

Maria Webb

The Penns & Peningtons of the seventeenth century in their domestic and religious life

ISBN/EAN: 9783337719173

Printed in Europe, USA, Canada, Australia, Japan

Cover: Foto ©Lupo / pixelio.de

More available books at **www.hansebooks.com**

THE

PENNS & PENINGTONS

OF

The Seventeenth Century,

IN THEIR

DOMESTIC AND RELIGIOUS LIFE:

ILLUSTRATED BY

ORIGINAL FAMILY LETTERS:

ALSO INCIDENTAL NOTICES OF THEIR FRIEND

THOMAS ELLWOOD,

WITH SOME OF

His Unpublished Verses.

By MARIA WEBB,
Author of "The Fells of Swarthmoor Hall and their Friends."

PREFACE.

THIS work originated in the belief that a volume depicting the religious and domestic life of Isaac Penington, of William Penn, and of Thomas Ellwood would be especially useful at the present time. Their lives were bright examples of the ennobling and strengthening influence of true religion. They differed materially in natural character from one another; but in each may be seen the distinguishing marks of the followers of the Lord Jesus carried into their varied spheres of operation; for their religion was practical as well as spiritual. And in their wives we have a beautiful exemplification of Christian matrons aiding and cheering their husbands amid trials and persecutions; and rejoicing in their faithfulness, notwithstanding the frowns of the world.

Tender-hearted and womanly, yet active and enduring, they show us what such women can do, in filling the blanks at home occasioned by their husbands' unavoidable absence.

These eminent Friends unitedly stand forth as noble examples of the conduct and principles which graced the earlier days of Quakerism, in the church, in the family, and in the general community.

It has been my endeavour as far as possible, in tracing their religious principles and spiritual experience, to let them express their feelings in their own words: hence the numerous extracts from their letters.

Theirs was an age of great religious excitement, and gave rise to a vast amount of controversial writing, to which Friends very largely contributed. Those who wish for information on this subject are referred to the laborious and exhaustive Catalogue of Quaker authors and their works which Joseph Smith, of Oxford-street, Whitechapel, London, has now in course of publication.

In collecting materials for this volume I have received assistance from many friends, to whom I take this opportunity of expressing my grateful

Preface.

acknowledgments; as well as to the members of the London Morning Meeting, who have kindly supplied me with copies of such of the documents under their care as were likely to suit my purpose; and more especially to those who corresponded with me in relation to them.

I am also greatly indebted to the Friends who have supplied me with materials from their private manuscript collections of old documents; and to those residing in the neighborhood of the localities referred to in this work, who have spared no pains to give me information respecting them.

In taking leave of this work, which in its progress has been a source of deep interest to the writer, hallowed memories connected with its origin present themselves. Some who rejoiced to hear of its commencement are no longer here to welcome its introduction to the public. Of the loved and valued friends removed during that interim to a higher and holier sphere, there is one name which I desire especially to associate with this book. It is that of my beloved brother, the late Joshua Lamb, of Peartree-hill, near Lisburn, than whom I never knew any one who more fully appreciated William Penn's mind, and the value of his religious writings. It was by his recommendation I was first led to study Penn's *Address to Protestants*, a work which, in a somewhat condensed form, might with great advantage be republished in the present day, in which Ritualism on the one hand, and Calvinism on the other are making such inroads upon the pure doctrines of Christianity.

M. W.

7, Palmerston-road, Dublin,
  28th of Fourth-month, 1867.

NOTE ON THE PORTRAIT OF GULIELMA MARIA PENN.

The original of this portrait is a painting on glass in the possession of the descendants of Henry Swan of Holmwood, Dorking, who died in 1796. It was given to him by John Townsend of London, at an unknown date, and along with it one of William Penn. Jemima Swan, the present owner of these portraits, kindly gave permission to have copies of them engraved for this work. The artist had the portrait of the lady nearly completed, when my friend John Thompson, of Hitchin, informed me that he had engravings of the great-grand-parents of the late Joseph John Gurney in his possession, closely resembling the photographic copies of the reputed portraits of William and Gulielma Penn, and he very kindly took them out of their frames and sent them for my inspection. I found points of dissimilarity as well as of resemblance.

The busts were different, and there was some difference in the attitude of the lady; but the dresses were so exactly alike,—each button, fold, and slope being the same,—that there was evidently some original connection between the paintings and engravings. A correspondence ensued between John Thompson and Daniel Gurney, the senior representative of the Gurney family, from which it was ascertained that the portraits of the Gurneys were first engraved in 1746, and that subsequently two copies of different sizes were executed. These engravings have always been regarded by the family as authentic likenesses, but they have never known of the existence of any paintings from which they were taken. Two sets of engravings were executed in the lifetime of Joseph and Hannah Middleton Gurney; but without their names, and probably without their knowledge; the first set being styled *A Sincere Quaker* and *A Fair Quaker*. Family tradition speaks of Hannah Middleton Gurney as having been surpassingly handsome.

Joseph Gurney and his wife were contemporaries of the Penns, and though much their juniors in age, it is probable that up to the time of their marriage in 1713, the style of their dress was not materially different from that of the Penns. From all these circumstances it appears to me most likely that both sets of *portraits* are genuine as regards the heads and faces, but that the *dresses* of the Gurneys, except hat and hood, are copied from those of the Penns, possibly because he who employed the artist had only *busts* of the Gurneys.

I am aware of the statement made by Granville Penn, and repeated by other writers, that the portrait of William Penn in armour, painted in Dublin in 1666, was the only likeness of him ever executed. But a second portrait might be in existence without his knowledge; as it is not probable any likeness of William Penn, accompanying (as this does) that of his first wife, should come into the possession of the children of his second wife, from whom Granville Penn was descended. Any such portraits would naturally be left to Letitia Aubrey, Gulielma's only daughter; and as she died childless and always remained amongst Friends, is it not most likely that after her death they became the property of the Friend who gave them to Henry Swan?

With this view of the case I leave the question to those who can follow it to a more certain conclusion. It is worth further scrutiny, as the Swan portraits, if really those of the Penns, would be a most interesting illustration of their history, especially as they give us a likeness of the Pennsylvanian legislator in the prime of life.—M. W.

CONTENTS.

CHAPTER I.

1623-1658.

The Chalfont Grange.—Isaac Penington settles there.—Alderman Penington and the Commonwealth.—Isaac Penington's politics.—His religious feelings.—Memoir of Mary Proude.—The Puritans.—The Springetts.—William Springett's home-life.—His removal to Cambridge.—Becomes a law-student.—Is knighted.—Mary Proude's religious difficulties.—Forsakes the Church of England.—Joins the Puritans.—Sir William Springett returns home.—Marries Mary Proude.—Birth and baptism of their first child.—Sir William joins the Parliamentary army.—His promptness in raising troops.—Wounded at the battle of Newbury.—His ability as a soldier.—His death and burial...........................Page 17 to 46

CHAPTER II.

1640-1658.

Sir William Springett's character.—Change in his religious opinions.—Puritan iconoclasts.—Aid to Irish Protestants.—Domestic characteristics.—Monument to his memory.—Birth of Gulielma Maria Springett.—Her mother's religious feelings about infant baptism.—Character of Madam Springett.—Her useful life.—Her medical skill. Expenditure of her income.—Herbert Springett.—His monument in Ringmer church.—Lady Springett's dissatisfaction with the religionists around her.—Withdrawal.—Tries fashionable life.—Her retrospect of that period.—Acquaintance with Isaac Penington.—Their marriage.—First acquaintance with the Quakers.—William Simpson and Thomas Curtis visit the Peningtons.—They are convinced of the truth of Quaker doctrines.—Religious joy and comfort.—Establishment in the truth..Page 47 to 76

CHAPTER III.

1658-1661.

The Ellwoods' visit to the Peningtons at Chalfont.—Their impressions of their Quaker friends.—James Nayler and Edward Burrough at the Grange.—Discussion on the doctrine of election.—Isaac Penington's account of his early religious feelings and views.—His later spiritual experience.—Letters to his father, the Alderman.—Alderman Penington's impeachment as a regicide.—Charles the Second's declaration from Breda.—Alderman Penington's condemnation.—Imprisonment in the Tower and confiscation of his estates.—Sir John Robinson's cruelty.—Alderman Penington's death....................Page 77 to 106

CHAPTER IV.

1642-1661.

Thomas Ellwood's early life.—His second visit to Chalfont.—His convincement.—Joins the Friends—His father's displeasure—The Peningtons' visit to Crowell.—Young Ellwood returns with them to the Grange.—He is arrested for travelling on the first day of the week.—Quaker and Presbyterian views of the Sabbath.—Thomas Ellwood returns to Crowell.—Is imprisoned in Oxford under keeping of the Marshal.—Isaac Penington writes to him from Aylesbury jail, and Thomas Loe from that of Oxford.—Ellwood is released.—Isaac Penington's letter from Aylesbury to his wife.—His trials and difficulties. —Is released from prison.............................Page 107 to 137

CHAPTER V.

1662.

Thomas Ellwod's desire to cultivate his knowledge of Latin.—His introduction to John Milton.—He finally leaves Crowell and settles in London.—Becomes reader to Milton.—His enjoyment of that privilege. —Is imprisoned with other Friends in Old Bridewell.—Trial.—Imprisonment in Newgate.—Crowded state of that jail.—Prison life.—

Inquest at Newgate.—Removal to Old Bridewell.—Is released.—
Visits his friends in Newgate.—Visits Milton.—Goes to Chalfont.—
Is engaged as tutor at the Grange.—His grief at the death of Edward
Burrough..Page 138 to 164

CHAPTER VI.

1662-1669.

Ellwood a tutor at Chalfont.—Gulielma Maria Springett.—His portrait
of her character.—Her suitors.—Ellwood's cautious demeanour towards her.—"He for whom she was reserved."—William Penn.—
Penn's Oxford experience.—Is expelled the University.—His father's
displeasure and severity.—Continental travel.—Returns home.—
Becomes a law student.—The plague in London.—Sent to the Duke
of Ormond's court in Dublin.—His first and last military exploit.—
Settles at Shangarry Castle, near Cork.—Visits the Friends' meeting
there, and hears Thomas Loe preach.—Is imprisoned with the
Quakers.—Released by order of Lord Ossory and summoned to London.—Interview with his father.—Sir William turns his son out of
doors.—Penn becomes a religious writer.—First interview with Guli
Springett.—Controversy.—Imprisonment in the Tower.—Writes *Innocency with her Open Face.*—Is released.—Acquaintance with the
Peningtons.—His letter to Isaac Penington on the death of Thomas
Loe.—Goes again to Ireland..............................Page 165 to 199

CHAPTER VII.

1665-1671.

Further persecution of the Friends.—The plague in London.—John
Milton removes to Chalfont.—Magisterial tyranny.—Penington and
Ellwood imprisoned.—The latter, on being released, visits Milton.—
The manuscript of *Paradise Lost* handed to him to read.—*Paradise
Regained* suggested by Ellwood.—Earl of Bridgwater imprisons Isaac
Penington.—Penington's letter to his wife from Aylesbury jail.—
Penington writes from prison to the Earl of Bridgwater.—A respite.
—Another letter to his wife.—Writes to the Amersham Friends from
Aylesbury jail,—and to George Fox.—Penington's letter to his uncle
—to his cousin.—Removed by Habeas Corpus to London.—Dismissed by proclamation.—Purchases Woodside.—Rebuilding of the
old house.—Imprisonment of Isaac Penington in Reading jail.—Is
released.—Christian influence in prison..................Page 200 to 232

CHAPTER VIII.

1666-1669.

Quaker meeting at Hedgerly.—Ambrose Bennett, the magistrate, breaks it up.—Judith Parker, the doctor's wife, remonstrates.—Bennett again imprisons Friends.—Release from prison.—Solemn meeting of Friends for the restoration of those who had been drawn away by John Perrot.—Perrot's mission to the Pope.—His imprisonment in Rome.—Release and return home.—Extravagant proceedings.—Establishment of meetings for discipline by George Fox.—Ellwood's choice of a wife.—Details of his courtship.—Is accepted.—Adventurous journey with Gulielma M. Springett.—Ellwood's bravery.—Gulielma's return home.—Ellwood's marriage.—Isaac Penington's son lost at sea.—Ellwood's grief.—His poetical effusions..................Page 233 to 260

CHAPTER IX.

1670.

William Penn ccralled from Ireland.—Reconciliation with his father.—Decline of the Admiral's health.—Conventicle Act.—William Penn a prisoner with William Meade.—His letter to his father from prison.—Penn and Meade at the bar.—Indicted for a riot.—The jury refuse to bring them in guilty.—The Recorder repeatedly insists that they must reconsider their verdict.—They persist in presenting the same.—Are confined to the juryroom for two nights and two days without food.—Ultimate triumph of jury, and liberation of the prisoners.—Jurymen and prisoners committed for pretended contempt of court.—Penn's letters from prison to his dying father.—Release from prison.—The jurymen bring an action against the Recorder for false imprisonment.—Triumph of the jury.—Death of Admiral Sir William Penn.—His last advice to his son.—The Admiral's monument.—William Penn's ability as a controversialist..................Page 261 to 289

CHAPTER X.

1672-1679.

Sir John Robinson again imprisons William Penn.—Sends him to Newgate.—State of that prison.—Penn's prison occupation.—Release.

—Visits the Continent.—His marriage.—Settles at Ruscombe.—Visit of the Swarthmoor family.—Imprisonment of George Fox.—William Penn writes to his friend in prison.—Controversy between Penn and Baxter.—Penn as a controversialist.—As an arbitrator.—Quaker trusteeship in connection with New Jersey.—Purchase of land from the Indians.—Government of New Jersey.—The Penns settle at Worminghurst.—Family concerns.—Another Continental visit.— Penn's speeches before the Parliamentary Committee.—His address to Protestants..Page 290 to 320

CHAPTER XI.

1673-1682.

Cessation of Isaac Penington's religious persecution.—Penington's letters —to his brother Arthur, a Roman Catholic—to Joseph Wright respecting his brother—to his sister Judith—to the Countess of Conway.—Peace and happiness at Woodside.—Isaac and Mary Penington visit their property in Kent.—Isaac Penington's death.—Mary Penington's memorial of her husband.—She anticipates her own decease. —Arranges her outward affairs and makes her will.—Takes her sons to school at Edmonton.—Her illness there.—Returns home.— Continued illness.—Her resignation, patience, and peace of mind.— She visits Worminghurst, and dies there.—Thomas Ellwood's lines on the death of his friends Isaac and Mary Penington. Page 321 to 342

CHAPTER XII.

1681-1684.

William Penn applies to Charles II. for a grant of land in America.— Obtains a charter for Pennsylvania.—Penn's motives in this undertaking.—His code of laws.—His coadjutors in the work.—Algernon Sidney.—Penn's letter to Sidney.—Hepworth Dixon on the early Quakers.—Death of Lady Penn.—Penn's farewell letters on leaving England.—Emigration to Pennsylvania.—His treaty of peace with the Indians.—Purchases of land from them.—Gulielma Penn in her husband's absence.—Poetical address by Thomas Ellwood to his friend in America.—Letter from Gulielma Penn to Margaret Fox.—William Penn's return.—His letter to Margaret Fox..............Page 343 to 373

CHAPTER XIII.

1684-1693.

William Penn's difficulties about the boundary line of his province.—His outlay without due return.—His influence with James II.—Is accused of being a Jesuit.—His correspondence with Dr. Tillotson.—William Penn at Chester during the King's progress.—King James driven from the Throne.—The Prince and Princess of Orange invited to assume the Crown.—William Penn suspected of treasonable correspondence with the exiled James II.—Letter from Gulielma Maria Penn to Margaret Fox.—Death of George Fox.—William Penn arrested.—Examined before the King and Privy Council.—Is imprisoned.—His writings during his seclusion.—His province sequestrated.—Confiscation of his Irish estates.—Is restored to liberty.—Death of Gulielma Penn............Page 374 to 397

CHAPTER XIV.

1694-1847.

William Penn's testimony respecting George Fox.—Penn applies successfully to Queen Mary for a restoration of his chartered rights in Pennsylvania.—Springett Penn's illness.—His death and character.—Removal of the Penn family to Bristol.—William Penn and his son visit Ireland.—He removes with his family to Pennsylvania.—Is cordially welcomed.—Pennsbury past and present.—Slaves employed there.—Efforts in England to break Penn's charter.—Is obliged to return to defend it.—William Penn jun. in Pennsylvania.—His conduct and character.—Philip Ford's fraudulent claims.—Logan's opinion of him.—Penn in the Fleet prison.—Efforts which led to his release.—The Provincial Assembly of Pennsylvania.—Prosperity of the settlement.—William Penn is attacked by paralysis.—Its effect on his mind during succeeding years.—Thomas Story at Ruscombe.—Death of William Penn.—His will.—Death of William Penn, jun.—His descendants.—Death of Hannah Penn.—Her descendants.—Descendants of the Peningtons.—Death of Thomas and Mary Ellwood............Page 398 to 446

THE
PENNS AND PENINGTONS,
&c.

CHAPTER I.
1623–1658.

The Chalfont Grange.—Isaac Penington settles there.—Alderman Penington and the Commonwealth.—Isaac Penington's politics.—His religious feelings.—Memoir of Mary Proude.—The Puritans.—The Springetts.—William Springett's home-life.—His removal to Cambridge.—Becomes a law-student.—Is knighted.—Mary Proude's religious difficulties.—Forsakes the Church of England.—Joins the Puritans.—Sir William Springett returns home.—Marries Mary Proude.—Birth and baptism of their first child.—Sir William joins the Parliamentary army.—His promptness in raising troops.—Wounded at the battle of Newbury.—His ability as a soldier.—His death and burial.

MORE than two hundred years have passed away since Isaac Penington, eldest son to Alderman Penington of London, brought his family to reside at the Grange, in the parish of St. Peter's, Chalfont, Buckinghamshire. Of the original old building in which they dwelt only a small portion is now standing; on its site a modern villa has been erected, and that part of the ancient house still in existence does not present itself to view in front.

The Grange was a happy home in those by-gone times. It was an abode where mental refinement, literary taste, and evidences of an abiding sense of God's presence pervaded the resident family. The Peningtons settled there in the year 1658—the same year in which Oliver Cromwell died.

The rustic beauty of the Chalfont vallies must have made that quiet neighborhood delightful to them, when contrasted with the social unrest and persecuting intolerance of which they had recently seen so much in the metropolis. The Grange was the family mansion which belonged to the paternal estate that Isaac Penington inherited from his ancestors. His father Alderman Penington had given up to his eldest son the property in question, on his marriage with Lady Springett. The few years that had elapsed from that event to their settlement at the Chalfont Grange, had been chiefly spent in London and its vicinity, where the highest circles were open to them.

Alderman Penington had inherited a handsome property from his father, who was Robert Penington, a London merchant. He also commenced life as a merchant, but being in easy circumstances he soon devoted himself to civic duties, and became an active, earnest politician. He was married to Abigail, daughter of John Allen of London. In 1638 he served as high sheriff of London, and in 1640 he was elected Member of Parliament for the city, and made himself very conspicuous in the House by his advocacy of the rights of the Parliament and the people. In 1642 he was chosen Lord Mayor of London, and afterwards was appointed Lieutenant of the Tower. He was one of the Commissioners of the High Court of Justice for the trial of Charles I., but he did not sign the warrant for his execution. He received the honour of knighthood from the Speaker of the House of Commons; and in 1649 was made a member of the Council of State.

At the time Alderman Penington served as High Sheriff of London, his son Isaac Penington, junr. was twenty-two years of age. We may conceive from the above glance at his father's career, what opportunities for worldly aggrandizement the intervening twenty years, from 1638 to 1658, must have spread before the son of that popular, wealthy, democratic politician. But of no such opportunities did he avail himself; the aspirations of the son were not directed by ambition; they were deep and earnest, but not worldly; more of the maternal than the paternal type. His mother's heartfelt desires were rather for the religious welfare, and the establishment of the Christian character of her children, than for their elevation in the world; and these feelings met a cordial response in the mind of her eldest son. It is true he did not ignore the importance of the great political questions which so much engrossed his father's attention, and which were so earnestly debated in that day. But whenever he wrote on them, which was not often, he discussed them in a reasonable and Christian spirit, untinctured by partizan bitterness.

One of his publications, written in 1651, which treats of matters connected with national government, is entitled *The Fundamental Right, Safety, and Liberty of the People.* In that he says, alluding to a limited monarchy, "Though I shall not plead for the resettlement of kingly government (for I am not so far engaged in my affections to it, as it yet hath been) yet I would not have any blame laid upon it beyond its desert; for doubtless it hath its advantages above any other government, on one hand; as it hath also its disadvantages on the other hand." "Kingly power did pass its limits—we may now speak of it." He then goes on to query, "Doth parliament now keep within its right limits?" … "and if things should yet devolve lower, into the great and confused body of the people, is it likely they would keep their limits?" He shows that in establishing justice the impossibility of the people acting for themselves, and the impropriety of their representatives in parliament assuming both legislative and administrative powers. But under no circumstances would his conscience allow him to bind himself to a party. He says, "There is not one sort of men on the face of the earth to whom I bear any enmity in my spirit; but I wish with all my heart they might all attain and enjoy as much peace, prosperity, and happiness as their state will bear; and there are not any to whom I should envy the power of government. But whoever they are whom I saw fitted for it, and called to it, they should have my vote on their behalf." He goes on to show that where the spirit of selfishness holds its natural place in men's hearts, their government will not promote spontaneously true freedom for others who are under them; for when the selfish man has great power, it will be exerted in promoting his own aggrandizement, and the freedom of others only in so far as it suits his selfish ends. Therefore he maintained it was alone the change of heart from sinful selfishness, to the desire after the promotion of Christian righteousness among the national governors, that could secure true justice to those they governed.

Openly declaring such views, Isaac Penington did not attach himself to any section, in that way which would prevent him from pointing out what he thought wrong in their proceedings. We cannot wonder under these circumstances, that he was not welcomed as a political writer by any of those who were struggling for power; politics in their worldly constructions and acceptations could not be long pursued by such a mind as his. Religion was his home; and it was on religious subjects that his heart and pen were chiefly engaged for many years —labouring to promote righteousness in all things.

But in these efforts he met with much that was disheartening, and finally his hopes became so much depressed by the conclusions he drew from the Calvinistic theology that had been presented to him as gospel truths, that his energies for a time seemed totally prostrated. In this depressed state he providentially made the acquaintance of Lady Springett. Her mind had more natural cheerfulness than his; but, like his, was deeply impressed with the consciousness that nothing on earth was worth living for if the heart be not fixed in its trust in the Lord, and in its desire to do his will on earth above all things. With these feelings in her soul, she was moving about amid the amusements and fashions of London life, when she first became acquainted with Isaac Penington. Before she met with him, she had had many trying experiences in her search after spiritual life. She was the widow of Sir William Springett, who died when she was about twenty years of age; and now she was about thirty, Isaac Penington being eight years older.

Penington's acquaintance with Lady Springett soon ripened into confidential friendship, and a loving attachment succeeded. In 1654 they were married. During the interval between their marriage and removal to the Grange in 1658, they first became acquainted with the Quakers, or Friends of Truth, as they originally designated themselves.

Thoroughly to understand Mary Penington's character, we must turn to the account she wrote of her own early life. It is comprised in two documents; one left to her daughter, Gulielma Maria Penn; the other a letter addressed to her grandson, Springett Penn. The information in these autobiographical sketches I shall endeavour to combine so as to form a continuous personal history, as much as conveniently can be adhering to the writer's own words.*

THE CHILDHOOD AND EARLY LIFE OF MARY
PROUDE, ULTIMATELY PENINGTON.

MARY PROUDE was born about the year 1624, and was the only child of Sir John Proude, a native of Kent, in which county he had valuable landed property. He entered into the military service of the States of Holland under the Prince of Orange, and was one of the officers killed at the siege of Groll in Guelderland. Her mother's death took place either immediately after or shortly before that of her father; so that the little girl was left without either of her parents at the age of three years. She was brought up in a Protestant family, where the ordinances of the Episcopal Church were recognized. Speaking of their habits, she says they were "a kind of loose Protestants, who minded no religion, though they went to their place of wor-

---

* I believe I have studied Mary Penington's autobiographical letters in all the forms they have been brought forward—comparing the printed selections in this country, and also the American edition in its fulness, with the manuscript copy which has been transcribed by private hands.

ship on First-days, to hear a canonical priest preach in the morning, and read common prayers in the afternoon. They used common prayers in the family, and observed superstitious customs, and times, and days of fasting and feasting. At that time, when I was afraid in the night season of such things as spirits walking, and of thieves, I would often say over, as I had been taught, that which is called the Lord's Prayer, hoping by that means to be delivered from the things I feared." She used, as many a child has done, the words of that beautiful comprehensive prayer as a charm to ward off evil, without entering into its spirit, or at all comprehending its meaning. But when she was about eight years of age, and still living with the *loose Protestants* she speaks of, she heard a sermon preached, the text of which made a more intelligible religious impression on her mind. It was the declaration of the Lord Jesus, "Blessed are they that hunger and thirst after righteousness, for they shall be filled." This, she says, was the first scriptural text of which she ever took serious notice, and who can imagine what a stay and blessing it proved in keeping alive religious hope in many an hour of discouragement and depression in after years? It appears to have served as a divine anchor, made so secure in that early time that no storm could afterwards entirely unsettle it.

When she was about nine years of age, the little orphan girl, who seems to have been the ward of

Sir Edward Partridge, was removed to his residence. He had a large mixed family; for beside his own immediate household, he had a sister, Madam Springett, a young widow lady, with her three children and their servants, who boarded in his house. Madam Springett joined her brother's family at meals, but had a private suite of apartments for her own family to retire to. She was a superior woman in every respect, and of her attention and kindness little Mary Proude appears to have largely partaken. She had a daughter Catherine, a little older than Mary, and two sons, William and Herbert. With these children Mary was educated under the roof of Sir Edward Partridge, until the boys were sent to a public school. Towards their uncle's ward the young Springetts, who were noble youths, acted with a chivalrous and most kind consideration, that made them the very best of friends. William was about two years and a half older than Mary. She thus speaks of his early habits:—

"He was of a most courteous affable carriage towards all. He was most ingeniously inclined from a very lad; carving and forming things with his knife or tools; so industriously active that he rarely ever was idle. For when he could not be employed abroad in shooting at a mark with a gun, pistol, crossbow, or longbow; or managing his horses, which he brought up and trained himself— teaching them boldness in charging, and all that was needful for service—when he could not, I say, be thus engaged abroad, then he would fence within doors; or make crossbows, placing the sight with that accurateness as if it had been his trade; and make bow-strings, or cast bullets for his carbines, and feather his arrows. At other times he would pull his watch to pieces to string it, or to mend any defect; or take to pieces, and mend, the house clock. He was a great artist not only in shooting but in fishing—making lines, and arranging baits and things for the purpose. He was also a great lover of coursing, and he managed his dogs himself. These things I mention to show his ingenuity and his industry in his youth. But his mind did not run into any vanity about such things after it was engaged in religion."

So long as mere childhood lasted under such care and with such companionship and bright surroundings, Mary's life must have passed on smoothly and pleasantly. Of the general religious habits and tone of the Partridges, she says they seemed to be more religious than the other family she had previously lived with. "They would not admit of sports on the First day of the week, calling it the Sabbath; and they heard two sermons on that day of a priest who was not loose in his conversation; he used a form of prayer before his sermon, and read common prayer. When I was about eleven years of age, a maid-servant who tended on me and the rest of the children, and was zealous in that way, would read Smith's and Preston's sermons on First-day between the sermons. I diligently heard her read, and liking not to use the Lord's Prayer only, I got a Prayer-book and read prayers mornings and nights, according to the days and occasions. About this time my mind was serious about religion, and one day, after we came from the place of public worship, this forementioned maid-servant read one of Preston's sermons on the text, "Pray continually." Much was said of the excellency of prayer—that it distinguished a saint from the world; for that in many things the world and hypocrites could imitate a saint, but in prayer they could not. This wrought much in my mind all the time she read, and it seemed plain to me that I knew not right prayer; for what I used as a prayer an ungodly man might do by reading it out of a book, and that could not be the prayer which distinguished a saint from a wicked one. As soon as she had done reading, and all gone out of the chamber, I shut the door, and in great distress flung myself on the bed, and oppressedly cried out aloud, 'Lord, what is prayer?' At this time I had never heard any, nor of any that prayed otherwise than by reading, or by composing and writing a prayer, which they called a form of prayer. This thing so wrought in me, that, as I remember, the next morning or very soon after, it came into my mind to write a prayer of my own composing to use in the mornings. So, as soon as I was out of bed, I wrote a prayer, though I then could scarcely join my letters, I had so little a time learned to write. It was something of this nature; that, as the Lord commanded the Israelites to offer up a morning sacrifice, so I offered up the sacrifice of prayer, and desired to be preserved during that day. The use of this for a little time gave me some ease, and I soon left off using my books, and as the feelings arose in me, I wrote prayers according to my several occasions."

The time when the circumstances above related marked the experience of this thoughtful little girl, was when the spirit of Puritanism began to be manifested in the churches. The reading of the common prayers of the Church of England Prayer-book, both in public and private worship, was one of the practices to which objection began to be raised by some of the most strictly religious people of that time; and there were other practices also, in both the Episcopal and Presbyterian Churches, to which these Puritans—as they were in ridicule called—objected. Mary Penington thus continues:—

"The next prayer I wrote was for an assurance of pardon for my sins. I had heard one preach how God had pardoned David his sins of His free grace; and as I came from our place of worship, I felt how desirable a thing to be *assured* of the pardon of one's sins; so I wrote a pretty large prayer concerning it. I felt that it coming of grace, though I was unworthy, yet I might receive pardon, and I used earnest expressions about it. A little after this I received some acknowledgments from several persons of the greatness of my memory, and was praised for it. I felt a fear of being puffed up with that praise; so I wrote a prayer of thanks for the gift of memory, and expressed my desires to use it to the Lord, that it might be sanctified to me, and that I might not be puffed up by it. These three prayers I used with some ease of mind for a time, but not long; for I began again to question whether I prayed right or not. I knew not then that any did pray extempore, but it sprung up in my mind that to use words according to the sense I was in of my wants, was true prayer, which I attempted to do, but could not; sometimes kneeling down a long time, but had not a word to say. This wrought great trouble in me, and I had none to reveal myself to, or advise with, but bore a great burthen about it on my mind; till one day, as I was sitting at work in the parlour, a gentleman that was against the superstitions of the times came in, and looking sorrowful, said 'it was a sad day.' This was soon after Prynne, Bastwick, and Burton were sentenced to have their ears cut, and to be imprisoned. It sunk deep into my spirit, and strong cries were in me for them, and for the innocent people in the nation. It wrought so strongly in me, that I could not sit at my work, but left it, and went into a private room, and, shutting the door, kneeled down and poured out my soul to the

Lord in a very vehement manner, and was wonderfully melted and eased. I then felt peace and acceptance with the Lord, and was sure that this was prayer [in spirit and in truth], which I never was in like manner acquainted with before, either in myself or from any one else."

The persecution and cruel punishment of Prynne, Bastwick, and Burton, which called forth the deep sympathy and the earnest prayers of this young girl, occurred during the year 1637. Neal, in his History of the Puritans, tells us that Prynne was prosecuted for writing a book entitled *Histriomastrix*, against plays, masques, dancing, etc., and was condemned by the Court of Star Chamber to be degraded from his profession of the law; to be pilloried at Westminster and in Cheapside, at each place to lose an ear; to be fined £5,000; and to suffer perpetual imprisonment. Burton was a parish priest who published two sermons against the late innovations in the church. Bastwick was a physician who wrote a book entitled *Eleucis religionis Papistica*. They were all three fined £5,000 each, had their ears cut off, and were condemned to perpetual imprisonment. Archbishop Laud was present at the passing of the sentence. Of course such persecution and cruelty had the effect of weakening the attachment of great numbers to the Establishment, and eventually of causing them to separate from the church which promoted it.

It is evident that during the period of early religious exercise alluded to above, Mary Proude did not open her mind to any person. One would think she might have done so to her friend Madam Springett; but on the subject which chiefly engrossed her feelings it is probable she perceived that lady felt no special difficulties, such as had taken hold of her mind respecting prayer. Madam Springett at the period in question nominally belonged to the Church of England, but had largely given her religious confidence to the Puritan section of the Church, as is evinced by her choosing a Puritan tutor for her sons when she sent them to College.

In relation to her son William the narrative says, " She sent him to Cambridge, as being accounted more sober than Oxford, and placed him in a Puritan college called St. Catherine's Hall, where was a very sober tender Master of the house, and a grave sober tutor; for she appointed him one Ellis, who was accounted a Puritan; she having brought him up in his youth, and had used her influence to get him the preferment of a Fellow in that College."

Relative to her own experience, M. Penington proceeds thus :—" Word having been brought to the house that a neighbouring minister, who had been suspended by the bishops for not being subject to their canons, had returned to his people again, and that he was to preach at the same place where he had preached three years before, I desired to go. For this I was reproved by those who had the care of me, as being not fit to leave my parish church. I could not comply with their mind, but felt I must go. When I came, I found the minister was indeed one of those called Puritans. He prayed fervently, and with much sense of feeling. I felt that his was that sort of prayer which my mind had pressed after, but that I could not come at it in my own will; only had just tasted of it that time I have just mentioned. Now I knew this was true prayer, and I mourned sorely that I still kneeled down morning after morning, and night after night, but had not a word to say. I was exercised with this a great time; I could not go to hear the common prayer that was read in the family at nights, nor could I kneel down when I went to their worship-house. I could but read the Bible, or some other book, whilst the priest read common prayer.

At length I could neither kneel nor stand up to join with the priest in prayers before the sermon; neither did I care to hear him preach; but my mind ran after the hearing of the Nonconformist before-mentioned. By constraint I went with the family in the morning, but could not be kept from going to hear the Puritan preacher in the afternoon. I went through much suffering to secure this, being forced to go on foot two or three miles, and none permitted to go with me. However, a servant out of compassion would sometimes run after me, least I should be frightened by going alone. I was very young, but so zealous in this, that all their reasonings and

Displeasure of friends. 33

threatenings could not keep me back; and in a short time I would not go to hear the parish priest at all, but went, wet or dry, to the other place. I would go in with the family to hear the Scriptures read; but if I did happen to go in before they had done the prayers, I would sit while they kneeled. These things wrought much trouble in the family, and there were none to take my part but two of the maid servants, who were inclined to mind what I said against the reading of their prayers, and so refused to join with them in it. This the governors of the family were much disturbed at, and they made me the subject of their discourse in company, saying that I professed to pray with the spirit, but rejected godly men's prayers; that I was proud, and a schismatic." This was hard enough against a conscientious tender-spirited girl of seventeen; but we must remember how trying it was to her guardians to see one so young taking such a stand against established forms, and against what they regarded and had adopted as the right and truly authorized course in family worship.

When to the above was added the suspicion that she went to hear the Puritan preacher, only to obtain more liberty to meet with some young men whose acquaintance she was not likely to form in the house of her guardian, no wonder its injustice hurt her much, and that her sense of delicacy was wounded to the quick. In the family of Sir Edward Partridge she had abundant opportunities of meeting with gay

3

company; and a beautiful young heiress as she was, with the advantages of wealth and educated taste, attracted, as we may well understand, numerous suitors; but from the special attentions thus directed to her she turned coldly away. Her heart was too much absorbed in the great search after truth, and longing for spiritual communion with God, to be moved by such attentions from any one who was not similarly interested. Thus she speaks of her feelings at that time :—

"I minded not those marriages that were propounded to me by vain persons, but having desired of the Lord that I might have one who feared Him, I had a belief, though then I knew none of my own outward rank that was such an one, that the Lord would provide one for me. In this belief I continued, not regarding the reproaches of them that said to me, no gentleman, none but mean persons were of this way, and that I would marry some mean one or other. They were disappointed in that, for the Lord touched the heart of him who was afterwards my husband, and my heart cleaved to him for the Lord's sake." This was William Springett. During the previous seasons of deep trial through which his uncle's ward had been passing, William had been at Cambridge pursuing his studies there, and afterwards at the Inns of Court studying law. As his uncle, Sir Thomas Springett, was his guardian, it is probable the nephew had his uncle's house as a second home, and had thus been entirely removed from the scene of Mary's trials when they were most bitterly felt; and it doubtless was through the influence of this uncle, who was a steady royalist, that William Springett was knighted by the king, that honour having been conferred on him at a very early age—most probably when he was a law student and under Sir Thomas Springett's immediate care and patronage.

It seems that as soon as William heard through his mother's letters how the case stood with Mary Proude, that he lost no time in hastening home, deserting all the attractions of London, and forsaking the law courts, to which he never returned as a student. As the object of his most cherished affection, he asked Mary to give him the right to protect and shield her, to which she consented with all her heart; for to her great joy she found what she scarcely ventured to hope or expect, that his religious feelings, notwithstanding the adverse society to which his London life had been exposed, corresponded very nearly with her own. Hence she says, " My heart cleaved to him for the Lord's sake." They were married a few months after William's return, when Mary was about eighteen, and he not yet twenty-one.

The youthful husband, with the utmost zeal, adopted and carried out the same objections to the use of forms of prayer and to other Church of England observances which his young wife had done previously. She says, speaking of that early time,

"We scrupled many things then in use amongst those that were counted honest, good people. We found that songs of praise with us must spring from the same thing as prayer did—the feelings of the heart—and so we could not in that day use any one's song any more than their prayer." And she adds, respecting her husband, "Being so zealous against the use of common prayer and superstitious customs, made him a proverb amongst his intimates and relations. Indeed, he was so sensible of blind superstition concerning what they called their churches, that, to show his abhorrence of their placing holiness in the house, he would give disdaining words about their church timber. When we had a child, he refused to allow the midwife to say her formal prayer, but prayed himself, and gave thanks to the Lord in a very sweet and melting way; which caused great amazement. He never went to the parish church, but went many miles to hear Wilson, the minister I before mentioned; nor would he go to prayers in the house, but prayed, morning and evening, with me and his servants; which wrought great discontent in the family, whilst we lodged with his uncle, Sir Edward Partridge. He would not let the parish priest baptize the child, but, when it was eight days old, had it carried in arms to this Wilson, five miles distant. There was great seriousness and solemnity observed in doing this; we then looked upon it as an ordinance of God. Notes were sent to professing people round about, for more than ten miles, to come to seek to the Lord at such a time, for a blessing upon his ordinance. No person was to hold the child but the father, whom the preacher desired to take it as being the fittest person to have charge of him. It was a great cross and a new business, which caused much gazing and wonderment for him, a gallant and very young man, in the face of so great an assembly to hold the child in his arms. He received large charge about educating his child, and his duty towards him. He was the first person of quality in this country that refused the common mode, which he did in his zeal against the formality and superstitions of the times.

"He took the Scotch Covenant against all popery and popish innovations, and was in the English engagement when the fight was at Edge Hill, which happened when his child was about a month old. He had a commission sent him to be colonel of a regiment of foot, and he raised eight hundred men without beat of drum, most of them religious professors and professors' sons. There were near six score volunteers in his own company; himself going a volunteer, taking no pay. He was afterwards made a deputy-lieutenant of the county of Kent, in which position he was zealous and diligent for the cause.

"Within a few days after his regiment was enrolled, there was a rising in the vale of Kent of many thousands; to suppress which, he and his newly gathered, undisciplined soldiers were commanded from their rendezvous at Maidstone. He, having placed his men in such order as their inexperience and the time would permit, came to take his leave of me before encountering the enemy. When he came, he found me in danger of being put out of the house in case the enemy proceeded so far; and it put him to great difficulty to provide for my safety, and to return to his regiment at the time appointed, it being reported Prince Rupert was coming over to join the risers. But, being of such quick capacity, he soon devised a course that effected it; fetching a stage coach from Rochester in the night, he carried me and my child and maid to Gravesend; and there, hiring a barge for us to go to London, he took a solemn leave of me, and went post to his regiment. When I came to London I found the whole city in alarm, nothing but noise of drums and trumpets, with the clattering of arms, and the loud cry, 'Arm! arm! for the enemy is near.' This was at the time of that bloody fight between the Parliament forces and the King's at Hounslow heath.

"The risers being dispersed in Kent, my husband came to London, having behaved very approvably in getting restored the cattle and horses to the persons that had been plundered by the risers, who had taken a great quantity, which, on their being dispersed, came into possession of the soldiers. He applied himself to have them all restored to those that were oppressed by the plunderers, but there were other officers associated with him who endeavored to enrich themselves by retaining them. He afterwards went upon several services with his regiment; he was at the taking of Lord Craven's house in Surrey, where several of his own company of volunteers were of the forlorn hope. He was also at the fight at Newbury, where he was in imminent danger; a bullet hitting him severely, though it had lost its force to enter. He lay for some nights on the field in Lord Robert's coach; there being neither time nor convenience to pitch his own tent which he had with him. For some days he lived on candied citron and biscuit. After being in several other engagements, he went back with his regiment into Kent.

"Not long after he had returned to Kent, his own native county, Sussex, was in danger from the Cavalier party, which had taken Arundel, and fortified the town and castle. Sir William Walker was commander-in-chief against them, his assistance having been sought by the associated counties. My husband looked upon this engagement as a particular service to his own county, and with great freedom went to Arundel, where they had a long siege before the town. After they had taken it, they besieged the castle; it was very difficult service, but, being taken, he and Colonel Morley had the government of the castle committed to them.

A few weeks after this, the calenture, a disease that was then amongst the soldiers of the town and castle, seized upon him in his quarters near Arundel; from whence, in the depth of frost and snow, he sent for me to London to come to him. This was very difficult for me to accomplish, it being a short time before the birth of our second child. The waters being up at Newington and several other places, we were forced to row in a boat on the highway, and take the things out of the coach into the boat with us. Springs were fastened to the bridles of the horses, and they swam over and brought the coach with them. The coachmen were so sensible of all the difficulties and the badness of the way between London and Arundel, at that time of the year, that in all the neighboring streets they refused to come with me. Only at length one widow woman, who kept a coach for hire, and had taken a deal of our money, undertook to let her servant go, even though he should hazard the horses. So I gave him a very great price (twelve pounds) to carry me down, with liberty to return whether I was with him or not, within a day's time. It was a very tedious journey; we were benighted, and in the dark overthrown into a hedge. When we got out, we found there was on the other side hardly room to get along, for fear of falling down a very steep precipice, where we would have been all broken to pieces. We had no guide with us but he who had come to me with the message from my husband, who riding on a white horse, we could see him on before. Coming to a garrison late at night, we had to stop the coach to give the commander notice by firing a gun, which was done by the sentinel. The colonel came down immediately to invite me to stay; and, to encourage me, said my husband was likely to mend, beseeching me not in my situation to run such a hazard. The coachman, being sensible of the difficulties still to be undergone, would needs force me to lodge in the garrison, saying his horses could not hold out. To which I replied that I was to pay for all the horses if they suffered, and that I was resolved not to go out of the coach unless it broke down, until it came so near the house that I could compass it on foot. So, seeing my resolution, he pushed on.

"When we came to Arundel we saw a most dismal sight—the town depopulated—the windows all broken from the firing of the great guns—the soldiers making use of the shops and lower rooms for stables, and no light in the town but what came from the stables. We passed through the town on to his quarters. Within a quarter of a mile of the house the horses came to a standstill. As we could not see the reason of it, we sent the guide forward for a light and assistance. Upon which the report reached my husband that I was come; but he assured them they were mistaken, that he knew I could not come, in the situation I was in. Still they affirmed that I had certainly come. 'Then,' said he, 'raise me up in the bed, that I may be able to see her when she enters.' But the wheel of the coach having pitched close into the root of a tree, it was some time before it could be loosened. It was twelve o'clock at night when I arrived; and as soon as I put my foot into the hall, from which the stairs ascended to his chamber, I heard his voice saying, 'Why will you lie to me? If she be come, let me hear her voice.' This struck me so, that I had not power to get up stairs, but had to be helped up by two. On seeing me, the fever having taken to his head, he in a manner sprang up as if he would come out of the bed, saying, 'Let me embrace thee, my dear, before I die. I am going to thy God and to my God.' I found most of his officers about the bed attending on him, with signification of great sorrow for the condition he was in, they greatly loving him. The purple spots had come out on him the day before, and now were struck in, and the fever had got to his head, which caused him to be in bed, they not having before been able to persuade him to go to bed, though his illness had been for five days before the spots came out. Seeing the danger of his condition, and that so many Kentish men, both commanders and others, had died of it in a week's time near his quarters, they entreated him to keep his chamber. But such was the activeness of his spirit, and the stoutness of his heart, that they could not get him to yield to the illness so as to stay within, till they covenanted with him that he might shoot birds with his crossbow out of the window; and he did do it till the spots went in, and the fever got to his head. He then became so violent, being young and strong, that they were forced to sit round the bed to keep him in. To my doctor, whom I brought down with me, he spoke seriously about dying, and to me most affectionately. To the officers who were around the bed striving to keep him in, he spoke no evil words; but wittily remarked to the marshal and others about keeping up a strict watch, or their prisoner would escape, and how they were to repair the breach when he thrust his limbs from under the clothes.

"Discerning my lips to be cool, he would hardly suffer me to withdraw them from his burning face so as to take breath, crying out, 'Oh, don't go from me!' at which the doctor and my maid were very much troubled, looking upon the infection to be so high that it endangered my life and the child's. Two hours at a time I sat by him thus, and after a little pause he called upon me again to lay my mouth to his, and that he would be very quiet. At length, while I was in that posture, he fell asleep; which they that were by observing, constrained me to go to bed. Considering my condition, and that I might have my maid with him, who could bring me an account, I was prevailed with, and went to bed. When he awoke he seemed much refreshed, took great notice of the servant, and said, 'You are my wife's maid. Where is your mistress? How does my boy? Go to my wife, and tell her I am ready to embrace her, I am so refreshed with my sleep.' She came and gave me this account, and I would have arisen and gone down, but she persuaded me not, saying he would go to sleep again, and my going would only hinder it. So I sent her with a message to him, and went to rest. Thinking from the description she gave he was recovering, I lay late in the morning. When I went down I saw a great change, and sadness upon every face about him, which stunned me. He spoke affectionately to me, with several serious and weighty expressions. At last he said, 'Come, my dear, let me kiss thee before I die,' which he did with that heartiness as if he would have left his breath in me. 'Come once more,' said he, 'let me kiss thee, and take my leave,' which he did as before, saying, 'No more now. No more ever.' He then fell into a great agony, and that was a dreadful sight to me.

"The doctor and my husband's chaplain, and some of the chief officers who were by, observing his condition, they concluded that they must either persuade me, or take me by force from the bed; his great love to me, they said, and his beholding me there being the occasion of it. Upon which they came and asked me to go from the bedside to the fire; that while I staid where I was he could not die. This word *die* was so great with horror, that I, like an astonished, amazed creature, stamped

His death.

with my foot, and cried, 'Die! die! must he die? I cannot go from him.' Upon this two of them gently lifted me in their arms, and carrying me to the fire, which was at a distance from the bed, they prevented me from going to him again. At that time I wept not, but stood silent and struck. After I was brought from the bed, he lay for a time very still; at length they said his sight was gone, and then they let me go to him. And standing there by his bedside I saw on him the most amiable, pleasant countenance I ever beheld—just like that of a person ravished with something he was looking at. He lay about an hour in this condition. Towards sunset he turned quickly about, and called upon a kinsman of his, 'Anthony, come quickly,' at which very instant Anthony came riding into the yard, having come many miles to see him. Soon after this he died, and then I could weep; but, fearing injurious consequences, they immediately took me up into another chamber, and suffered me no more to look at him."

Sir William Springett's remains were next morning taken privately by his officers and soldiers to Ringmer, and there deposited in the family vaults where several of his ancestors lay, intending that a public funeral should follow as soon as arrangements could be made for it in London. But those who had the management of his pecuniary affairs, discovering that he had expended so much of his own private property that was not likely to be refunded, in equipping, maintaining, and paying the soldiers, declared against it. To meet the heavy cost for the public service, he had not only mortgaged to a considerable extent his own estates, but he had used all the ready money (£1,600) which he had got with his wife. So much being thus sunk, the executors prudently determined not to allow further outlay; and this deciding the question about the public funeral, Sir William Springett's remains were accordingly left to repose at Ringmer, in his own native county of Sussex. In Ringmer church a handsome mural monument was erected to his memory, which is still in perfect preservation.

CHAPTER II.

1640–1658.

Sir William Springett's character.—Change in his religious opinions.—Puritan iconoclasts.—Aid to Irish Protestants.—Domestic characteristics.—Monument to his memory.—Birth of Gulielma Maria Springett.—Her mother's religious feelings about infant baptism.—Character of Madam Springett.—Her useful life.—Her medical skill. Expenditure of her income.—Herbert Springett.—His monument in Ringmer church.—Lady Springett's dissatisfaction with the religionists around her.—Withdrawal.—Tries fashionable life.—Her retrospect of that period.—Acquaintance with Isaac Penington.—Their marriage.—First acquaintance with the Quakers.—William Simpson and Thomas Curtis visit the Peningtons.—They are convinced of the truth of Quaker doctrines.—Religious joy and comfort.—Establishment in the truth.

WHEN dwelling on Sir William Springett's character and religious convictions, his wife mentions some points on which a change had gone forward in his mind, from the time when with so much solemnity he had carried his infant son to the baptismal font. Having in vain looked for any declaration in the New Testament that recommends infant baptism, he at length came to the conclusion that it was an unauthorized rite. Again arose the thought, if infant baptism be incorrectly looked on as producing regeneration—the being born again—without which, our Lord declared to Nicodemus, "a man cannot enter into the Kingdom of God," then it was not merely an uninfluential and unauthorized rite, but, by giving a false meaning to Christian regeneration, it had become a positive evil. Its tendency and influence, leading away from the true meaning of scriptural regeneration, had done great harm in the church.

With respect to the sacramental rite of the Lord's supper, not having experienced it to bring his mind, as he had hoped it would have done, into any closer spiritual communion with the Lord, he was startled. Striving to discover the cause of this, he came at length to the conclusion that there existed a wrong construction of our Lord's words, which had led to its establishment in the Church as a congregational religious rite. As he dwelt on this subject, carefully examining the texts of Scripture that bore on the point, this conviction continued to deepen in his mind till he felt constrained to discontinue partaking of it. Respecting his having turned from the use of forms of prayer, his wife says, "This turning in him proceeded from a glimpse of the dawning of the day when prayer is to be offered up in the spirit and with the understanding; also that there was a spirit of prayer and supplication, in which any one who felt it might mentally engage without form, yet with true acceptance to God, seems to have been made clear to him. "He also saw," she says, "in the little measure of light accorded him, that priests were not to preach for hire, but were to be sent of the Lord to reach the consciences of the hearers. This made him decline false dead ways, and cleave in heart to the people called Puritans (for in that day those that heard the Lord were nick-named Puritans). Amongst them it was his delight to be exercised in the worship of God, and to mingle in their chaste conversation."

Sir William Springett was one of those indomitable soldiers of the Covenant, who, in their zeal for the Lord, brought their energies into action against the use of priestly vestments as well as against Papal idolatry. The Puritanical glasses they looked through in that day represented almost every work of art as dangerous, that had been imported from any country under the Papacy; hence much was sacrificed which in another age would have been spared. Sir William's wife tells us her husband commanded his soldiers to break down and destroy every vestige of those objects that he regarded as Popish idols, whether crosses, statues, pictures, or gold ornaments. It mattered not with what exquisite art the marble figure had been chiseled, or with what elaborate and successful skill the painting represented life, if it depicted or attempted to embody fanciful representations of the Lord Jesus, of his apostles, or of Romish saints, from the fury of the Puritan soldier nothing could shield it. "Be they ever so rich," says Lady Springett, "he destroyed them, and reserved not one for its comeliness or costly workmanship." Looking back from our stand-point upon that wholesale destruction of works of artistic genius, some of us may be more inclined to cry out against the iconoclastic furor of our Puritan forefathers, than to commend their destructive proceedings. Whatever we may think, wives like Lady Springett in that day regarded them as evidences of Christian faithfulness, and no doubt they did imply faithfulness to the conscientious views they had adopted. In Sir William's crusade against idolatry there was not only true conscientious earnestness, but a commendable impartiality—not saving what was his friend's property and destroying his enemy's; as is manifested by the following statement from his wife:—"I find freedom," she says, "to mention one passage in this pursuit of destroying Popish relics and pictures. There was a Parliament-man who was also a deputy-lieutenant of the county, a great stirrer in the Parliament cause, and his wife a zealous Puritan. This man was assisting him (Sir William) and was his companion in the searching of Popish houses, and in destroying their pictures and trumpery. Going one day to their house to visit them, as he passed through the hall, he spied several superstitious pictures, as of the crucifixion of Christ, his resurrection, and such like; very large pictures they were, and a great ornament to the hall. They had been moved out of the parlour to manifest neglect. He, looking upon it as a very unequal thing to destroy such things in Popish houses, and have them in those of their opposers, drew out his sword, and cut them all out of their frames, and, spearing them on the sword's point, he went into the parlour with them. The mistress of the house being there, he said to her, 'What a shame that thy husband should be so zealous a prosecutor of Papists, and spare such things in his own house! But,' saith he, 'thou seest I have acted impartially, and have destroyed them here also.'"

His wife says, and no doubt she had good reason to say it, that he was just and merciful in doing the work which as a soldier he had to do, never in any case converting confiscated property or sequestered estates to his own use. She adds, "He even refused to buy any goods that were plundered from the enemy; nor ever made any use of one pound's worth, I dare aver, that belonged to them who were conquered. He had very great offers from persons in power, of houses and goods both in London and elsewhere, of those called delinquents; all which he refused, and rather chose, whilst his family was with him in the city, to pay twenty shillings a week for lodgings than touch any of them. One considerable place offered him was Leeds Castle in Kent. It was seized by the Parliament party, and made a garrison, and he was intended to be the commander of it, and greatly pressed to make use of the goods and furniture, and have his family live in the Castle, but he refused it. Another house offered him was

Hollingborn, which was very well furnished, and within a few miles of Leeds Castle; but he refused it also, giving them an answer to this effect, that he durst not make use of any man's estate or goods, nor dwell in any man's sequestered house, much less this, which was his uncle Sir Thomas Culpeper's. His mind throughout life was ever for the exercise of compassion and charitableness, of which there have been many instances given me by persons who have observed him in the places where he was quartered, beside what I have seen myself, and I had converse with him from the time he was twelve years old to his dying day. One instance I shall mention that I had from the Mayor of Maidstone, in Kent. He brought me a bill for three pounds after his death, with my husband's hand to it, telling me that as he was walking in the street with him, a poor man was had to prison, who made miserable moan; whereat Sir William stopped the bailiff, and asked what they were taking him to prison for? He answered, for debt. He replied, 'You shall not carry him there. Mr. Mayor, lay you down the money, and I will see it discharged.'

"He was very generous to the Irish Protestants who came over after the massacre in Ireland; also to the plundered ministers and maimed soldiers that were wounded in the army. He rarely gave less than a twenty-shilling piece at the private fasts where these sufferings were presented before him, and that was constantly once and sometimes twice a week. I shall mention a remarkable instance of his charity for the sufferers in Ireland. We were at a fast at Milk-street in London, where Thomas Case, a Puritan preacher, set forth the great distress the Irish Protestants were in, and the need they stood in of assistance to get over to England. He related it so affectingly that it pierced my husband greatly, and as he was taking down the sermon after him, he felt an engagement in his mind to give twenty pounds"—a sum in that day probably equal to a hundred pounds at the present time—" Afterwards he considered that, as this was determined when he was warmed with a clear sense of their misery, and as he grew cooler that he might change, whereupon he took his notebook, and wrote in it a solemn engagement before the Lord to perform it when he came home. When all was over, there was appointed at the door two men of quality to stand with basins, to receive the collections for the Irish Protestants; and some others that were officers were appointed to receive for the maimed soldiers. My husband, as he passed out, put in five pieces of gold to the Irish, and one piece into the other basin; and said nothing to me about it till we came to our lodgings; then he refused to sup, but went up to writing. After some time he called me to fetch him fifteen pounds in a bag. When I brought it, he then spoke to me to this purpose:—'Now that I have made sure of the thing, I will acquaint thee what it is to do;' so he told me

the business, and read to me the engagement in his
book, and the letter he had written to Thomas
Case, giving him an account how it was, but not
setting his name to it; declaring that he had given
it to the Lord, and desired to remain unknown.
The footboy was sent away with the letter and
money sealed up, with the order to turn his coat
before he came in sight of the place, that they
could not see what livery he wore, and on deliver-
ing the money and letter into his hands for whom
they were sent, not to stay to be asked any questions.

"He was most affectionately tender to me and
his child—beyond what I had known in any, considering his youth. I do not remember that he
ever let an opportunity slip of acquainting me with
his condition when absent. He hath often writ
letters when he baited, on purpose to send to me
by travellers that he might meet on the road.
After the battle of Newbury he gave the messenger he was sending to the Parliament to acquaint
them with the issue of the battle, a piece, only to
knock at the door of my lodgings in Blackfriars,
and leave word that he saw him well after the
battle—there being time for no more; which message in all probability saved my life—I being then
sick of the measles, which could not come out
because of the exercise of my mind by reason of
my having heard of the battle. The message was
left between three and four o'clock in the morning;

at the hearing of which the oppression was rolled off my spirits, like the removal of a great stone, and the measles came forth.

"I must add that, in addition to such gentleness, sweetness, compassion, affableness, and courtesy, thy grandfather had a courage that was without harshness or cruelty; and an undaunted spirit such as was rarely found with the forementioned excellencies. He was also very hospitable; his generous mind delighted in entertaining those that were engaged in the cause with him,—not in excess, but with great freedom and heartiness, always seasoned with savoury and edifying discourse,—making mention of the Lord's gracious dealings with them."

Thus closes Mary Penington's retrospective description of the husband of her youth, in the letter she addressed to her grandson, Springett Penn. As a true and altogether reliable, unadorned history, it constitutes, I think, one of the finest and most touching descriptions of a noble gallant young Puritan soldier which the seventeenth century has bequeathed to us. The men of Sussex might well be proud of him as a native of their county, and doubtless they would be so if they only understood his character. But, during the lapse of ages, one generation dying out, and another coming in, each cherishing its own favorites for the time being, true and accurate knowledge of the good and the noble sons of past centuries is liable to be forgotten even in their native place. And, were it not for some favourable circumstances, this history of Sir William Springett's short life would have been lost like many another. His wife's most tender and graphic description, addressed to his daughter and to his grandson, and the careful preservation of her letters among the Friends, brings him now before us in life-like colours after the lapse of so many ages. Probably few in Sussex at this day know aught about him, save what the mural tablet in the church of Ringmer sets forth. The inscription on the monument in question is as follows:—

Here lyeth the body of

SIR WILLIAM SPRINGETT, KNT.,

Eldest son and heir of Herbert Springett of Sussex,
Who married Mary Proude, the only daughter and heir of
Sir John Proude, Knt., Colonel in the service of the United Provinces,
And of Anne Fagge, his wife, of the co-heirs of Edward Fagge
of Ewell, near Feversham, in the County of Kent, Esq.

He had issue by Mary, his wife, one sonne, John Springett, and one daughter, Gulielma Maria Posthuma Springett.

He, being Colonel in the service of the Parliament at the taking of Arundel Castle in Sussex, there contracted a sickness of which he died February the 3d, Anno Domini
1643, being 23 years of age.

His wife, in testimony of her dear affection to him, hath erected this monument to his memory.

A few weeks after the death of Sir William Springett, the bereaved widow was roused from the depth of her desolation and sorrow, by her maternal feelings on the birth of an infant daughter.

This was Gulielma Maria, above mentioned.* Her Heavenly Father had in this darling child sent another claim on her affections, another tie binding her to life, and her energy arose to meet surrounding circumstances. In the name Gulielma Maria given to the infant, those of both parents were united. Her mother-in-law, now the chief earthly friend left to the young widow, came to reside with her, and she remained there during the residue of her life, which only lasted about four years after the death of her son William.

Lady Springett had adopted the same views which her husband had arrived at, respecting the unscriptural character of infant baptism, and the injury that had resulted to Christian life from the popular construction put on water-baptism. She therefore refused to allow her little daughter to be baptised. When reflecting on the rite of baptism, as practised in the Church, the declaration of the Apostle relative to another ritual observance, which was abolished under the new dispensation, was so continually in her mind as a case in point, that she could in no degree yield to the entreaties of her friends and relatives. It was very trying to maintain her ground against all their persuasion; but hard above all it must have been to stand out against the expressed desire of her loved and honor-

---

* As *February*, old style, was the last month of the year, it may be presumed Gulielma was born in 1644, but we have no exact record of the date.

ed mother-in-law; nevertheless, singlehanded and conscientious, she withstood all who endeavoured to persuade her to have her child formally baptised. She says, "That scripture in the last of the Galatians, of circumcision or uncircumcision availing nothing, but a new creature, was so often in my mind, that I could not but resolve that it [the baptismal rite] should not be performed. This brought great reproach on me, and made me as a byword among the people of my own rank in the world, and a strange thing it was thought to be by my relatives and acquaintance. Those who were accounted able ministers, and such as I formerly delighted to hear, were sent to persuade me; but I could not do it and be clear. My answer to them was, 'He that doubts is damned if he do it." She did doubt, and she believed that she had good reason to doubt of infant baptism being an institution authorized by Jesus, and therefore the little Gulielma Maria was never taken to the baptismal font.

It seems marvellous of two such young persons, and yet it does really appear as if Sir William Springett and his wife were at that time, when these views became fixed in their minds, standing *totally alone* when declining to receive the popular idea of water baptism, as being the essential baptism which accompanies regeneration and salvation. It is very certain that Mary Penington says nothing about having studied any writings on the question, save those of the New Testament; or of having any example before her of any one who altogether on scriptural grounds disapproved of the rite as practised in the Churches, except her deceased husband. It does not appear that the views advocated by them were the same as those held by the Baptists, who, though disapproving of infant baptism, insist on adult water baptism as essential, and as that which was commanded by Christ. George Fox did not commence his ministry for several years after the death of Sir William Springett; it was not therefore from the Friends' ideas they had been brought to that conclusion. But it is true that about the time of Guli's birth and after it, there was a minister who held an official place in the University of Cambridge, who entertained very decided convictions against the notions of water baptism which prevailed in the Church of England, of which he was a member. This was William Dell, Master of Gonville and Caius College, Cambridge. How far he had sufficient Christian faithfulness to preach in that persecuting age the views he set forth in his writings, which were afterwards published, I know not. He seemed to have but little hope of the age he lived in taking a right scriptural view of the doctrines in question, because he says it was "so rooted and built up in the doctrines of men." Hence he appealed to and wrote especially for the next generation. So far as I can ascertain, his excellent work on *The Doctrine of the Baptisms* was not published for eight or ten years after the period in question; and in his preface to the reader, introducing the work *On Baptisms*, he warns him that he would "speak much otherwise than all former or later writers whatever, that he had met with."

Within the four years which elapsed from the death of Sir William Springett to that of Madam Springett, John, his first-born child and only son, seems to have also died, though the child's mother has left us no specific account of the event. Circumstances indicate that it was within that time his brief life closed.

Of her mother-in-law's high moral worth and great ability and usefulness, Mary Penington gives her grandson a beautiful account. Speaking of both great-grandparents she says, " Thy dear mother's father was of religious parents; his father (thy great-grandfather) though a lawyer, was religious and strict, as I have heard of him, in those things wherein the ministration of that time consisted, and in the exercise of what in that day of dim light was accounted holy duties. He died of consumption, leaving thy great-grandmother with two sons and a daughter [born after her father's death]. She was married to him about three or four years, and left a widow about twenty-two years of age. She was an excellent woman; and had a great regard to the well-being of her children, both in the inward and outward condition; and that she might the better bring them up, she lived a retired life; refusing all other marriage, though frequently offered, as I have heard her say. She suffered pretty hard things of his two executors, his brother Sir Thomas Springett, and a brother-in-law; who thought that she, being so very young a widow, would marry again. Through their jealousy on this point, they refused her the management of the education of her children, and put her upon suing them for it; which she at last obtained, with charges, after some years' suit.

"She lived a virtuous life,—constant in morning and evening prayer by herself, and often with her children; causing them to repeat to her what they remembered of sermons they had heard, and of scriptures. I lived in the house with her from nine years of age, till after I was married to her son; and after he died, she came and lived with me, and died at my house. In all which time I never, as I remember, heard her say an improper word, or saw her do an evil action. She spent her time very ingeniously; and in a bountiful manner bestowed great part of her jointure yearly upon the poor, in providing physic and surgery. She had a yearly jointure of about twelve score pounds, and with it she kept a brace of horses, a man, and a maid. She boarded with her only brother, Sir Edward Partridge. She kept several poor women constantly employed simpling for her in the summer; and in the winter preparing such things as she had use for in physic, and surgery, and for eyes; she having eminent judgment in all three, and admirable success; which made her famous and sought to out of several counties by the greatest persons, as well as by the low ones. She was daily employing her servants in making oils, salves, and balsams; drawing of spirits; distilling of waters; making of syrups and conserves of many kinds, with pills and lozenges. She was so rare in her ability in taking off cataracts and spots on eyes, that Hopkins, the great oculist, sent many to her house when there was difficulty of cure, and that he could not attend or spare so much time as was necessary to compass it. She cured many burns and desperate cuts; also dangerous sores that came by thorns; likewise broken limbs; many afflicted with the king's evil; taking out bones. One case of great difficulty I especially remember—a child's head that was so burnt that its skull was like a coal; she brought it to have skin and hair again, and invented a thin pan of beaten silver covered with bladder to preserve the head in case of a knock or a fall. She frequently helped in consumptious cases beyond the skill of doctors to help, through her diligence and care.

"In the villages about her lodged several patients, that had come there some hundreds of miles to be under her care; and sometimes would remain there, away from their homes, for a quarter of a year at a time. She has sometimes had twenty persons in a morning—men, women, and children

—to attend to. I have heard her say she spent half her revenue in making the medicines which she needed for these cures. She never would take presents of much value from any one; only this she would do—if the patients were able, she gave them a note of what things they could buy, and they brought them to her, and she made up the medicine for them; her man-servant writing the directions she gave, and packing up the salves and medicines.

" In the place where she dwelt she was called in her religion, of latter times, a Puritan; afterwards she was called an Independent. She had an Independent minister in her house, and gave liberty to people to come there twice a week to hear him preach. She constantly set apart the Seventh-day, about three or four o'clock in the afternoon, for her family to leave all their occasions, and this minister preached or prayed with them as a preparation for the morrow. She was a most tender and affectionate mother to thy grandfather, and greatly delighted in his love to me, and always shewed great kindness to me. Indeed, she was very honourable in counselling her son not to marry for an estate, urging him to consider what would make him happy in his choice ['many great offers' having been made to draw him into marriage alliance]. She would discourse to him in this wise, that she knew me, and we were known to one another, and said she would choose me for his wife if I had no portion. She lived to see thy mother three or four years old, and was very affectionate to her, and took great delight in seeing her wisdom." Thus closes her daughter-in-law's account of that admirable Puritan matron.

Her husband Herbert Springett, barrister-at-law, who died in 1621, was at his death, as is stated on the mural monument to his memory in Ringmer church,

> In the sixtie and sixe year of his age.
> A friend to virtue, a lover of learning,
> Of prudence great, of justice a furtherer.
> Redress he did the wrongs of many a wight,
> Fatherless and widdows by him possess their right.
> To search into each cause, and thus end all strife,
> With patience great he spent his mortal life.

Mary Penington describes her own religious feelings as being at this time in a very unsatisfied state. She says she changed her ways often, going from one notion to another. In fact, she went the whole round of the popular sects of that day; heard their preachers on all occasions; made the acquaintance of high religious professors; attended their lectures, their fasts, their thanksgivings, their prayer meetings; watched their private walk in life, and noticed the position they took in the world. Instead of meeting with the spiritual instruction and seeing the realization of the Christian life of which she had been in quest, she turned away heartsick, under the impression of a prevading empty show that had assumed the name of religion.

At length she made up her mind to abandon all outward forms of religious worship, and to hold herself unconnected with any section of Christians, relying on the ultimate fulfilment of the promise of the Lord, "Blessed are they that hunger and thirst after righteousness, for they shall be filled."

Having found no abiding comfort amid religious professors, she at length determined to try the gay world. She says, "I then had my conversation much among people of no religion, being ashamed to be counted religious, or to do any thing that was called religious; and I began to loathe whatever profession of that sort any one made, holding the professors of every sort worse than the profane, they boasted so much of what I knew they had not attained; I having been zealous in whatever they pretended to, yet could not find purging of heart, nor an answer from the Lord of acceptation. In this restless state I let in every sort of notion that rose in that day, and for a time applied myself to examine them, and get out of them whatever good could be found; but still sorrow and trouble was the end of all. I was at length ready to conclude that though the Lord and His Truth were certain, yet that they are not now made known to any upon earth; and I determined no more to enquire or look after God, for that it was in vain to seek him. So for some time I took no notice of any religion, but minded recreation, as it is called; and went after it into many excesses and vanities—as foolish mirth, carding, dancing, and singing. I frequented music assemblies, and made vain visits where there were jovial feastings. I delighted in curiosities, and in what would please the vain mind, and satisfy the lust of the eye and the pride of life; frequenting places of pleasure, where vainly dressed persons resorted to show themselves and to see others in the like excess of folly; and riding about from place to place in an airy mind. But in the midst of all this my heart was often sad and pained beyond expression."

After a round of such fashionable recreations as above specified, she tells us that, taking with her none but little Guli and her maid, she would often in disgust forsake for a time city life, and seek entire seclusion in the country, where she would give way to her feelings of distress. She says, " I was not hurried into those follies by being captivated by them, but from not having found in religion what I had sought and longed after. I would often say within myself, what are they all to me? I could easily leave all this; for it hath not my heart, it is not my delight, it hath not power over me. I had rather serve the Lord, if I could indeed feel and know that which would be acceptable to Him. One night in my country retirement I went to bed very sad and disconsolate; and that night I dreamed I saw a book of hieroglyphics of religion respecting things to come in the Church, or religious state. I dreamed that I took no delight at all in them; and felt no closing of my mind with them, but turned away greatly oppressed. It being evening, I went out from the company into the open air, and lifting up mine eyes to the heavens I cried out, 'Lord, suffer me no more to fall in with any false way, but show me the truth.' Immediately I thought the sky opened, and a bright light like fire fell upon my hand, which so frightened me that I awoke, and cried out. When my daughter's maid (who was in the chamber) came to the bed-side to see what was the matter with me, I trembled a great time after I was awakened."

Her mind having fully realized the superficial and unsatisfying character of the fashionable amusements of the gay world, her thoughts again and again turned to the religious feelings of former days. She still clung to the belief that though she had run into vanity, she was yet under her heavenly Father's care, and that He who had made the blessed promise to that state, knew of the hungering and thirsting after righteousness which often had such possession of her mind. But above all things she abhorred hypocrisy and religious presumption in any one, and therefore she often distrusted herself, and these feelings. She could not for a long time entertain the idea that it was the Holy Spirit which was giving her these gleams of light and trust. and tendering her heart in prayerful feeling towards God. Thus she details circumstances that unfold her state of mind :—

"One day, when going through the city from a country-house, I could not make my way through the crowd that filled the street (it being the day whereon the Lord Mayor was sworn) but was forced to go into a house till it was over. Being burdened by the vanity of their show, I said to a professor that stood by me, 'What benefit have we now by all the blood that has been shed, and by Charles being kept out of the nation, seeing all these follies are again allowed?' He answered, none that he knew of, save the enjoyment of their religion. To which I replied, 'That is a benefit to you who have a religion to be protected in the exercise of, but it is none to me.'" Looking back on that period, when she would not allow to herself that she had any religion at all, she says it was wonderful to her to remember how she, notwithstanding, confided in the goodness and care of God. "That help I frequently had from Him whilst in the most confused and disquieted state I ever knew. Trust in the Lord was richly given me in that day when I durst not own myself to have any religion I could call true; for if I were but taking a servant, or doing any outward thing that much concerned my condition in the world, I never feared, but retired, waiting to see what the day would bring forth, and as things were offered to me closed with them, if I felt my heart answered thereto." At this very time she says, "In anguish of spirit I could but cry to the Lord, 'If I may not come to thee as a child, because I have not the spirit of sonship, yet thou art my Creator; and as thy creature I cannot breathe or move without thee. Help is only to be had from thee. If thou art inaccessible in thy own glory, and I can only get help where it is to be had, and thou only hast power to help me, what am I to do?'

"Oh! the distress I felt in this time, having never dared to kneel down, as formally going to prayer, for years, because I feared I could not call God Father in truth; and I durst not mock Him as with a form. Sometimes I would be melted into tears, and feel an inexpressible tenderness; but not knowing what it was from, and being ready to misjudge all religion, I thought it was some influence from the planets which governed this body. But I durst not regard any thing in me, being of or from God; or that I felt any influence of His spirit on my heart. I was like the parched heath for want of rain, and like the hunted hart longing for water, so great was my thirst after that which I did not know was near.

"In the condition I have mentioned, of weary seeking and not finding, I married my dear husband Isaac Penington. My love was drawn to him because I found he saw the deceit of all mere notions about religion; he lay as one that refused to be comforted until He came to His temple 'who is truth and no lie.' All things that had only the *appearance* of religion were very manifest to him, so that he was sick and weary of show, and in this my heart united with him, and a desire was in me to be serviceable to him in this his desolate condition; for he was as one alone, and felt miserable in the world. I gave up much to be a companion to him. And, oh! the secret groans and cries that were raised in me, that I might be visited of the Lord, and brought to a clear knowledge of his truth and way; that my feet might be turned into that way before I went hence, even if I never should take one step in it that would bring joy or peace; yet that I might assuredly know myself to be in it, even if my time were spent in sorrow.

"I resolved never to go back into those formal things I had left, having found death and darkness in them; but would rather be without a religion until the Lord manifestly taught me one. Many times, when alone, did I reason thus :—'Why should I not know the way of Divine life? For if the Lord would give me all in this world, it would not satisfy me.' 'Nay,' I could cry out, 'I care not for a portion in this life: give it to those that care for it: I am miserable with it. It is acceptance with God, of which I once had a sense, that I desire, and that alone can satisfy me.'

"Whilst I was in this state, I heard of a new people called Quakers, but I resolved not to inquire after them nor the principles they held. For a year or more after I had heard of them in the north, I heard nothing of their ways except that they used *thee* and *thou* to every one; and I saw a book written about plain language by George Fox, which I remember I thought very ridiculous; so gave no attention either to the people or the book, except it were to scoff at them and it. Though I thus despised this people, I had sometimes a desire to attend one of their meetings, if I could go unknown, and hear them pray. I was quite weary of hearing doctrines discussed, but I believed if I were with them when they prayed, I would be able to feel whether they were of the Lord or not. I endeavoured to stifle this desire, not knowing how to get to one of their meetings unknown; and if it should be known, I thought it would be reported that I had joined them." An opportunity for acquaintance with the "Friends of Truth" by and by presented itself unsought for, as Mary Penington thus states :—

"One day, as my husband and I were walking in a park, a man that for a little time had frequented the Quakers' meetings saw us as he rode by, in our gay vain apparel. He spoke to us about our pride, at which I scoffed, saying, 'He a public preacher indeed!—preaching on the highways!' He turned back again, saying he had a love for my husband, seeing grace in his looks. He drew nigh to the pales, and spoke of the light and grace of God that had appeared to all men. My husband and he having engaged in discourse, the man of the house coming up invited the stranger in. He was but young, and perceiving my husband was too able for him in the fleshly wisdom, said he would bring a man next day who would better answer all his questions and objections; who, as I afterwards understood, was George Fox. He came again the next day, and left word that the Friend he intended to bring could not well come; but some others he believed would be with us about the second hour; at which time came Thomas Curtis and William Simpson. My mind had been somewhat affected by the discourse of the night before; and though I thought the man weak in the management of the arguments he brought forward to support his principles, yet many scriptures which he mentioned stuck with me, and felt very weighty. They were such as showed me the vanity of many of my practices; which made me very serious, and soberly inclined to hear and consider what these other men had to say. Their solid and weighty carriage struck a dread over me, for they came in the authority and power of the Lord to visit us. The Lord was with them, and all we who were in the room were made sensible at that time of the Divine power manifestly accompanying what they said. Thomas Curtis repeated a scripture that struck out all my enquiries and objections, 'The doctrine is not mine, but His that sent me. If any man will do His will he shall know of the doctrine, whether it be of God, or whether I speak of myself.' Immediately it arose in my mind, if I would for certain know whether or not it was truth which these people upheld, I must do what I knew to be the

Lord's will. Much that was contrary thereto in me was set before me to be removed. I was shown my want of obedience to what Christ required; and that I must join in with what I knew, before I would be in a capacity to receive and understand what they laid down for their principles."

The effect upon Mary Penington's mind of this application of the text quoted by Thomas Curtis, was not of a transient character. Such of her practices as were contrary to the teaching and commands of the Lord Jesus were brought in review before her by the Holy Spirit, now at work in her heart. The axe being unsparingly brought down on the root of the evil that was within, much painful exercise succeeded. She says:—"Terrible was the Lord against the vain and evil inclinations in me, which made me night and day in sorrow; and if it did cease a little, then I grieved for fear I should again be reconciled to the things which I felt under judgment, and which I had then a just detestation of. Oh! how I did long not to be left secure or quiet till the evil was done away! How often did this run through my mind, 'Ye will not come to me, that ye may have life.' It is true I am undone if I come not to thee, but I cannot come unless I leave that which cleaveth close unto me, and how can I part with it? I saw the Lord would be just in casting me off, and not giving me [divine] life, if I would not come from my beloved lusts to Him for that life. I never had peace or quiet from sore exercise of mind for many months, till I was by the Lord's judgments brought off from all those things which I found His light made manifest to be deceit, bondage, vanity, and the spirit of the world. The giving up of these things cost me many tears. I felt that by the world I would be regarded as a fool, and that my honourable position must be sacrificed if I took up the cross, and acted contrary to the fashions and customs that prevailed in the world and among my acquaintances. My relations made this cross a very heavy one; but at length I gave up all."

During the mental struggles above alluded to, Mary Penington does not appear to have sought or maintained any intimate acquaintance with the Friends, or to have made a practice of attending their meetings; but it is most probable she had been reading some of their writings. She states, "A little while after the visit of the Friends before mentioned, one night on my bed it was said to me, 'Be not hasty to join these people called Quakers.'" And after she had given up all her worldly reasoning against the pointing of her own enlightened conscience, she adds, "I then received strength to attend the meetings of this despised people, which I had intended never to meddle with. I found they were truly of the Lord, and my heart owned them and honoured them. I then longed to be one of them, and minded not the cost or pain; but judged it would be well worth my utmost cost and pains

Love and acceptance.

to witness in myself such a change as I saw in them—such power over the evil of human nature. I had heard it objected against them, that they could work no miracles, but I said they did work great miracles, in that they produced such changes, turning them that were in the world and in the fellowship of it from worldly things.

"In taking up the cross, I received strength against many things that I once thought it not possible to deny myself. But oh! the joy that filled my soul at the first meeting held in our habitation at Chalfont. To this day I have a fresh remembrance of it, and of the sense the Lord gave me of His presence and ability to worship Him in that spirit which was undoubtedly His own. Oh! long had I desired to worship Him in the full assurance of acceptation, and to lift up my hands and heart without doubting, which I experienced that day. In that assembly I acknowledged His great mercy and wonderful kindness, for I could then say, 'This is what I have longed and waited for, and feared I never should have experienced.'

"Many trials have I been exercised with since then; and all that came by the Lord's ordering strengthened my life in Him, and hurt me not. But once my mind running out in prejudice against some Friends, it did sorely hurt me. After a time of deep and unknown sorrow the Lord removed the prejudice, and gave me a clearness of sight and love and acceptance with His beloved ones.

The Lord hath many a time refreshed my soul with His presence, and given me an assurance that I knew that state which He will never leave nor suffer me to be drawn from. Though infirmities beset me, my heart cleaveth to the Lord, in the everlasting bond that cannot be broken. Whilst I see and feel these infirmities, I also feel that faith in Him which gives the victory, and keeps me low under a sense of my own weakness. By that grace which is sufficient, I feel and know where my strength lieth; so that when I have slipped in word or thought, I have recourse to my Advocate, and feel pardon and healing, and a going on to overcome in watching against that which easily besets me. I do believe the enemy cannot prevail, though he is suffered to prove me, that I may have my dependence fixed on the Lord; and be kept on the watch continually, knowing that the Lord alone can make successful war against the dragon. I am thus instructed, by the discovery of my own weaknesses, to be tender towards those who also are tempted, and taught to watch and pray against temptation. Sweet is this state, though low; for in it I receive my daily bread, and enjoy that which the Lord handeth forth continually."

CHAPTER III.

1658–1661.

The Ellwoods' visit to the Peningtons at Chalfont.—Their impressions of their Quaker friends.—James Nayler and Edward Burrough at the Grange.—Discussion on the doctrine of election.—Isaac Penington's account of his early religious feelings and views.—His later spiritual experience.—Letters to his father, the Alderman.—Alderman Penington's impeachment as a regicide.—Charles the Second's declaration from Breda.—Alderman Penington's condemnation.—Imprisonment in the Tower and confiscation of his estates.—Sir John Robinson's cruelty.—Alderman Penington's death.

MARY PENINGTON'S narrative brought us in the last chapter to the point from which we first started—1658—four years after her marriage with Isaac Penington. Their family at that time consisted of three other children besides Gulielma Maria Springett, then in the fifteenth year of her age, a lovely, graceful girl, the delight of her family and friends.

Thomas Ellwood gives us a peep into the home of the Peningtons at this period, through his graphic description of the first visit he and others of his father's family paid them, after they had settled at Chalfont. The Ellwoods had made the acquaintance of Lady Springett and her daughter in London, several years before her marriage with Isaac Penington. Thomas Ellwood, who was a few years older than Guli, speaks of having been her playfellow in former times, and of having been often drawn with her in her little coach through Lincoln's-inn Fields by Lady Springett's footman. Ultimately the family left London, and settled at Crowell in Oxfordshire, on the Ellwood estate. Hearing that the Peningtons had moved to Chalfont, the Ellwoods, father and son, went to visit them; and the latter in his autobiography speaks of the occasion as follows:—

"I mentioned before, that during my father's abode in London, in the time of the civil wars, he contracted a friendship with the Lady Springett, then a widow, and afterwards married to Isaac Penington, Esq. To continue the acquaintance, he sometimes visited them at their country residence at Datchet, and also at Causham Lodge, near Reading. Having heard that they were come to live on their own estate at Chalfont in Buckinghamshire, about fifteen miles from Crowell, he went one day to visit them there and to return at night, taking me with him; but very much surprised we were when, being come thither, we first heard, then found, they were become Quakers—a people we had no knowledge of, and a name we had till then scarcely heard of. So great a change from a free, debonair, and courtly sort of behaviour, which we formerly had found them in, to so strict a gravity as they now received us with, did not a little amuse, and disappoint our expectation of such a pleasant visit as we used to have, and had now promised ourselves. Nor could my father have any opportunity, by a private conference with them, to understand the ground or occasion of this change, there being some other strangers with them, related to Isaac Penington, who came that morning from London to visit them also.

"For my part I sought, and at length found means to cast myself into the company of the daughter, whom I found gathering flowers in the garden, attended by her maid, who was also a Quaker. But when I addressed myself to her after my accustomed manner, with intentions to engage her in some discourse which might introduce conversation, on the ground of our former acquaintance, though she treated me with a courteous mien, yet, young as she was, the gravity of her look and behaviour struck such an awe over me, that I was not so much master of myself as to pursue any further converse with her. Wherefore, asking pardon for my boldness in having intruded into her private walks, I withdrew, not without some disorder of mind.

"We stayed dinner, which was very handsome, and lacked nothing to recommend it but the want of mirth and pleasant discourse, which we could neither have with them, nor, by reason of them, with one another amongst ourselves; the weightiness that was upon their spirits and countenances keeping down the lightness that would have been up in us. We stayed, notwithstanding, till the rest of the company had taken leave of them, and then we, also doing the same, returned, not greatly satisfied with our journey, nor knowing what in particular to find fault with.

"Some time after this, my father, having gotten some further account of the people called Quakers, and being desirous to be informed concerning their principles, made another visit to Isaac Penington and his wife at the Grange, in St. Peter's Chalfont, and took both my sisters and me with him. It was in the Tenth-month, in the year 1659, that we went thither on that occasion. We found a very kind reception, and tarried some days, at least one day the longer, because while we were there, a meeting was appointed at a place about a mile from thence, to which we were invited to go, and willingly went. It was held in a farm house, called the Grove, which having formerly been a gentleman's seat, had a very large hall, and that was well filled. To this meeting came Edward Burrough, beside other preachers, as Thomas Curtis and James Nayler; but none spake at that time but Edward Burrough, next to whom, as it were under him, it was my lot to sit, on a stool by the side of a long table on which he sat, and I drank in his words with desire, for they not only answered my understanding, but warmed my heart with a certain heat which

I had not till then felt from the ministry of any man.

When the meeting was ended, our friends took us home with them again; and after supper, the evenings being long, the servants of the family who were Quakers, were called in and we all sat down in silence. But long we had not so sat before Edward Burrough began to speak, and though he spake not long, yet what he said did touch, as I suppose, my father's copyhold, as the phrase is. He, having been from his youth a professor, though not joined in what is called close communion with any one sort, and valuing himself upon the knowledge he esteemed himself to have respecting the various notions of each profession, thought he had now a fair opportunity to display his knowledge; and thereupon began to make objections against what had been delivered. The subject of the discourse was, 'The universal free grace of God to all mankind.' To this he opposed the Calvinistic tenet of particular and personal predestination; in defence of which indefensible notion he found himself more at a loss than he expected. Edward Burrough said not much to him upon it, though what he said was close and cogent. But James Nayler interposing, handled the subject with so much perspicuity and clear demonstration, that his reasoning seemed to be irresistible; and so I suppose my father found it, which made him willing to drop the discourse.

As for Edward Burrough, he was a brisk young man, of a ready tongue, and might have been, for aught I then knew, a scholar; but what James Nayler said had with me the greater force, because he looked like a plain, simple countryman, having the appearance of a husbandman or shepherd. As my father was not able to maintain the argument on his side, so neither did they seem willing to drive it on to an extremity on their side; but, treating him in a soft and gentle manner, did after a while let fall the discourse, and then we withdrew to our respective chambers.

"The next morning we prepared to return home (that is my father, my younger sister, and myself; for my elder sister was gone before by the stage-coach to London), when, having taken leave of our friends, we went forth, they with Edward Burrough accompanied us to the gate, where he directed his speech in a few words to each of us severally, according to the sense he had of our several conditions. When we were gone off, and they gone in again, they asked him what he thought of us; he answered them, as they afterwards told me, to this effect:—"As for the old man he is settled on his lees, and the young woman is light and airy; but the young man is reached, and may do well if he does not lose it."

Isaac Penington's religious experience and his religious conclusions, before his settlement at Chal-

font, are unfolded by his own words. He says:—
"My heart from my childhood was pointed towards the Lord, whom I feared and longed after from my tender years. I felt that I could not be satisfied with, nor indeed seek after the things of this perishing world, but I desired a true sense of, and unity with, that which abideth for ever. There was something still within me which leavened and balanced my spirit almost continually; but I knew it not distinctly so as to turn to it, and give up to it entirely and understandingly. In this temper of mind I earnestly sought after the Lord, applying myself to hear sermons, and read the best books I could meet with, but especially the Scriptures, which were very sweet and savoury to me. Yea, I very earnestly desired and pressed after the knowledge of the Scriptures, but was much afraid of receiving men's interpretations of them, or of fastening any interpretations upon them myself; but waited much, and prayed much, that from the Spirit of the Lord I might receive the true understanding of them, and that He would endue me with that knowledge which I might feel to be sanctifying and saving.

"And indeed I did sensibly receive of His love, of His mercy, and of His grace, and at seasons when I was most filled with the sense of my own unworthiness, and had least expectation of the manifestations of them. But I became exceedingly entangled about election and reprobation; having drunk in that doctrine according as it was then held forth by the strictest of those that were termed Puritans, fearing lest, notwithstanding all my desires and seeking after the Lord, He might in His decree have passed by me. I felt it would be bitter to me to bear His wrath, and be separated from His love for evermore; yet if He had so decreed, it would be, and I should, notwithstanding fair beginnings and hopes, fall away, and perish at last."

Under the gloom of that awful perversion of Christ's gospel to man, Isaac Penington's sensitive mind suffered fearfully for years. Gleams of hope and spiritual brightness at times shone through the clouds, and brought some comfort to his mind; but no settled peace, no full abiding sense of his Heavenly Father's loving care kept possession of his soul, so long as an apprehension of the truth of that God-dishonouring doctrine continued to find any place in his mind.* But at length the time arrived when the triumph of Christian truth drove hence that baneful error, which, under one phase or another, had tended in Penington's mind to destroy a right sense of the supreme justice, love, and mercy

---

* I have again and again thought over the appellation of *God-dishonouring doctrine*, as given above, to the doctrine of Unconditional Election and Reprobation, to try if I might not soften it, seeing that it is believed in by many who would be shocked at the thought of entertaining any opinions that are dishonouring to God. But my conviction is so strong of this being its true character, that I cannot think it right to make any alteration which would lessen the force or fullness of the expression.

of the Lord. They who were made instrumental in bringing about this happy change were not among the learned theologians of that day, but belonged to the Christian body before alluded to, and which in an especial manner rejected the systematic theology taught by the professors of the popular divinity. He describes the result of his intercourse with the Quakers as follows:—

"At first acquaintance with this people that which was of God in me opened, and I did immediately in my spirit own them as children of my Father, truly begotten of His life by His own spirit. But the wise reasoning part presently rose up, contending against their uncouth way, for which I did disown them, and continued a stranger to them, and a reasoner against them, for about twelve months. By weighing and considering things in that way, I was still further and further off from discerning their leadings by the Spirit of God into those things. But at length it pleased the Lord to draw out His sword against that part in me, turning the wisdom and strength thereof backward; and again to open that eye in me wherewith He had given me to see the things of His kingdom in some measure from a child. And then I saw and felt them grown in that Life and spirit which I, through the treachery of the fleshly-wise part, had been estranged from. And now, what bitter days of mourning I have had over this, the Lord alone fully knows. Oh! I have known it indeed to be a bitter thing to follow this wisdom as that which could make me truly to understand the Scriptures. The Lord hath judged me for it, and I have borne a burden and condemnation for that which many at this day wear as their crown."

In another place he speaks of having "now at length met with the true way, and walked with the Lord therein, wherein daily certainty, yea, full assurance of faith and of understanding, is obtained." " Blessed be the Lord ? there are many at this day who can truly and faithfully witness that they have been brought by the Lord to this state. We have thus learned of Him not by the high, striving, aspiring mind, but by lying low, and being contented with a little ; if but a crumb of bread, yet bread ; if but a drop of water, yet water. And we have been contented with it, and thankful to the Lord for it. Nor was it by thoughtfulness and wise searching, or deep considering with our own wisdom and reason that we obtained this; but in the still, meek, and humble waiting have we found it."

There was in Isaac Penington's religious experience much spiritual feeling; and occasionally we find in his writings an amount of figurative expression which has sometimes been called mysticism. Whether it has a right to be so called, or not, depends on the meaning we attach to the word. If by mysticism in religion, we only mean an earnest longing after, and very high enjoyment of inward spiritual communion with God, and, in writing, frequent allusions to such spiritual experience, mingled with figurative phrases, we need not demur to its application to Penington. But if, as is more commonly understood, we mean by religious mysticism an ecstatic state of feeling, leading into what is unpractical and mysterious, instead of a calming influence that acts on the conscience and regulates the whole moral life, Penington was no mystic. That mysticism which looks at Bible history and Gospel teaching through a haze that resolves them into fanciful types and figures, dissipating the simple truth and the obvious meaning of Holy Scripture, could not correspond in any degree with Penington's religion. He, though contemplative and retiring, was a true practical Christian. In common with the early Friends, he avoided using terms which had originated in the dogmatic theology. With them he wished to keep to Scripture language, and to avoid artificial terms which were liable to unscriptural constructions.

It will be observed that he regarded that which is now called Calvinism as having led his mind into serious error, and away from the reverential caution of his earlier days. It is in relation to its teachings that he says, " I have known it, indeed, to be a bitter thing to follow this wisdom as that which could make me truly to understand the Scriptures." In some other instances he uses still stronger language, when describing the mental suffering and perplexities which had resulted from his having been influenced by such doctrine, instead of seeking and waiting reverentially and trustingly for the enlightening influence of the Holy Spirit. This he afterwards found to make clear whatever was necessary to be cleared, in order to "God's will being truly made known to the heart—savingly, livingly, powerfully."

The unsatisfied feeling with regard to spiritual communion with God, which for so many years was endured both by Isaac Penington and his wife, does not appear to have arisen out of, or to have been accompanied by, a sense of unforgiven sin. Circumstances indicate that in both cases the Lord was leaving them to pass through necessary experiences, until that degree of insight was acquired which prepared them to fill their allotted positions in the church. Isaac Penington became an eminent preacher of the Gospel among the Friends, and also an indefatigable writer. He was ever ready to put forth his literary powers and gentle persuasive influence, in defence of that spiritual religion and gospel Truth which had brought so much comfort to his own soul. Mary Penington seems to have been in an especial manner fitted to be a true helpmate to him; her practical business capacity supplying what was less active in him. Unitedly they went forward with abiding trust in their Heavenly Father's love and care, their spiritual life being made strong in the Lord. To the inquiry, years after he had joined the Friends, if he were yet truly satisfied with the spiritual privileges he enjoyed, Isaac Penington replied, " Yes, indeed; I am satisfied at the very heart. Truly my heart is now united to Him whom I longed after, in an everlasting covenant of pure life and peace."

Of the early Puritans he retained a high appreciation and affectionate remembrance; but he regarded them as having eventually missed their way in some religious matters of great importance to spiritual life. He says, "There was among them great sincerity, and love, and tenderness, and unity in that which was true; minding the work of God in themselves, and being sensible of grace and truth in one another's hearts, before there was such a rent among them." " By degrees forms and different ways of worship grew among them, and the virtue and power of godliness decreased, and they were swallowed up in high esteem of, and contending each sort for their own forms, whilst themselves had lost a sense of what they were inwardly to God, and what they had inwardly received from God in the days of their former zeal and tenderness. Oh! that they could see this. Oh! that they could return to their early Puritan state, to the love and tenderness that was then in them. May the Lord open again the true spiritual eye in them, and give them to see therewith!"

When Isaac Penington had anchored on what he felt to be gospel Truth, he was indefatigable in his efforts to draw others into that state which had brought him so much consolation and clearness of spiritual vision. Especially dreading that teaching which did not dwell on or lead to a consciousness of the absolute necessity of the purification of the heart and conduct, he became very close and earnest in pressing home the worthlessness of *religious belief* which did not bring forth *holiness of life*. Many of his letters addressed to acquaintances under these feelings are still extant. Some of them were to persons now quite unknown, and various others to his own relations. Those letters to his father which have been preserved are remarkable productions. They seem to have followed each other uninterruptedly, but only two of them have dates, and these belong to 1658, the year in which Isaac Penington and his wife fully joined the Friends. I shall place those which I select in the order of time, as nearly as this can be ascertained from internal evidence. The manuscripts from which I have copied these letters are preserved in the Friends' Library, Devonshire House, London. Believing that if given in full they would be found tedious by the general reader, I have avoided the repetitions and omitted some paragraphs. Their character and tone of deep feeling will, I trust, be appreciated from the following copious extracts:—

No. I.—*Isaac Penington to his father, Alderman Penington, on the religion of the latter.*

"Ah, dear father, how strong and tender my affections have been to thee from my childhood, and how they have grown upon me of late years, the Lord knows and will in due time make manifest. My breathings have been strong after thy soul, my sorrow great concerning it, my prayer constant and very vehement for thee. Indeed there was somewhat in my heart which still caused me to fear concerning thy religion, through its beginning and its growth, of its not being what thou took it to be, nor able to effect in the end what thou expectest from it. Now let my love speak freely, and be not offended, for the Lord knows I would not speak one word to grieve or trouble thee, were there not an exceeding great cause."

"Thy religion began in the wrong part; thy fear was raised, and thy affection stirred, so thou didst bend thyself to seek after God to avoid the wrath thou wast afraid of. By this means thou fell in with that religion which was obvious to thee, and hast taken up duties and practices which the understanding and affections have drawn into. Here thou hast raised up a building, and here lies thy life and thy hope; thy confidence arises but from the temper of the natural part in thyself."

"Now, dear father, what hath thy religion effected? Is thy soul redeemed from sin? Art not thou a captive to this day to many lusts? If thou knewest that power wherein is the lawful strife against sin, thy bonds would be broken. But striving against sin in the part wherein sin's strength lies can never bring victory. But oh! dear father, there is power in the death of Christ; power to bridle the tongue and the passions; power to bridle prejudices; yea, and to cut down that in which these things stand. If thou knewest the Truth of Christ, the living Truth, which the Apostles knew and preached, thou wouldst say by experience, this is able to make free from sin, for it takes possession of the heart where sin's throne is; it is stronger than sin, and its strength would appear if it were but hearkened to and turned to.

"Oh! that thou knewest that Egypt, that Sodom, that Babylon which the Lord calls out of, and that Canaan, that Sion, that Jerusalem which He calls to, that thou mightest set thy face thitherward; for thy soul must leave the one, and come to the other, or thou wilt miss what thou hopest for in the end. Therefore [seek] to know the Word in thy heart, to know the living Christ, to know the voice of the living God; to know that which smites thee in secret; and let not the wound be healed slightly. Let not the deceiver cry, 'Peace! peace!' where there is no peace;' but know the destruction of that wicked one in thee to whom God will never be reconciled. And do not hearken to teachers who teach in the wisdom which is out of the life, which is in the fallen understanding; for in that state they themselves cannot but perish, and their doctrine is not able to save any. Therefore, dear father, seek the true Teacher, which is He that smiteth in secret. Oh! how often hath He knocked at the door of thy heart: do at length let Him in. He comes with the true knowledge, with true life, with true power. Do not thrust Him away, but make peace with Him; give up His enemy to Him; let Him beat down the high and lofty one, and raise up the poor, the meek, even that of God in thee which is in captivity. Let not thy talent lie hid in the napkin, or thou wilt not be able to answer for it to God."

"I remain thy dearly loving son, filled with grief and sorrow for thy soul.

"J. P."

No. II.—*Isaac Penington to his father, Alderman Penington, on gospel ministry.*

" Dear Father,

"The gospel is the power of God unto salvation; it is the glad tidings of freedom from sin, and of the baptism of the Spirit, that we may serve God in holiness and righteousness all the days of our life. The ministers of the gospel are those who in the spirit of Christ, by the gift and inspiration thereof, preach these tidings to the poor and needy, to the captives, to those that groan under the pressure of the body of corruption.

"This gospel, through the great mercy of God, I have at length heard preached. Though thou, through prejudice, calls this speaking of the Spirit through servants and handmaids, *prating*, yet the Lord can forgive thee; for surely if thou knew what thou didst herein, thou wouldst not thus offend the Lord—extolling preaching by man's wisdom, from a minister made by man, for gospel preaching; and condemning the preaching of persons sent by God under the immediate inspiration of his Spirit.

"As for those whom thou callest ministers, if I were to speak concerning them the very truth from the Lord, thou couldst not receive it; yet I am far from accounting them the 'off-scouring of the earth;' for I look upon them as wise and knowing, and as of great beauty in earthly learning and wisdom; but surely not as having 'the tongue of the learned,' in the gospel sense, 'to speak a word in season to him that is weary.' [Yet they abundantly examine] the Scriptures, and toss them about, and wrest them in their uncertain reasonings and guessings concerning the sense, and in the various doubtful interpretations they give.

"And whereas I am blamed for not putting a difference between the profane and scandalous ministers and the reverend and godly sort, my answer is: they are united in one form of ministry. The question is not concerning the persons, but the ministry, in which they are one, and their standing and power of government one, which is not by the power and presence of the Spirit, but by the strength of the magistrate. The true gospel ministry is spiritual, and cannot be upheld by that which is carnal in its call, its maintenance, or its government. When Christ came in the flesh, the severe words He pronounced were not so much against the profane and scandalous among the Scribes and Pharisees, as against those that appeared most strict, and were accounted among the Jews the most reverend and godly. And were it not for the appearance of godliness in these men, the persecution of the present times had not been so hot, and the good old work of reformation so much overturned as it is at this day."

No. III.—*Isaac Penington to his father, Alderman Penington, combating the accusations of the latter against "The Friends of Truth."*

"Ah, dear father, why dost thou so often give me occasion of mourning before the Lord, because of hard and unrighteous charges from thee. How often have I solemnly professed that there never was any desire in me, nor endeavours used by me, to draw my father to this way [the Friends' way] which my father will not equally consider, but will have his own apprehension go for granted! All the desire that is in my soul is this, that my father might have the true knowledge of Christ, and not set up another thing instead of it; that he might indeed hear His sayings, and do them, and not set up his own or other men's fancies and invented meanings instead of the sayings of Christ. Now, though I am not for ways, or opinions, but only for Christ, the living power of God felt in the heart, yet because my father stumbleth at these things, I cannot but say somewhat more. My father lays down three reasons why he cannot believe this way to be of God, viz. :—

"1st. '*God's way is a way of love, peace, and unity.*'

"*Answer.*—If my father had that eye opened that can see the things of God, and did apply himself to look therewith, he might see that peace, that love, that unity among this people which other men do but talk of; but if he takes things by the report of the enemies both to God and them, he shall be sure to hear and believe bad enough. They have no war with any thing but unrighteousness; and with that they cannot have peace, no, not though it be in their dearest relations. They love the souls of their enemies, and think no pains or hazard too great for the saving of them. Being persecuted, they bless; being reviled, they entreat and pray for their persecutors. They are at unity with whatever is of God; but with the seed of the serpent they cannot be at unity; for they freely witness against the generation of vipers in this present age, under their several painted coverings, as Christ and his Apostles did against the Scribes and Pharisees. The spirit of the Scribes and Pharisees is now in the world; and the Spirit of Christ and His apostles is also in the world, and they cannot but fight, each with its proper weapons: the one with stocks, whips, fines, prisons, etc., the other with the spiritual armour of Christ. Thus the one wrestles with flesh and blood, fights with the creature, hurts that: the other loves the creature, seeks the saving of it, and fights only against the power of darkness which rules the creature."

" 2nd. *God's way is a way of humility.*'

" *Answer.*—If they had not been broken and humbled by God, they could never have been entered into this way, which the lofty fleshly part abhors. Nor is this a voluntary humility; but a true Christian humility, which crosseth and breaketh the will [that is opposed to God] all the day long."

" 3rd. *That God is a God of order, not of confusion.*'

" *Answer.*—Blessed be the Lord, who hath recovered for us some of the true church's order, and delivered out of the confusion of Antichrist. We know that order which is of the Spirit of Christ; but that which man in his wisdom calls order is but Antichrist's order. To have man's spirit speak, and God's Spirit stopt, is the order of all the Antichristian churches and congregations. But to have man's spirit stopt and God's Spirit speak is the order of Christ's church, and this order we know and rejoice in."

" The last part of the letter consists of very harsh and unrighteous charges, mixed with bitter expressions which I pass over, appealing to God who is able to clear me. Only I confess it is somewhat hard to *one part of me*, that my own father should deal thus with me."

" About not having comfort in me, and wishing me more comfort in *my* son, I must needs say this —If that eye were opened which could see the work of God in and upon me, this might afford comfort; and if the Lord ever vouchsafe to give me such a cause of comfort in any of my children, it will be the joy of my soul. If I were in any *formal* way of religion, I might be a comfort to my father, for he could at least bear with that; but because the Lord hath seized upon my heart by the power of His Truth, and I can bow to none but Him,—no, not to my most dear father—now I am no comfort.

" 14th of Twelfth Month, 1658."

From the above letters it will be evident how diametrically different were the religious views and feelings of the father and son. Two other letters also exist from the latter to the former; but to enter into their details would rather fatigue than edify most of my readers. One of them is very long, and from the tenor of both it seems that the Alderman had continued to speak disparagingly, even fiercely, of the Friends and of his son's religion and had proceeded to show how much of Holy Scripture he could cite in behalf of the religious views which he himself relied on as sustained by gospel Truth. Isaac Penington makes very plain remarks to his father on his religion, as not producing the fruits of righteousness—such remarks as no proud or self-satisfied spirit could patiently bear, and then he takes up each of the texts referred to, and gives that exposition which he thinks the true one. With the following words he enters on the consideration of the texts in his fourth letter: " My father in his letter mentioneth many Scriptures which raise his confidence. It is upon my heart to consider of them in dear love to my father's soul."

The texts alluded to by Alderman Penington are as follows :—Luke, xix. 10; John, i. 12; John, iii. 16, 17; Rom. viii. 30; Rom. x. 4; 1 Cor. i. 30; 2 Cor. v. 19, 21; Gal. iv. 4, 5, 6; Eph. ii. 13, 14, 16; Col. i. 21, 22; 1 Tim. i. 15; Tit. ii. 14; Heb. i. 3; 1 John, i. 7; 1 John, ii. 1, 2, 5; Rev. i. 5. 6.

No one can doubt the earnest, loving, truthful feelings which induced Isaac Penington to write the letters in question to his father; though some may doubt the probability of such letters producing conviction under the circumstances, whilst others will question the correctness of Isaac Penington's assertion in the first letter, that his father's religion "began in the wrong part." Doubtless it began very differently to what his did. His did not begin in fear of divine wrath, but in longing after purity of heart. But the first spiritual awakening and early religious convictions of various minds begin so variously, that it does not seem to be for any one to speak dogmatically as to where or how they must begin.

But we are certainly warranted in judging the tree by its fruits, and judging the genuineness of religion by its results. Our Lord has expressly directed our attention to the test, *men do not gather grapes of thorns, or figs of thistles.* Any one who is living under the influence of the Holy Spirit must in life and conduct be governed by truth.

It is quite evident that the dominion of the Spirit of Truth, and the absolute truthfulness which accompanied that dominion in the hearts and lives of Isaac Penington and his wife, suffered no compromise in judging their own conduct or that of another, whether that other was father, friend or enemy. To speak to his father with the plainness which marks his expressions in these letters, must have been to such a nature as Isaac Penington's a great difficulty. But, being among those whom Jesus had "sanctified through the Truth," he was ready to sacrifice all that he believed it called for. A writer of eminence in our own days truly expresses, in the following declaration, what such sacrifices involves:—

"The sacrifice which God requires from us first and foremost is the sacrifice to Truth. Not to authority, not to freedom, not to popularity, not to fear, but to Truth. It is no doubt a hard sacrifice which is thus required. Long inveterate custom, cherished phrases bound up with some of our best affections, the indolent respect of persons, or acquiescence in common usage—these are what Truth again and again compels us to surrender. But this is precisely the sacrifice which God demands from us at His altar, this is precisely the sacrifice which in our solemn act of self-dedication we declare that we are ready to offer—'that we will always prefer Truth to custom;' that we will give to Truth not the second or the third, but the first place; that antiquity, novelty, prejudice, fashion must give way before the claims of Truth, wherever it be found. Dear no doubt is tradition; dear is the long familiar recollection; dear and most sacred in its own place and measure is venerable antiquity on the one hand, or bold originality on the other; but dearer than any of these, dearer and higher in human things, dearer and higher yet in things divine, is Truth; the duty of seeking and speaking the Truth in love, in the unshaken faith that Truth is great and will in the end prevail. And may He whose name is Truth be with our humblest efforts to teach the Truth, and honour the Truth everywhere!"

The latest date in any of Isaac Penington's letters to his father is in the last month of 1658. An event was then approaching in the nation's history which must have claimed the utmost attention and interest of Alderman Penington. Whether amid that anxiety the correspondence between him and his eldest son extended any further, or was ever renewed, it is now impossible to ascertain.

When Richard Cromwell had proved himself unequal to the task of holding the reins of government which had been placed in his hands, one popular change succeeded another without any consolidation of central authority. Most of those who had sat as the late king's judges could read in the signs of the times the probable restoration of the Stuart dynasty. That thought brought more terror to many hearts than they were inclined to manifest. At length the crisis came, and on the first day of May, 1660, the famous declaration of Charles the Second from Breda was presented by his commissioner to both Houses of Parliament; and also to the city authorities, and through them to the nation. The royal promise of indemnity which it contained raised for a few days the drooping hopes of those who had most to fear. Thus the indemnity clause announced:—" We do by these presents declare that we do grant a free and general pardon, which we are ready on demand to pass under our great seal of England to all our subjects whatever, who within forty days after the publishing hereof shall lay hold on this our grace and favour, and shall by any public act declare their doing so, and that they return to the loyalty and obedience of good subjects; excepting only such persons as shall hereafter be excepted by parliament—those only to be excepted. Let all our subjects, how faulty soever, rely upon the word of a king solemnly given by this present declaration, that no crime whatsoever committed against us, or our royal father, before the publication of this, shall ever rise in judgment, or be brought in question against any of them, to the least endamagement of them either in their lives, liberties, or estates, (as far as lies in our power) or so much as the prejudice of their reputations."

Of the original members of the Parliamentary High Court of Justice, which condemned the late King, forty-eight were still living; and nineteen of these, relying upon *the word of a king* so solemnly set forth, delivered themselves up as accepting pardon and promising allegiance to Charles the Second. Of the remaining twenty-nine, who could not rely on the royal promise as sufficient to ensure pardon, a few secreted themselves in England —the others immediately went abroad. Alderman Penington was one of the nineteen who, relying on the word of the King, came in before the expiration of the forty days. On the 8th of

May the two Houses of Parliament proclaimed Charles the Second, King of England, Scotland, and Ireland, and on the twenty-fifth he arrived at Dover.

Before the arrival of the King, the Parliament, anxious to prove to him its great loyalty, decided that all they who had sat as his father's judges should be imprisoned and brought to trial; and also every one who in an official capacity had had anything to do with his accusation or execution. About three months after the kingdom was restored to Charles, twenty-nine persons were brought to trial, and condemned to death as regicides. Included in the twenty-nine were the nineteen trusting ones who had given themselves up on his declaration of indemnity. Of the nineteen, fourteen were respited from death, the punishment being changed to imprisonment for life, and all their property and estates were confiscated. Ten, among whom were six who had signed the king's death-warrant, and four officials, were condemned to death, and suffered execution.

Alderman Penington, with the thirteen others, was committed as a prisoner to that Tower over which he once ruled as an honourable and executive governor; but his durance there was cut short by hard usage. Sir John Robinson, Lieutenant of the Tower, was devoid of humanity and of principle; and the treatment to which he subjected the prisoners was consistent with his character. Lucy

Hutchinson, in the memoirs of her husband, Colonel Hutchinson, says:—" The gentlemen who were the late king's judges, and who were decoyed to surrender themselves to custody by the Houses' proclamation, were kept in miserable bondage under that inhuman, bloody jailer, the Lieutenant of the Tower, who stifled some of them to death for want of air; and, when they had not one penny but what was given them to support their families (all their estates being confiscated), exacted from them rates for bare unfurnished prison rooms; of some, forty pounds for one miserable chamber; of others, double; beside unjust fees, for to raise which their poor wives were obliged to engage their jointures, or make other miserable shifts. And yet this rogue had all this while three pounds a week paid out of the Exchequer for every one of them." This unscrupulous man, Sir John Robinson, will come under our notice again.

It was in October that the regicides were condemned and their estates confiscated. In the State Papers belonging to that period, which have recently been published, I find this entry, "December 7th, 1660: Petition of George, Bishop of Worcester, to the King, for the grant of a lease of tenements in Whitefriars belonging to the bishopric, value eighty pounds a year, forfeited by Isaac Penington, late Alderman of London." And again, " August 8th, 1661; Grant to George, Bishop of Worcester, of five houses, etc. in Whitefriars, near Fleet-street, lately belonging to Isaac Penington, attainted of treason." In the *Gentleman's Magazine* it is stated that Alderman Penington's estates, among which was the seat of the Sharlows, called The Place, being confiscated, were given by Charles the Second to the Duke of Grafton.

Finally, we have in the State Papers, under the date of " Dec. 19th, 1661; Warrant to Sir John Robinson, Lieutenant of the Tower, to deliver the corpse of Isaac Penington, who died in prison there, to his relations."

Neither record nor relic beyond what has been introduced, have I been able to discover of the condemned alderman, Isaac Penington, except that his silver drinking cup has for many years been in possession of his American descendants. It is now the property of Edward Penington of Philadelphia. It has on it the Tower stamp, the initials I. P., and the date 1642, the year in which he was chosen Lord Mayor of London.

CHAPTER IV.

1642–1661.

Thomas Ellwood's early life.—His second visit to Chalfont.—His convincement.—Joins the Friends—His father's displeasure—The Peningtons' visit to Crowell.—Young Ellwood returns with them to the Grange.—He is arrested for travelling on the first day of the week.—Quaker and Presbyterian views of the Sabbath.—Thomas Ellwood returns to Crowell.—Is imprisoned in Oxford under keeping of the Marshal.—Isaac Penington writes to him from Aylesbury jail, and Thomas Loe from that of Oxford.—Ellwood is released.—Isaac Penington's letter from Aylesbury to his wife.—His trials and difficulties.—Is released from prison.

THE tutor whom Isaac Penington had heretofore employed to teach his three eldest children English, being unable to give them instruction in Latin, another had to be looked for. He who succeeded as teacher at the Grange was Thomas Ellwood, already introduced as the youthful friend of Gulielma Springett; and who with his father, as before related, had visited the Peningtons on their settlement in Buckinghamshire. As he continued to be tutor to the children and an honoured inmate of the family for the seven following years, his personal history during that period is much interwoven with theirs. It becomes an interesting element in the social and religious life at Chalfont, and we must therefore glance at his antecedents.

Ellwood's father was an estated gentleman of honourable descent, whose property and family residence were at Crowell, about three miles eastward from Thame, in Oxfordshire. Thame Park was the abode of Lord Wenman, whom he speaks of as his relative, and a person of great honour and virtue—at whose table he was always received as a welcome guest. Ellwood says, "I have cause to think I should have received from this lord some advantageous preferment, had I not been called into the service of the best and highest Lord, and thereby lost the favour of all my friends, relations, and acquaintances of this world."

Thomas was the youngest of the family, and only about two or three years old when they all removed to London as a place of greater safety, on the commencement of the civil war. It was during the years which intervened before their return, that this amiable boy became the playmate of Lady Springett's lovely little daughter. He tells us, in his interesting fragment of autobiography, that till he was about fifteen years of age his health was so delicate and his stature so small, that fears were entertained lest he should prove a dwarf. But about that time his constitution and physical vigour underwent a change which banished all such fears. From being a small delicately knit, refined lad, he afterwards became a vigorous, middle-sized young man, delighting in athletic sports, but ever averse to what was coarse or vulgar in mind or manners. He relates the following characteristic incident which occurred at that period:—

"My father being in the commission of the peace, and going to a petty sessions at Watlington, I waited on him thither. When we came near the town, the coachman, seeing a nearer and easier way than the common road, through a corn-field, and that it was wide enough for the wheels to run without damaging the corn, turned down there. This being observed by a husbandman who was at plough not far off, he ran to us, and stopping the coach poured forth complaints in none of the best language for driving over the corn. My father mildly answered him, that if there was an offence committed, he must rather impute it to his servant than to himself, since he neither directed him to drive that way, nor knew which way he drove. Yet added, that he was going to such an inn in the town, whither if he came he would make him full satisfaction for whatever damage he had sustained thereby. And so on we went, the man venting his discontent in angry accents as he went back. At the town, upon inquiry, we understood that it was a way very often used without damage, being broad enough; but it was not the common road, which lay not far from it, and was also good enough, wherefore my father bid his man drive home that way.

"It was late in the evening when we returned, and very dark; this quarrelsome man, who had troubled himself and us in the morning, having gotten another lusty fellow like himself to assist him, waylaid us in the night, expecting we should return the way we went. But when they found we did not, but took the common way, angry that they were disappointed, and loath to lose their purpose, they coasted over to us in the dark, and laying hold on the horses' bridles, stopped them from going on. My father, asking the coachman the reason that he went not forward, was answered that there were two men at the horses' heads who held them back. Whereupon my father, opening the boot, stepped out, and I followed close at his heels.

"Going to the place where the men stood, he demanded of them the reason of this assault; they said we were upon the corn. We knew we were not on the corn, but on the common way, and so we told them; but they said they were resolved they would not let us go on any farther, but would make us go back again. My father endeavoured by gentle reasoning to persuade them to forbear, and not run themselves farther into danger of the law; but they rather derided him for it. Seeing therefore fair means would not work upon them, he spoke more roughly, charging them to deliver their clubs (for each of them had a great club in his hand, somewhat like those called quarter-staves); thereupon they, laughing, told him they did not bring them thither for that end. Whereupon my father, turning his head to me, said:—'Tom, disarm them.' I stood ready at his elbow, waiting for the word of command; for, being naturally of a bold spirit, full of youthful heat, and that fully aroused by the sense I had of the abuse and the insolent behaviour of those rude fellows, my blood began to boil, and my fingers itched, as the saying is, to be dealing with them. Wherefore, immediately stepping boldly forward to lay hold on the staff of him that was nearest to me, I said, 'Sirrah, deliver your weapon.' He thereupon raised his club, which was big enough to have knocked down an ox, intending no doubt to knock me down with it, as probably he would have done, had I not, in the twinkling of an eye, whipped out my rapier, and made a pass upon him. I could not have failed running him through up to the hilt had he stood his ground; but the sudden and unexpected sight of my bright blade, glistening in the dark night, did so amaze and terrify the man, that, slipping aside, he avoided my thrust; and, letting his staff sink, betook himself to his heels for safety; which his companion seeing fled also. I followed the former as fast as I could, but fear gave him wings, and made him swiftly fly; for, although I was accounted very nimble, I could not overtake him, which made me think he took shelter in some bushes, which he knew where to find though I did not. Meanwhile the coachman, who had sufficiently the outside of a man, excused himself for not intermeddling, under pretence that he durst not leave his horses, and so left me to shift for myself. I had gone so far beyond my knowledge that I understood not which way to turn, till by hallooing and by being hallooed to again I was directed where to find my company.

"We had easy means to find who these men were, the principal of them having been at the inn during the day-time, and both quarreled with the coachman and threatened to be even with him when he went back; but since they came off so badly in their attempt, my father thought it better not to know them than to oblige himself to prosecute them.

"At that time, and for a good while after, I had no regret upon my mind for what I had done, or had designed to do, in this case; but went on resolved to kill, if I could, any man that should make the like attempt, or put any affront upon us; and for that reason I seldom went afterwards upon those public services without a loaded pistol in my pocket. But when it pleased the Lord in His infinite goodness to call me out of the spirit and ways of the world, and give me the knowledge of His saving Truth, whereby the actions of my forepast life were set in order before me, a sort of horror seized upon me when I had considered how near I had been to staining my hands with human blood. And whensoever afterwards I went that way, and indeed as often since as the matter has come into my remembrance, my soul has blessed the Lord for my deliverance; and thanksgiving and praises have arisen in my heart, as they do now, to Him who preserved and withheld me from shedding man's blood.

"About this time my dear and honoured mother, who was indeed a woman of singular worth and virtue, departed this life; having a little time before heard of the death of her eldest son, who had fallen under the displeasure of my father, for refusing to resign his interest in an estate which my father sold. Thereupon my brother desired that he might have leave to travel, in hopes that time and absence might work reconciliation. He went into Ireland with a person powerful there in those times, by whose means he was quickly preferred to a place of trust and profit, but lived not long to enjoy it."

All the circumstances above related had taken place before Thomas Ellwood's first visit to the Peningtons at the Chalfont Grange. About a year elapsed between the first and the second visit of the Ellwoods, when the addresses of Edward Burrough and James Nayler made so deep an impression on Thomas's mind. That impression did not wear off on his return home; but it determined him to see more of the Friends. He says, "I had a desire to go to another meeting of the Quakers; and bid my father's man to inquire if there were any in the country thereabouts. He told me he had heard at Isaac Penington's that there was to be a meeting at High Wycombe on Thursday next. Thither therefore I went, though it was seven miles from me. And that I might be rather thought to go out a-coursing than to a meeting, I let my greyhound run by my horse's side." That meeting and what he heard there, he tells us acted like the clinching of a nail, confirming and fixing the good principles that had before sunk so deeply. Light burst in upon his mind, letting him see his inward state and condition towards God. His whole desires, feelings, and trains of religious thought in the succeeding weeks underwent a change. He observes:—"Now I saw that, although I had been in a great degree preserved from the common immoralities and gross pollutions of the world, yet the spirit of the world had hitherto ruled in me, and had led me into pride, flattery, vanity, and superfluity. I found there were many plants growing in me which were not of the Heavenly Father's planting; and that all of these, of whatsoever kind or sort they were, or how specious soever they might appear, must be plucked up."

The new spiritual birth and awakened perceptions that now arose in his soul brought with them both comfort, and true earnestness of desire to be conformed to the will of God in all things. Conflicts and trials succeeded, but strength was given adequate to the necessity on every occasion. An enlightened conscience, pointing in the gospel to the words of the Lord Jesus Himself, made it clear to him that the Friends were right in maintaining that the follower of Christ must live a life of truthfulness—must make it the great object of his life to be true to God, true to his fellow-man, and true to the convictions of his own conscience in all things; that God required from His children and would help them to maintain truth in heart, in word, and in deed; and that no one who is not governed by the Spirit of Truth and truthfulness, is pleasing God and serving Him aright. Then came the pinch in the application of this strict truthfulness to the current manners, popular language, and complimentary titles which prevailed in the world. The Friends had taken a decided stand against whatever they deemed untruthful in each of these, and young Ellwood, after examining every point, believed in his heart that the stand they had made was a right one; and thus believing, he acted upon it. So also he united with their views in giving up those things that he regarded as springing from a degree of human pride and vanity that should not be countenanced. Expensive personal decoration was discarded; gold rings, gold lace, and all such ornaments were cast off, and in language and manners the Quaker mode of using no merely complimentary titles was adopted by him.

The ceremonious uncovering of the head and bowing of the knee were seriously regarded by the Friends as marks of veneration that should not be offered to any mortal, but should be considered as due to God alone, and observed in prayerful approaches to Him. We cannot wonder that, viewing these observances in this light, no earthly consideration could induce them to comply with the fashionable usages. In these respects, also, Ellwood united with and adopted the principles and practice of the Quakers. He thus describes meeting with some of his former acquaintances after he had made that change, on an occasion when sent by his father to Oxford, with a message to his brother magistrates who sat on the bench during the sessions :—

"I went directly to the hall where the sessions were held, and had been but a very little while there before a knot of my old acquaintances espying me, came to me. One of these was a scholar in his gown, another a surgeon of that city (Oxford), both my schoolfellows and fellow-boarders at Thame school, and the third a country gentleman with whom I had long been very familiar. When they were come up to me, they all saluted me after the usual manner, putting off their hats and bowing, saying 'Your humble servant, sir,' expecting, no doubt, in return the same from me. But when they saw me stand still, not moving my cap nor bowing my knee in a way of congee to them they were amazed, and looked first one upon another, then upon me, and then one upon another again for a while, without a word speaking. At length the surgeon, a brisk young man, who stood nearest to me, clapping his hand in a familiar way upon my shoulder, and smiling on me said, 'What Tom! a Quaker?' to which I readily and cheerfully answered, 'Yes, a Quaker.' And as the words passed out of my mouth, I felt joy springing in my heart; for I rejoiced that I had not been drawn out by them into any compliance; and that I had strength and boldness given me to confess myself to be one of that despised people."

In that age men when dressed generally wore their hats in the house as well as out of doors, only removing them on occasions of ceremony. Young Ellwood had not only hats and caps taken from him, one after another, till all he possessed were gone, but also every means of procuring others. To this his father had recourse in order to put it out of his power ever to appear covered in his presence—when he found that other and most cruel treatment which he had recourse to was unavailing. But do or say what he would to his son, he found him immoveable in this, though he still acted towards him with filial deference in every thing, but what appeared to him as encroaching on the honour due to God. The courage manifested in his earlier days in disarming the ruffian who attacked his father's carriage, was not now exercised in defending himself; that would have been impossible, without exasperating one whom he most gladly would, if in conscience he could, have appeased. All his courage was now exercised in patient endurance of personal abuse from his father, having entered the service, and under the teaching of Him who, "when he was reviled, reviled not again."

Several months followed without in any degree reconciling the father to the changes that had taken place in the son, when to the joy of the latter their friends from Chalfont came to pay them a visit at Crowell; which Ellwood speaks of thus:—

"At length it pleased the Lord to move Isaac Penington and his wife to make a visit to my father, and see how it fared with me: and very welcome they were to me, whatever they were to him, to whom I doubt not they would have been more welcome had it not been for me. They tarried with us all night, and much discourse they had with my father, both about the principles of Truth in general, and in relation to me in particular, which I was not privy to; but one thing which I afterwards heard of was this: when my father and we were at their house some months before, Mary Penington in some discourse there had told him how hardly her husband's father, Alderman Penington, had dealt with him about his hat; which my father, little then thinking that it would, and so soon too, be his own case, did very much censure the Alderman for. He spared not liberally to blame him for it; wondering that so wise a man as he was should take notice of so trivial a thing as the taking off or keeping on of a hat. This gave her a handle to take hold of him by. And having had an ancient acquaintance with him, and he having always had a high opinion of and respect for her, she, who was a woman of great wisdom, of ready speech, and of a well-resolved spirit, did press so close upon him with this home argument, that he was utterly at a loss how to defend himself.

"After dinner next day, when they were ready to return home, she desired of my father that, since my company was so little acceptable to him, he would give me leave to go and spend some time with them, where I should be sure of a welcome. He was very unwilling I should go, and made many objections, all which she removed so clearly by her answers, that, not judging what further excuse to allege, he at length left it to me, and I soon turned the scale for going.

"We were come to the coach side before this was concluded on, and I was ready to step in, when one of my sisters privately put my father in mind that I had no hat on. That somewhat startled him, for he did not think it fit I should go from home so far, and to stay abroad, without a hat. Wherefore he whispered her to fetch me a hat, and he entertained them with some discourse in the meantime. But as soon as he saw the hat coming he would not stay till it came, lest I should put it on before him; therefore, breaking off the discourse, he abruptly took his leave of them.

"I had not one penny of money about me, nor indeed elsewhere; for my father as soon as he saw that I would be a Quaker, took from me both what money I had, and everything else of value that would have made money—as silver buttons, rings, etc., pretending that he would keep them for me till I came to myself again. But as I had no money, being among my friends, I had no need of any, nor ever honed after it; though upon one particular occasion I had like to have wanted it."

That occasion is worth noting for more than its quaint detail. It brings before us one of the characteristic enactments of the Commonwealth; suggesting the different views on the sabbath question that prevailed between the Puritan and the Quaker of the seventeenth century. We find nearly the same difference prevailing between the Presbyterians and the Friends of our own time, though it may be the chasm between the two in this day is scarcely so wide as formerly. Perhaps the Presbyterians do not now regard the Sunday as occupying exactly the same ground as the Jewish sabbath. The Friends, however, still hold that the first day of the week, though most necessary as a day of rest from usual labour, has no Christian warrant for being kept as the Jews were ordered to keep their sabbath. They believe that both the corporal and mental constitution of man require such rest. They also believe that on such a day of repose from toil, religious worship and religious instruction should be especially attended to. But they do not hold that the first day of the week is any more holy, in the Jewish sense, than any other day.

The occasion above alluded to occurred in 1660, a few weeks prior to the restoration of Charles the Second. "I had been at Reading," Ellwood says, "and set out from thence on the first day of the week, in the morning, intending to reach (as in point of time, I well might) to Isaac Penington's, where the meeting was to be that day; but when I came to Maidenhead, I was stopped by the watchman laying hold on the horse's bridle, and telling me I must go with him to the constable for travelling on Sunday. Accordingly I suffered him to lead my horse to the constable's door. When we got there, the constable told me I must go before the warden, who was the chief officer of the town; and he bid the watchman bring me on, himself walking before.

"Being come to the warden's door, the constable knocked, and desired to speak with Mr. Warden. He thereupon quickly coming to the door, the constable said: 'Sir, I have brought a man here to you, whom the watch took riding through the town.' The warden began to examine me, asking whence I came, and whither I was going. I told him I came from Reading, and was going to Chalfont.

He asked why I travelled on that day. I told him I did not know it would give offence to ride or to walk on that day, so long as I did not drive any carriage or horses laden with burthens. 'Why,' said he, 'if your business was urgent, did you not take a pass from the mayor of Reading?' 'Because,' I replied, 'I did not know nor think I should have needed one.' 'Well,' said he, 'I will not talk with you now—it is time to go to church —but I will examine you further anon;' and turning to the constable, 'Have him to an inn, and bring him before me after dinner.'

"The naming of an inn put me in mind that such public-houses were places of expense, and I knew I had no money to defray it, wherefore I said to the warden: 'Before thou sendest me to an inn, which may occasion some expense, I think it needful to acquaint thee that I have no money.' At that the warden stared, and turning quickly upon me said, 'How! no money! how can that be? you don't look like a man that has no money.' 'However I look,' said I, 'I tell thee the truth, that I have no money, and I tell it to forewarn thee that thou mayst not bring any charge upon the town.' 'I wonder,' said he, 'what art you have got that you can travel without money; you can do more, I assure you, than I can.'

"I making no answer, he went on and said, 'Well, well! but if you have no money, you have a good horse under you, and we can distrain him for the charge. 'But,' said I, 'the horse is not mine!' 'No! but you have a good coat on your back, and I hope that is your own.' 'But it is not,' said I, 'for I borrowed both the horse and the great coat.' With that the warden, holding up his hands, smiling said, 'Bless me! I never met with such a man as you are before! What! were you set out by the parish?' Then, turning to the constable, he said, 'Have him to The Greyhound, and bid the people be civil to him.' Accordingly, to The Greyhound I was led, my horse put up, and I put into a large room, and some account given of me, I suppose, to the people of the house.

"This was new work to me, and what the issue would be I could not foresee; but being left there alone I sat down, and retired in spirit to the Lord, in whom alone was my strength and safety; and of Him I begged support, even that He would be pleased to give me wisdom, and right words to answer the warden, when I should come to be examined before him again.

"After some time, having pen, ink, and paper about me, I set myself to write what I thought might be proper if occasion required, to give to the warden. While I was writing, the master of the house being come home from his worship, sent the tapster to me to invite me to dine with him. I bid him tell his master that I had no money to pay for dinner. He sent the man again to tell me I should be welcome to dine with him, though I had no money. I desired him to tell his master that I was very sensible of his civility and kindness, in so courteously inviting me to his table, but that I had not freedom to eat of his meat unless I could pay for it. So he went on with his dinner, and I with my writing. But before I had finished what I had on my mind to write, the constable came again, bringing with him his fellow constable. This was a brisk genteel young man, a shopkeeper in the town, whose name was Cherry. They saluted me very civilly, and told me they came to take me before the warden. This put an end to my writing, which I put into my pocket and went along with them.

"Being come to the warden, he asked me the same questions he had asked before, to which I gave him the like answers. Then he told me the penalty I had incurred; which he said was either to pay so much money, or lie so many hours in the stocks, and asked me which I would choose. I replied, 'I shall not choose either, and I have already told thee I have no money; though if I had money, I could not so far acknowledge myself an offender as to pay any. But as to lying in the stocks, I am in thy power, to do unto me what it shall please the Lord to suffer thee.'

"When he heard that, he paused awhile, and then told me he considered I was but a young man, and might not perhaps understand the danger I had brought myself into, and therefore he would not exercise the severity the law awarded upon me. In hopes that I would be wiser hereafter, he would pass by this offence and discharge me. Then, putting on a countenance of the greatest gravity, he said, 'But, young man, I would have you know that you have not only broken the law of the land, but also the law of God; and therefore you ought to ask of Him forgiveness, for you have highly offended Him.' 'That,' said I, 'I would most willingly do, if I were sensible I had offended Him by breaking any law of His.' 'Why,' said he, 'do you question that?' 'Yes, truly,' said I, 'for I do not know of any law of God that doth forbid me to ride on this day.' 'No! that is strange! Where, I wonder, were you bred? You can read, can't you?' 'Yes,' said I, 'that I can.' 'Don't you then read,' said he, 'the commandment, *Remember the Sabbath day to keep it holy. Six days shalt thou labour and do all thy work; but the seventh is the Sabbath of the Lord; in it thou shalt not do any work.*' 'Yes,' I replied, 'I have read it often, and remember it well. But that command was given to the Jews, not to Christians; and this is not that day; their Sabbath was the seventh day, but this is the first day of the week. 'How is it,' said he, 'you know the days of the week no better? You need to be better taught.'

"Here the younger constable, whose name was Cherry, interposing said, 'Mr. Warden, the gentleman is right as to that, for this is the first day of the week and not the seventh.' This the old warden took in dudgeon; and looking severely on the constable said, 'What! do you take upon you to teach me? I'll have you know I will not be taught by you.' 'As you please for that, sir,' said the constable, 'but I am sure you are mistaken on this point; for Saturday was the seventh day, and you know yesterday was Saturday.'

"This made the warden hot and testy, and put him so out of patience that I feared it would have come to a downright quarrel betwixt them, for both were confident, and neither would yield. And so earnestly were they engaged in the contest, that there was no room for me to put in a word between them. At length the old man, having talked himself out of wind, stood still awhile, as it were to take breath, and then bethinking of me he turned and said, 'You are discharged, and may take your liberty.' 'But,' said I, 'I desire my horse may be discharged too, else I know not how to go.' 'Aye, aye,' said he, 'you shall have your horse,' and, turning to the other constable who had not offended him, he said, 'Go see that his horse be delivered to him.'

"Away thereupon went I with that constable, leaving the old warden and the young constable to compose their difference as they could. Being come to the inn, the constable called for my horse to be brought; which done, I immediately mounted and began to set forward. But the hostler, not knowing the condition of my pocket, said modestly to me, 'Sir, don't you forget to pay for your horse's standing?' 'No truly,' said I, 'I don't forget it, but I have no money to pay it with, and so I told the warden before he sent him here.' 'Hold your tongue,' said the constable, 'I'll see you paid.' Then, opening the gate, they let me out, the constable wishing me a good journey, and through the town I rode without further molestation; though it was as much the Sabbath, I thought, when I went out, as it was when I came in.

"A secret joy arose in me as I rode away, that I had been preserved from doing or saying anything which might give the adversaries of Truth advantage against it, and against the Friends; and praises sprang up in my thankful heart to the Lord my Preserver. It added not a little to my joy that I felt the Lord near unto me by His witness in my heart to check and warn me; and that my spirit was so far subjected to Him as readily to take warning." With joy and thankful congratulations his friends at Chalfont welcomed his return. They had been anxious about him, knowing he intended to be with them at meeting that day.

In allusion to the visit he was then making at the Grange, he says, "Great was the love and manifold the kindness which I received from my worthy friends, Isaac and Mary Penington, while I abode in their family. They were indeed as affectionate parents and tender nurses to me in that time of my religious childhood. For, beside their weighty and seasonable counsels, and exemplary conversations, they furnished me with the means to go to the other meetings of Friends in that country, when the meeting was not in their own house. But that I might not, on the one hand, bear too much on my friends, nor, on the other hand, forget the house of thraldom, after I had staid with them some six or seven weeks, from the time called Easter to that of Whitsuntide, I took my leave of them, and returned home."

Before the close of 1660, both Isaac Penington and Thomas Ellwood were made prisoners for obeying their conscience. They were confined in separate prisons, the former in that of Aylesbury, the latter in Oxford, for continuing to attend their own religious meetings. This step resulted from the outbreak of the Fifth Monarchy Men,* and the

---

* These were "a sect of religionists, whose distinguishing tenet was a belief in the coming of a fifth universal monarchy, of which Jesus Christ was to be the head, while the saints, under his personal sovereignty, should possess the earth. They appeared in England towards the close of the Protectorate; and in 1660, a few months after the Restoration, they broke out into a serious tumult in London under their leader Venner, in which many of them lost their lives, some being killed by the military, and others afterwards executed. Several Fifth Monarchy Men also suffered death in 1662, on a charge (most probably unfounded) of having conspired to kill the king and the Duke of York, to seize the Tower, etc. They are the same who were sometimes called Millennarians, their notion being that the reign of Christ upon earth was to last for a thousand years. They seem also, from the extravagance and violence of conduct into which they occasionally broke out, to have been confounded, in the popular imagination, with the old Anabaptists of Munster."—*Penny Cyclopædia*.

discovery of some of their ulterior designs, which doubtless caused uneasiness to the King, though they came from a comparatively small and impotent body. It is plain his alarm was stimulated to the utmost by the dominant party, in order to bring about persecuting enactments throughout the nation, against all who would not conform to the Church of England mode of worship. All, except those attached to the Established Church, were forbidden under severe penalties to assemble together, lest whilst pretending to worship God they should plot against the government. This enactment the Friends did not think it was right to obey. They believed and acted on the belief that they must obey God rather than man, when man's laws were in conflict with those of God. They referred to the King's solemn pledge, that all should enjoy liberty of conscience; and pleaded, as well they might, for a reasonable discrimination, and not to allow the wild fancies of a small body of fanatics to establish such a system of national tyranny. But their pleadings were all in vain; they were only met with the tender of the oaths of allegiance and supremacy, which it was well known they would refuse to take, on the ground of their Lord and Master having commanded his followers to "swear not at all." Then followed their incarceration.

Thomas Ellwood was not imprisoned in the Castle at Oxford with the other Friends, but separately confined in custody of the marshal.

Thomas Loe, an Oxford Friend, and one of the prisoners in the Castle, hearing of the circumstance, wrote him a letter, in which he says, "A time of trial God hath permitted to come upon us to try our faith and love to Him, and this will work for the good of them that through faith endure to the end. I believe God will be glorified through our steadfastness in suffering, and His name exalted in the patience of His chosen ones. When I heard that thou wast called into this trial, with the servants of the Most High, to give thy testimony to the Truth of what we have believed, it came into my heart to write to thee. Well, my dear friend, let us live in the counsel of the Lord, and dwell in His strength, which gives power and sufficiency to endure all things for His name sake, and then the blessings of His heavenly kingdom shall be our portion. Oh! dear heart, let us give up all freely unto the will of God, that our God may be glorified by us and we comforted together in the Lord Jesus; which is the desire of my soul, who am thy dear and loving friend in the eternal Truth,

"THOMAS LOE."

"P.S. We are more than forty here, who suffer innocently for the testimony of a good conscience, because we cannot swear, and break Christ's commands. We are all well, and the blessing and presence of God are felt to be with us. Friends here salute thee. Farewell. The power and wisdom of the Lord God be with thee. Amen."

Ellwood speaks thus of the above letter, "Greatly was my spirit refreshed and my heart gladdened at the reading of this consolating letter from my friend; and my soul blessed the Lord for His love and tender goodness to me. But I had cause soon after to redouble my thankful acknowledgment to the Lord my God, who put it into the heart of my dear friend, Isaac Penington, also to visit me with some encouraging lines from Aylesbury jail, where he was then a prisoner, and from whence he thus saluted me:—

"Dear Thomas,

"Great hath been the Lord's goodness to thee, in calling thee out of that path in which thou wast running towards destruction; to give thee a living name and an inheritance amongst His people, which certainly will be the end of faith in Him and obedience to Him. And let it not be a light thing in thine eyes, that He now accounteth thee worthy to suffer amongst his chosen lambs. Oh! that the spiritual eye and heart may be kept open in thee, which seeth and feeleth the value of these things.

"Aylesbury Jail, 14th of the Twelfth Month, 1660."

"Though these epistolary visits," says Ellwood, "were very comfortable and confirming to me, and my heart was thankful to the Lord for them, yet I honed after personal conversation with my friends;

and it was hard, I thought, that there should be so many faithful servants of God so near me, yet that I should not be permitted to enjoy their company. For though my marshal-keeper was very kind to me, and allowed me the liberty of his house, yet he was not willing I should be seen abroad. Once, and but once, I prevailed on him to let me see my friends in the Castle; and it was on these conditions he consented—that I should not go forth till it was dark, that I should muffle myself up in my cloak, and that I would not stay out late: all which I punctually observed."

The magistrates, who had arranged for young Ellwood being kept apart from the Quaker prisoners in the castle, seem to have been influenced by the hope of his being ultimately induced by such means to give up his connection with the Friends. They could but little appreciate the depth of his convictions when they entertained the thought. His father had been from home when he was made prisoner, and at his intercession on his return he was promptly released. But the Friends in Oxford Castle and also those in Aylesbury jail, including Isaac Penington, remained in prison for several months.

The following letters are from the Penington Manuscripts, in the Devonshire House Library:—

Isaac Penington to his wife.

"Aylesbury Jail, 17th, 1st Month, 1661.

"My Dear,

"Yesterday I, with some few others, was sent for before the court. The judge asked me if I would take the oath. I delivered him a paper, which was an appeal to the court whether it was fitting for us, as the case stood, to take the oath. He thought it had been the paper delivered him before by Friends in other places, and so asked me again about the oath. I told him the paper was an appeal to him and the court, and desired it might be read, that the court should hear it, which he endeavoured to put off; but I pressing it hard as exceedingly necessary, he promised it should by and by, but called on some other business, and so we were ordered to withdraw for the present, but were called in no more. I am told we are appointed to appear to-morrow, at the sixth hour in the morning; what further they will propose to us I do not know. It is believed they will release some and detain others. William stays to know: whom I suppose thou mayst expect to-morrow night.

"My dear heart, my dear and tender love is to thee. I know thou dost believe that it is most just that the Lord should dispose of me, and will not desire me unless He please in the freedom of conscience that I return to thee. I am thine very much and desire to be thine even more, according to the purity and largeness of my love in the inner man. When the Lord pleaseth our innocence shall be cleared, and that which is now our reproach be our beauty and honour in the sight of all the world.

"My dear love to Guli, to A. H., and to all Friends in the family, and to my dear little ones.

"I. P."

Isaac Penington to his Wife.

"My dear,

"When I was called before the judge on the second day, he again asked me if I would take the oath. I answered I had put in an appeal to the court respecting it. He did not much press it on me, but took a paper of J. W. containing the substance of the oath, which the justices, as we were told, had looked into and confessed that it was the substance of the oath, and that there wanted nothing but the formality. At last he told me I must put in sureties for the peace, which I said I durst not do. The next morning I was brought before him again with J. W. and J. Brierly. Then he told me he would not require the oath of me, nor yet sureties for the peace, but he had heard I was the son of such a person, &c., and therefore could do no less than require sureties of me for the performance of what was promised in the paper, to wit, that I would neither plot nor conceal any plot which I knew or did certainly hear of. This, as far as I remember, was the substance. I was sore distressed, and had not a word to say for a long season; but my soul breathed to the Lord to preserve my innocence, and to make me willing to stand as a fool before them, if He did not give me wherewith to answer them. Indeed I felt that I could not do the thing; but how to avoid it, with the reasonableness and fair dealing which appeared to be on their side, I knew not. At length I told the judge that as to keeping out of plotting, &c., I could easily do that, but to come under such a bond I could not. Then he and the officers of the court much disdained and derided me, and asked if I did not take bond of my tenants, &c., which the Lord enabled me to bear with meekness and stillness of spirit. Then I told him that I could give under my hand what he required, which was more to me than a bond, but it weighed little with him. I likewise told him I was so far from plotting, notwithstanding that I had lost my whole estate, that I did never so much as grumble in my mind, or wish the change of government that I might enjoy my estate again. He seemed to be satisfied concerning my innocence, and said that he believed I would keep my promise, yet he could do no less than require this of me, considering what my father was.*

---

* It should be remembered that Alderman Penington was then a State prisoner in the Tower.

"So he committed me, referring me to the justices to be released either upon my own recognizance, or upon sureties. Since which time three of the justices sent for me to the White Hart, with whom I was a pretty season; they seemed very willing to release me, urging me much either to enter into bond myself, or put in sureties, but they were tied down to these by the judge's order, which they could not recede from. I told them I was innocent in the sight of the Lord, and did in my heart believe the Lord would justify me in this at the great day, but that I durst not do what did appear to me to cast any cloud or doubt over my innocency. I asked what I or the sureties were to be bound in; he said, I in £200, or the sureties in £100 each. I told him if I had any estate left me that was my own, I could freely subscribe myself willing to bear the penalty of £400, if I were found in any such thing. Nay, I did not care to what amount I ran, so free I was from any such danger, but to be bound in the way the case stood I could not. Since this last refusal I have found great peace and satisfaction from the Lord concerning this affair, and great rest in my spirit. Let all that love me bless the Lord for me in this, for I see clearly I had been a miserable man had I been suffered for the gaining of my liberty to have betrayed mine innocency."

We have no account of the precise time or circumstances under which Isaac Penington and his friends were released from imprisonment, but there are evidences which prove it must have been pretty early in 1661. Although he alludes in the above letter to all his estate having been confiscated, thus leaving him no property he could call his own, yet we find that he continued for years after this to reside at the Grange, which leads to the conclusion that there had been, after the death of Alderman Penington, some arrangement made or tacit permission given, by which the Chalfont estate was not claimed for the four or five following years.

CHAPTER V.

1662.

Thomas Ellwood's desire to cultivate his knowledge of Latin.—His introduction to John Milton.—He finally leaves Crowell and settles in London.—Becomes reader to Milton.—His enjoyment of that privilege.—Is imprisoned with other Friends in Old Bridewell.—Trial.—Imprisonment in Newgate.—Crowded state of that jail.—Prison life.—Inquest at Newgate.—Removal to Old Bridewell.—Is released.—Visits his friends in Newgate.—Visits Milton.—Goes to Chalfont.—Is engaged as tutor at the Grange.—His grief at the death of Edward Burrough.

WHEN relating his own history, Thomas Ellwood gives us a few glimpses into circumstances in the life of the poet Milton at the period which succeeded the Restoration. He thus tells of the occasion which led to their first acquaintance.

"I mentioned before that when I was a boy I had made good progress in [classical] learning, and lost it again before I became a man; nor was I rightly sensible of my loss therein until I came among the Quakers. But then I both saw my loss and lamented it, and applied myself with the utmost diligence at all leisure times to recover it; so false I found that charge which in those times was cast as a reproach on the Quakers, that they despised and decried all human learning, because they denied it to be essentially necessary to a Gospel ministry. But though I toiled hard, and spared no pains to regain what once I had been master of, yet I found it matter of so great difficulty, that I was ready to say, as said the noble Ethiopian to Philip, 'How can I, unless some man guide me?' This I had formerly complained of to my friend Isaac Penington, but now more earnestly, which put him upon considering and contriving a means for my assistance. He had intimate acquaintance with Dr. Paget, a physician of note in London, and he with John Milton, a gentleman of great repute for learning throughout the learned world. This person having filled a public station in former times lived now a private and retired/life in London, and having wholly lost his sight, kept always a man to read for him, who usually was the son of some gentleman of his acquaintance whom in kindness he took to improve in his learning.

"Thus by the mediation of my friend Isaac Penington with Dr. Paget, and of Dr. Paget with John Milton, was I permitted the liberty of coming to his house at certain hours when I would, and to read to him what books he should appoint me, which was the favour I desired. But this being a matter which required some arrangement to bring about, I in the mean time returned to my father's house in Oxfordshire.

"I had previously received directions by letters

from my eldest sister, written by my father's command, to sell off what cattle he had left about his house, and to discharge his servants, which I had done at the time called Michaelmas. All that winter when I was at home I lived like a hermit all alone, having a pretty large house and nobody in it but myself, especially at nights; an elderly woman, whose father had been an old servant in the family, came every morning and did whatever I had for her to do."

Finding through his sister's correspondence that his father had decided to reside no more at Crowell, but finally to dispose of the property, he determined not to lose time there, but hasten to carry out his favorite project. He says, "I committed the care of the house to a tenant of my father's who lived in the town, and, taking my leave of Crowell, went up again to my sure friend Isaac Penington; where, understanding that through the mediation used for my admittance to John Milton, I might come now when I would, I hastened to London. He received me courteously, as well for the sake of Dr. Paget who introduced me, as of Isaac Penington who recommended me; to both of whom he bore a good respect. Having inquired divers things of me with respect to my former progression in learning, he dismissed me to provide myself such accommodations as might be most suitable to my future studies. I went therefore, and took myself a lodging as near to his house, which was then in Jewyn-street, as conveniently I could. From thence forward I went every day in the afternoon, except on the first day of the week; and, sitting by him in his dining-room, read to him in such books in the Latin tongue as he pleased to hear me read.

"At my first reading to him, observing that I used the English pronunciation, he told me that if I would not only read and understand Latin authors, but be able to converse with foreigners either abroad or at home, I must learn the foreign pronunciation. To this consenting, he instructed me how to sound the vowels; so different from the common pronunciation used by the English, who *Anglice* their Latin.

"I had before, during my retired life at my father's, by unwearied diligence and industry so far recovered the rules of grammar, in which I had once been very ready, that I could both read a Latin author after a sort, and hammer out his meaning. But the change of pronunciation proved a new difficulty to me. It was now harder to me to read than it was before to understand when read. But

> Incessant pains
> The end attains;

and so did I; which made my reading the more acceptable to my master. For he, perceiving with what earnest desire I pursued learning, gave me not only all the encouragement but all the help he could. For, having a curious ear, he discerned by my tone when I understood what I read, and when

I did not; and would accordingly stop me, examine me, and open the most difficult passages to me.

"Thus went I on for about six weeks' time, reading to him in the afternoons, and exercising myself with my own books in my chamber in the forenoons. But, alas! London and I could never agree. My lungs, I suppose, were too tender to bear the city air; so I soon began to droop, and in less than two months time I was fain to leave both my studies and the city, and return to the country in order to preserve life; and much ado I had to get thither.

"I chose to go down to Wycombe to John Rance's house; both as he was a physician, and his wife a discreet and grave matron, whom I had a very good esteem for, and who I knew had a good regard for me. There I lay ill a considerable time, and in that degree of weakness that scarcely any one who saw me expected my life. But the Lord was both gracious to me in my illness, and was pleased to raise me up again, that I might serve him in my generation.

"As soon as I had recovered sufficient strength to be fit to travel, I obtained of my father (who was then at his house at Crowell to dispose of some things, and in my illness had come to see me) as much money as would meet all the expenses of my illness, which having paid I took leave of my friends there and returned to my studies in London. I was very kindly received by my master, who had conceived so good an opinion of me, that my conversation, I found, was acceptable to him, and he seemed heartily glad of my recovery and return; and into our old method of study we fell again, I reading to him, and he explaining to me as occasion required.

"But as if learning had been a forbidden fruit to me, scarcely was I well settled in my work when I met with another interruption. A sudden storm, arising from I know not what surmise of a plot, the meetings of Dissenters (such, I mean, as could be found, which perhaps were not many beside the Quakers) were broken up throughout the city, and most of the prisons filled with our friends. I was that morning, which was the 26th of the Eighth month, 1662, at the meeting at the Bull and Mouth by Aldersgate, when on a sudden a party of soldiers of the trained bands of the city rushed in with noise and clamour, being led by one called Major Rosewell, an apothecary, if I misremember not, and at that time under the ill name of a papist. As soon as he was come within the room, having a file or two of musketeers at his heels, he commanded his men to present his muskets at us, which they did; with intent I suppose to strike terror into the people. Then he made a proclamation, that all might depart if they would who were not Quakers.

"It so happened that a young man, an apprentice

in London, whose name was Dove—the son of Dr. Dove, of Chinnor near Crowell—came that day in curiosity to see the meeting, and finding me there whom he knew, sat down by me. As soon as he heard the noise of soldiers he was much startled, and asked me softly if I would not shift for myself, and try to get out. I told him no; I was in my place, and was willing to suffer if it was my lot. When he found the notice given, that they who were not Quakers might depart, he again solicited me to go. I told him I could not, for that would be to renounce my profession, which I would by no means do. But as for him, who was not one of us, he might do as he pleased. Whereupon, wishing me well, he turned away, and with cap in hand went out. And truly I was glad he was gone, for his master was a rigid Presbyterian, who in all likelihood would have led him a wretched life had he been taken and imprisoned among the Quakers.

"The soldiers came so early that the meeting was not fully gathered when they came, and when the mixed company were gone out, we were so few in that large room that they might take a clear view of us all, and single us out as they pleased. He that commanded the party gave us first a general charge to come out of the room. But we who came thither at God's requirings to worship Him, like that good man of old who said, 'We ought to obey God rather than man,' stirred not, but kept our places. Whereupon he sent some of his soldiers among us, with command to drag or drive us out, which they did roughly enough.

"When we came into the street, we were received there by other soldiers, who with their pikes holden lengthways from one to another, encompassed us round, as sheep in a pound; and there we stood a pretty time, while they were picking up more to add to our number. In this work none seemed so eager and so active as Major Rosewell. Which observing, I stepped boldly to him as he was passing, and asked if he intended a massacre: for of that in those times there was a great apprehension and talk. The suddenness of the question somewhat startled him; but, recollecting himself, he answered: 'No; but I intend to have you all hanged by the wholesome laws of the land.' When he had gotten as many as he thought fit, in number thirty-two, whereof two were caught in the street who had not been at the meeting, he ordered the pikes to be opened before us; and giving the word, 'March,' went himself at our head, the soldiers with their pikes making a lane to keep us from scattering.

"He led us up St. Martin's, and turned down to Newgate, where I expected he would lodge us. But to my disappointment he went on through Newgate, and turning through the Old Bailey, brought us into Fleet-street. I was then wholly at a loss to conjecture whither he would lead us, unless it were to Whitehall; for I knew nothing then of Old Bridewell; but on a sudden he gave a short turn, and brought us before the gate of that prison, where knocking, the wicket was opened, and the master with his porter stood ready to receive us.

"One of those two who were picked up in the street being near me, and telling me his case, I stepped to the major and told him that this man was not at the meeting, but was taken up in the street; and showed him how hard and unjust a thing it would be to put him into prison. I had not pleased him before in the question I had put to him about a massacre; and that I suppose made this expostulation less acceptable to him from me than it might have been from another. For, looking sternly at me, he said, 'Who are you that take so much upon you? Seeing you are so busy, you shall be the first that shall go into Bridewell,' and, taking me by the shoulders, he thrust me in.

"The porter, pointing with his finger, directed me to a pair of stairs on the further side of a large court, and bid me go up them, and go on till I could go no further. Accordingly I went up the stairs; the first flight whereof brought me to a fair chapel on my left hand, which I could look into through the iron grates, but could not have gone into if I would. I knew that was not the place for me; wherefore, following my direction, and the winding of the stairs, I went up a story higher, which brought me into a room that I soon perceived to be a court-room or place of judicature. After I had taken a view of it, observing a door on the further side I opened it, but quickly drew back, being almost affrighted at the dismalness of the place. For, besides that the walls quite round were laid all over from top to bottom in black, there stood in the middle of it a great whipping-post, which was all the furniture it had. In one of these rooms judgment was given, and in the other it was executed, on those who for their lewdness were sent to this prison and there sentenced to be whipped. It was so contrived that the court might not only hear, but see, their sentence executed. A sight so unexpected and withal so unpleasing gave me no encouragement to rest there; looking earnestly around, I espied on the opposite side a door which gave hopes of a further progress. I stepped hastily to it, and opened it. This let me into one of the fairest rooms that, as far as I remember, I was ever in; and no wonder; for though it was now put to this mean use, this house had for many ages been the royal palace of the Kings of England, until Cardinal Wolsey built Whitehall, and presented it as a peace-offering to King Henry the Eighth, who till then had held his court here; and this room was called the King's Dining-room. In length it was threescore feet, and had breadth proportionable. On the front side were very large bay windows, in which stood a large table. It had other very large tables in it, with benches round, and at that time the floor was covered with rushes.

"Here was my *nil ultra*, and here I found I

might set up my pillar. So, having followed my keeper's direction to the utmost point, I sat down, and considered that rhetorical saying that 'the way to heaven lay by the gate of hell;' the black room being regarded as bearing some resemblance to the latter, as this comparatively might in some sort bear to the former. But I was quickly put from these thoughts by the flocking in of the other Friends, my fellow-prisoners; amongst whom, when they were all come together, there was but one whom I knew so much as by face, and with him I had no acquaintance; for, having been but a little while in the city, and in that time kept close to my studies, I was by that means known to very few.

"As before hinted, it was a general storm which fell that day, but it alighted most heavily on Friends' meetings; so that most of the men Friends were made prisoners, and the prisons generally were filled. And great work had the women Friends to run about from prison to prison, to find their husbands, their fathers, their brothers, or their servants; for, according as they disposed of themselves to the various meetings, so were they dispersed to the various prisons. And no little care and pains had they, when they had found them, to furnish them with provisions and other necessary accommodations.

"An excellent order, even in those early days, was practiced among the Friends of London, by which there were certain individuals of either sex appointed to have the oversight of the prisons in every quarter, and to take care of all Friends, the poor especially, that should be committed thither. This prison of Bridewell was under the care of two honest, grave, discreet, and motherly women, whose names were Anne Travers and Anne Merrick, both widows. They, as soon as they understood there were Friends brought into that prison, provided some hot victuals, meat, and broth, for the weather was cold; ordering their servants to bring these things, with bread, cheese, and beer; came themselves also, and having placed all on a table, gave notice to us that it was provided for those who had not others to provide for them, or were not able to provide for themselves; and there was no deficiency among us of a competent number of such guests.

"As for my part, though I had lived as frugally as possibly I could, that I might draw out the thread of my little stock to the utmost length, yet had I by this time reduced it to tenpence, which was all the money I had about me, or anywhere else at my command. This was but a small estate to enter upon an imprisonment with; yet was I not at all discouraged at it, nor had I a murmuring thought. I had known what it was moderately to abound, and if I should now come to suffer want, I knew I ought to be content; and through the grace of God I was so. I had lived by Providence before, when for a long time I had no money at all; and I had always found the Lord a good provider. I made no doubt, therefore, that He who sent the ravens to feed Elijah, and who clothes the lilies of the field, would find means to sustain me with needful food and raiment.

"Although the sight and smell of hot food was sufficiently enticing, for I had eaten little that morning, and was hungry, yet, considering the terms of the invitation, I questioned my being included in it, and after some reasoning concluded that, while I had tenpence in my pocket, I should be but an intruder to that mess, which was provided for such as perhaps had not twopence in theirs. Being come to this resolution, I withdrew as far from the table as I could, and sat down in quiet retirement of mind till the repast was over, which was not long; for there were hands enough at it to make light work of it. When evening arrived, the porter came up the back-stairs, and opening the door told us that if we desired to have anything that was to be had in the house, he would bring it to us; for there was in the house a chandler's shop, where bread, beer, butter, cheese, eggs, and bacon might be had for money. Upon which many went to him, and spake for what of these things they had a mind to, giving their money to pay for them. Among the rest went I, and intending to spin out my tenpence as far as I could, desired him to bring me a penny loaf only. When he returned, we all resorted to him to receive our several portions;

when he came to me, he told me he could not get a penny loaf but two halfpenny loaves. This suited me better; wherefore, returning to my place again, I sat down and eat up one of my loaves, reserving the other for the next day. This was to me both dinner and supper; and so well satisfied was I with it, that I would willingly then have gone to bed, if I had one to go to; but that was not to be expected there, nor had any one bedding brought in that night. Some of the company had been so considerate as to send for a pound of candles, that we might not sit all night in the dark. Having lighted divers of them, and placed them in several parts of that large room, we kept walking to keep us warm.

"After I had thus warmed myself, and the evening was pretty far spent, I bethought me of a lodging, and cast my eye on the table which stood in the bay-window, the frame whereof looked, I thought, somewhat like a bedstead. Willing to make sure, I gathered up a good armful of the rushes wherewith the floor was covered, and spreading them under the table, crept in on them in my clothes, and keeping on my hat, laid my head on one end of the table's frame instead of a bolster. My example was followed by the rest, who gathered up rushes as I had done, made themselves beds in other parts of the room, and so to rest we went. Having a quiet, easy mind, I was soon asleep, and slept till about the middle of the night. Then awaking, and finding my legs and feet very cold, I crept out of my cabin and began to walk about. This waked and raised all the rest, who finding themselves cold as well as I, got up and walked about with me till we had pretty well warmed ourselves, and then we all lay down again and rested till morning.

"Next day all they who had families or belonged to families in the city, had bedding brought in of one sort or other, which they disposed at the ends and sides of the room, leaving the middle void to walk in. But I, who had nobody to look after me, kept to my rushy pallet under the table for four nights, in which time I did not put off my clothes; yet, through the goodness of God to me, I rested and slept well, and enjoyed health, without taking cold. In this time divers of our company, through the solicitations of some of their relations or acquaintances to Sir Richard Brown, who was at that time Master of Misrule in the city, and over Bridewell more especially, were released; and among these one William Mucklow, who lay on a hammock. He having observed that I only was unprovided, came very courteously to me, and kindly offered me the use of his hammock. This was a providential accommodation to me, which I received thankfully, both as from the Lord and from him. From thenceforward I thought I lay as well whilst I staid there as ever I had done in my life.

"Among those that remained, there were several

young men who cast themselves into a club, and laying down every one an equal portion of money, put it into the hand of our friend Anne Travers, desiring her to lay it out for them in provisions, and send them in every day a mess of hot meat; and they kindly invited me to come into their club with them. They saw my person, and judged me by that, but they saw not my purse, nor understood the lightness of my pocket. But I, who alone understood it, knew I must sit down with lower commons. Wherefore, without giving them the reason as fairly as I could, I excused myself from entering at present into their mess. And before my tenpence was quite spent, my Heavenly Father, on whom I relied, sent me a fresh supply.

"William Penington, a brother of Isaac Penington, a Friend, and a merchant in London, at whose house before I came to live in the city I was wont to lodge, having been at his brother's that day on a visit escaped the storm, and so was at liberty; and understanding when he came back, what had been done, bethought himself of me, and hearing where I was, came in love to see me. In discourse amongst other things he asked me how it was with me as to money: I told him I could not boast of much, and yet I could not say I had none; though what I then had was indeed next to none. Whereupon he put twenty shillings into my hand, and desired me to accept of that for the present. I saw the Divine hand in thus opening in this manner to me his heart and hand; and I received it with thankful acknowledgment, as a token of love from the Lord and from him.

"On the Seventh-day he went down again as usual to Chalfont; and in discourse gave an account of my imprisonment. Whereupon, on his return the Second-day following, my affectionate friend Mary Penington sent me forty shillings, which he soon after brought me. Not many days after this I received twenty shillings from my father, who, understanding I was a prisoner in Bridewell, sent me this money to support me there. Now was my pocket, from the lowest ebb, risen to a full tide. I was at the brink of want, next door to nothing, yet my confidence did not fail, nor my faith stagger; and on a sudden came plentiful supplies, shower upon shower, so that I abounded; yet in humility could say, 'This is the Lord's doings.' And without defrauding any of the instruments of the acknowledgments due unto them, mine eye looked over and beyond them to my Heavenly Father, whom I saw was the author thereof, and with thankful heart I returned praises and thanksgivings to Him. And this goodness of the Lord to me I thus record, to the end that all into whose hands this may come, may be encouraged to trust in Him whose mercy is over all his works, and who is indeed a God near at hand to help in the needful time. Now I durst venture myself into the club to which I had been invited, and accordingly (having by this time gained acquaintance with them) took an opportunity to cast myself among them; and thenceforward, so long as we continued prisoners together, I was one of their mess.

"The chief thing I now wanted was employment, which scarcely any wanted but myself, for the rest of my company were generally tradesmen, and of such trades as could set themselves to work there. Of these, divers were tailors—some masters, some journeymen—and with these I most inclined to settle. But because I was too much a novice in their art to be trusted with any of their work, I got work from a hosier in Cheapside; which was to make night-waistcoats of red and yellow flannel, for women and children. And with this I entered myself among the tailors, sitting cross-legged as they did; and so spent those leisure hours with innocency and pleasure, which want of business would have made tedious."

Thus circumstanced, these prisoners were continued in Bridewell for two months, without being brought before any magistrate to have accusation made against them. And when at last they were brought up, it seemed merely to have the oaths of allegiance and supremacy tendered. The prisoners complained of the illegality of their imprisonment, and desired to know what they had lain so long in prison for. To this the Recorder replied, "If you think you have been wrongfully imprisoned you have your remedy at law, and may take it if you think it worth your while. The court may send for any man out of the street, and tender him the oath; so we take no notice of how you came hither, but, finding you here, we tender you the oath of allegiance, which if you refuse to take we shall commit you, and at length premunire you." Accordingly, as each of the Friends was brought up, and declined to take the oaths, he was set aside and another called. The final process of declaring them outlaws, to be imprisoned for life, was left for a future occasion. When all were gone over, instead of being sent back to Bridewell, they were committed to Newgate, where a circumstance occurred which I shall leave Thomas Ellwood to narrate. His description brings strikingly before us the crowded state of the London prisons, showing the recklessness of that spirit of religious persecution which filled them. No marvel that, eventually, at its culmination, plague and pestilence swept over the city. He says:—

"When we came to Newgate we found that side of the prison very full of Friends, who were prisoners there before us; as indeed were all the other parts of that prison, and most of the other prisons about the town; and our addition caused a still greater throng on that side of Newgate. We had the liberty of the hall, which is on the first story over the gate, and which in the daytime is common to all the prisoners on that side, felons as well as others. But in the night we all lodged in one room, which was large and round, having in the middle of it a great pillar of oaken timber, which bore up the chapel that is over it. To this pillar we fastened our hammocks at one end, and to the opposite wall on the other end, quite round the room, in three stories one over the other; so that they who lay in the upper and middle row of hammocks were obliged to go to bed first, because they were to climb up to the higher by getting into the lower ones. And under the lower range of hammocks, by the wall sides, were laid beds upon the floor, in which the sick and weak prisoners lay. There were many sick and some very weak, and though we were not long there, one of our fellow-prisoners died.

"The body of the deceased, being laid out and put in a coffin, was set in a room called 'The Lodge,' that the coroner might inquire into the cause of his death. The manner of their doing it is this. As soon as the coroner is come, the turnkeys run into the street under the gate, and seize upon every man that passes till they have got enough to make up the coroner's inquest. It so happened at this time, that they lighted on an ancient man, a grave citizen, who was trudging through the gate in great haste, and him they laid hold on, telling him he must come in and serve upon the inquest. He pleaded hard, begged and besought them to let him go, assuring them he was going on very urgent business. But they were deaf to all entreaties.

When they had got their complement, and were shut in together, the others said to this ancient man. 'Come, father, you are the oldest among us; you shall be our foreman.' When the coroner had sworn the jury, the coffin was uncovered, that they might look upon the body. But the old man said to them, 'To what purpose do you show us a dead body here? You would not have us think that this man died in this room! How shall we be able to judge how this man came by his death, unless we see the place where he died, and where he hath been kept prisoner before he died? How know we but that the incommodiousness of the place wherein he was kept may have occasioned his death? Therefore show us the place wherein this man died.'

This much displeased the keepers, and they began to banter the old man, thinking to beat him off it. But he stood up tightly to them: 'Come, come,' said he, 'though you made a fool of me in bringing me hither, ye shall not find me a child now I am here. Mistake not; for I understand my place and your duty; and I require you to conduct me and my brethren to the place where this man died. Refuse it at your peril!' They now wished they had let the old man go about his business, rather than by troubling him have brought this trouble on themselves. But when he persisted in his resolution, the coroner told them they must show him the place.

"It was evening when they began, and by this

time it was bed-time, with us, so that we had taken down our hammocks, which in the day hung by the walls, and had made them ready to go into and were undressing, when on a sudden we heard a great noise of tongues and trampling of feet coming towards us. By and by one of the turnkeys, opening our door, said: 'Hold! hold! do not undress; here is the coroner's inquest coming to see you.' As soon as they were come to the door (for within it there was scarcely room for them to come) the foremen who led them, lifting up his hands, said: 'Lord bless me, what a sight is here! I did not think there had been so much cruelty in the hearts of Englishmen to use Englishmen in this manner! We need not now question,' said he to the rest of the jury, 'how this man came by his death; we may rather wonder that they are not all dead, for this place is enough to breed an infection among them. Well,' added he, 'if it please God to lengthen my life till to-morrow, I will find means to let the King know how his subjects are dealt with here.'

"Whether he did so or not I cannot tell; but I am apt to think he applied himself to the mayor or the sheriffs of London; for the next day one of the sheriffs, called Sir William Turner, a woollen draper in Paul's-yard, came, and ordering the porter of Bridewell to attend him to Newgate, sent up a turnkey amongst us, to bid all the Bridewell prisoners come down to him; for they knew us not, but we knew our own company. Being come before him in the press-yard, he looked kindly on us, and spake courteously to us. 'Gentlemen,' said he, 'I understand the prison is very full, and I am sorry for it. I wish it were in my power to release you and the rest of your friends who are in it. But, since I cannot do that, I am willing to do what I can for you. And therefore I am here to inquire how it is. I would now have all you who came from Bridewell return thither again, which will give better accommodation to you; and your removal will give more room to those that are left behind; and here is your old keeper, the porter of Bridewell, to attend you thither.'

"The sheriff bidding us farewell, the porter of Bridewell came and told us we knew our way to Bridewell without him, and he would trust us; therefore he would not stay nor go with us, but left us to take our own time, so that we were in before bed-time. Then went we up again to our friends in Newgate, and gave them an account of what had passed; and having taken a solemn leave of them, we made up our packs to be gone.

"We walked two and two abreast, through the Old Bailey into Fleet-street, and so to Old Bridewell. It being about the middle of the afternoon, and the streets pretty full of people, both the shopkeepers at their doors and passengers in the way would stop us, and ask what we were, and whither we were going. When we told them we were prisoners going from one prison to another, from Newgate to Bridewell, 'What!' said they; 'without a keeper?' 'No,' said we, 'for our word which we have given is our keeper.'"

This was indeed a welcome change to the Bridewell prisoners, though in connection with it Thomas Ellwood felt deep sorrow in leaving behind in Newgate some of his very dear friends, especially Edward Burrough, who, though a young able man when sent there, in a few weeks from this time fell a victim to the pestilential atmosphere of the place. Just a few days before his death the Bridewell prisoners were liberated, without any further examination or explanation; the probable inference being that the King had interfered on having had his attention drawn to it by the earnest appeal of Margaret Fell. Her letter to the King at this juncture, and her allusion to the liberation of the Quaker prisoners, will be found in the sixteenth chapter of *The Fells of Swarthmoor Hall*. Before many weeks of 1663 had passed, all the prison doors of the metropolis were opened, and the Quaker prisoners suffered to return home. But the respite was only a short one; their enemies found means of again assailing them, and giving the King to understand that the city authorities and episcopal clergy would not put up with his interference in connection with the metropolitan prisons and their inmates. Till the plague came with all its horrors, the King never again interfered; but then at last, when pestilence had overspread the city, he authoritatively declared, probably at the instigation of the court physicians, that no more Quakers should be sent to the metropolitan jails.

I must allow Thomas Ellwood to finish his personal history for 1662 in his own words. He says, " Being now at liberty, I visited my friends that were still in prison, and particularly I visited my friend and benefactor William Penington, at his house; and then went to wait upon my master Milton; with whom I could not yet propose to enter upon my intermitted studies, until I had been in Buckinghamshire, to visit my worthy friends Isaac Penington and his wife, with other Friends in that country. Thither therefore I betook myself, and the weather being frosty, and the ways by that means clean and good, I walked it through in a day, and was received by my friends with such demonstrations of kindness as made my journey every way pleasant to me.

" I had intended only a visit hither, and therefore purposed, after I had staid a few days, to return to my lodging and former course in London; but Providence ordered it otherwise. Isaac Penington had at that time two sons and one daughter, all then very young; of whom the eldest son, John Penington, and the daughter, Mary, the wife of Daniel Wharley, are yet living while I write this. And being himself both skilful and curious in pronunciation, their father was very desirous to have them well grounded in the rudiments of the English tongue; to which end he had sent for a man out of Lancashire, whom he had heard of, and who was undoubtedly the most accurate English teacher that ever I met with or have heard of. His name was Richard Bradley. But as he pretended no higher than the English tongue, and had led them to the highest improvement they were capable of in that, he had taken his leave of them, and gone to London to teach an English school of Friends' children there. This put my friend to a fresh strait. He had sought for a new teacher to instruct his children in the Latin tongue, but had not yet found one. Wherefore, one evening, as we sat together by the fire in his bedchamber, he asked me, his wife being by, if I would be so kind to him as to stay a while till he could hear of such an one as he aimed at, and in the meantime enter his children in the rudiments of Latin.

"This question was not more unexpected than surprising to me; the more because it seemed directly to thwart my former purpose of endeavouring further to improve myself by following my studies with my master Milton. But the sense I had of the manifold obligations I lay under to these worthy friends of mine shut out all reasoning, and disposed my mind to an absolute resignation to their desire, that I might testify my gratitude, by a willingness to do them any friendly service I was capable of. And though I questioned my ability to carry on the work to its due height, yet as only an initiation was proposed, I consented; and left not that position till I married, which was in the year 1669, near seven years from the time I came thither. During which period, having the use of my friend's books as well as of my own, I spent much of my leisure hours in reading, and not without improvement to my private studies; which, with the good success of my labours bestowed on the children, and the agreeable conversation which I found in the family, rendered my undertaking the more satisfactory.

"But alas! not many days had I been there, ere we were almost overwhelmed with sorrow for the unexpected loss of Edward Burrough, who was justly very dear to us all. This not only good, but great good man, by a long, and close, and cruel confinement in Newgate, was taken away by sudden death, to the unutterable grief of very many, and the unspeakable loss of the Church of Christ in general."

Thomas Ellwood gave expression to his sorrow in sundry verses on the death of his venerated friend, one of which was an acrostic, *Ellwood's Lament for his endeared Edward Burrough*, for which the reader is referred to the author's autobiography.

CHAPTER VI.

1662–1669.

Ellwood a tutor at Chalfont.—Gulielma Maria Springett.—His portrait of her character.—Her suitors.—Ellwood's cautious demeanour towards her.—" He for whom she was reserved."—William Penn.—Penn's Oxford experience.—Is expelled the University.—His father's displeasure and severity.—Continental travel.—Returns home.—Becomes a law student.—The plague in London.—Sent to the Duke of Ormond's court in Dublin.—His first and last military exploit.—Settles at Shangarry Castle, near Cork.—Visits the Friends' meeting there, and hears Thomas Loe preach.—Is imprisoned with the Quakers.—Released by order of Lord Ossory and summoned to London.—Interview with his father.—Sir William turns his son out of doors.—Penn becomes a religious writer.—First interview with Guli Springett.—Controversy.—Imprisonment in the Tower.—Writes *Innocency with her Open Face*.—Is released.—Acquaintance with the Peningtons.—His letter to Isaac Penington on the death of Thomas Loe.—Goes again to Ireland.

ALTHOUGH the spring of 1663 brought some respite to the Friends from the cruel assaults of their enemies, both in the metropolis and the surrounding counties, yet, as the year waned, religious persecution began to rage with renewed violence. That party in the Episcopal Church which believed that the terror of physical suffering would succeed in bringing the conscience and conduct of dissenters into conformity with their demands, again determined to try their strength in a fresh struggle with every phase of nonconformity. The Friends were the only dissenters who in this emergency persistently continued to meet publicly for divine worship in their own fashion. They felt bound thereto by allegiance to God, notwithstanding the law of man which interposed to prevent them; consequently they again became the chief victims. In London, Hertfordshire, and the north of England this fresh storm of persecution chiefly raged. The Friends at Chalfont, during the years 1663 and 1664, seem to have remained in the peaceful exercise of their own religious worship.

Meantime the young tutor at the Grange appears to have made his way steadily with the education of the junior Peningtons. To their sister Guli he was as an attached elder brother, one on whom she could depend for all those little acts of manly courtesy and care which to a nature like his it was a heartfelt pleasure to yield; often accompanying her in equestrian expeditions over the country, and in her walks of exploration through the surrounding woods and fields. In 1664 Gulielma was twenty years of age, and was as remarkable for her goodness and piety as for her beauty and native gracefulness. We are told that her hand was sought by men of all classes, peers and commoners, courtiers and Puritans. But I must allow her friend, who was acquainted with her so intimately from childhood, to tell us of her at this period, and of his own demeanour towards her. Thomas Ellwood says:—

"While I remained in that family various suspicions arose in the minds of some concerning me, with respect to Mary Penington's fair daughter, Guli. For she, having now arrived at a marriageable age, and being in all respects a very desirable woman—whether regard was had to her outward person, which wanted nothing to render her completely comely; or to the endowments of her mind, which were every way extraordinary; or to her outward fortune, which was fair, and which with some hath not the last nor the least place—she was openly and secretly sought and solicited by many, some of almost every rank and condition, good and bad, rich and poor, friend and foe. To whom in their respective turns, till he at length came for whom she was reserved, she carried herself with so much evenness of temper, such courteous freedom, guarded with the strictest modesty, that, as it gave encouragement or ground of hope to none, so neither did it administer any matter of offence or just cause of complaint to any.

"But such as were thus engaged for themselves, or advocates for others, could not, I observed, but look upon me with an eye of jealousy; and a fear that I would improve the opportunities I had of frequent and familiar conversation with her, to work myself into her good opinion, and her special favour, to the ruin of their pretences. And according to the several kinds and degrees of their fears of me, they suggested to her parents ill surmises against me. Some were even inclined to question the sincerity of my motives in first coming among the Quakers, urging with a 'Why may it not be that the hope of obtaining so fair a fortune may have been the chief inducement?' But this surmise could find no place with those worthy friends of mine, her father-in-law and her mother, who, besides the clear sense and sound judgment they had in this case, knew very well the terms and motives on which I came among the Friends; how strait and hard the passage was to me; how contrary to all worldly interest, which lay fairly another way; how much I had suffered from my father for it; and how regardless I had been of seeking any such thing these three or four years I had been amongst them.

"Some others, measuring me by their own inclinations, concluded I would steal her, run away with her, and marry her; which they thought I might be easily induced to do, from the opportunities I frequently had when riding and walking abroad with her, by night as well as by day, without any other company than her maid. But such was the confidence her mother had in me, that she felt her daughter was safe from the plots or designs of others if I were with her. And so honourable were her thoughts of me, that she would not admit any suspicion.

"Whilst I was not ignorant of the various fears which filled some jealous heads concerning me, neither was I so stupid or so divested of human feeling as not to be sensible of the real and innate worth and virtue which adorned that excellent dame, and attracted the eyes and hearts of so many, with the greatest importunity, to seek and solicit her hand. But the force of truth and sense of honour suppressed whatever would have arisen in my heart beyond the bounds of friendship. And having observed how some others had befooled themselves by misconstruing her common kindness, expressed in innocent, open, free conversation, springing from the abundant affability, courtesy, and sweetness of her natural temper, to be the effect of singular regard and peculiar affection for them, I resolved to shun the rock on which I had seen so many run and split; remembering that saying of the poet,

Felix quem faciunt aliena pericula cautum,

I governed myself in a free yet respectful carriage towards her, and thereby preserved a fair reputation with my friends, and enjoyed as much of her favour and kindness in a virtuous and firm friendship, as was fit for her to show or for me to seek."

"*He for whom she was reserved*"—the fortunate one thus alluded to by Ellwood—was then a total stranger to Gulielma, and at that very time, 1664, like herself, had only just completed his twentieth year. At the period in question, he was very differently surrounded to what she was. Instead of rural life in its cultivated beauty like that which lay around her, and the peace and happiness of a truly Christian home which she enjoyed, he was studying life in continental courts, or making acquaintance with the rank and fashion of France.

Before he was eighteen years of age William Penn had been sent to the Continent by his father, Admiral Penn, for the purpose not only of ordinary travel, but especially to have spread before him the allurements of gay courtly life in their most fascinating forms. By this means the father hoped to supplant and drive away the serious impressions his mind had received when an Oxford student, from the Quaker preaching of Thomas Loe, whose prison letter to Ellwood has already been quoted. Young Penn was expelled the University for refusing to wear the college cap and gown; for discussing among his fellow students the wickedness and absurdity of religious persecution; and, more especially, for asserting the scriptural truth of Quaker doctrines. No gentle measures awaited his return home after this expulsion. But it was in vain that the stern authoritative admiral insisted on the abandonment of every new religious idea the son had taken up. Personal flagellation and solitary confinement followed, till the father became aware that the religious convictions even of a youth of sixteen or seventeen were not so to be overcome. At length, when severity failed, continental travel was resolved on; and no arrangements were spared that could render it attractive. William accordingly went abroad under the highest auspices, and with companionship which his father entirely approved of. The courtly life to which he was introduced in Paris, and the brilliant fairy-like scenes that floated before him in the elegant chateaux of French nobles and the ducal palaces of Northern Italy, for a time raised up other desires and other visions in the mind of the youth, which were more in unison with those of his ambitious father.

In little more than two years young Penn returned without any visible remains of the Quaker predilections of his Oxford life. He had acquired the air and bearing of a noble young cavalier, and withal manifested such powers of thought and conversational ability in speaking of what he had observed abroad, that his father and mother were delighted. It was evident he had just seen enough of courtly life to be transiently dazzled by its exterior graces, without having been tainted by its vices. A considerable portion of those two years had been spent in perfecting his theological studies in France, under the guidance of Moses Amyrault, a learned professor of divinity of the Reformed French Church. And now that he had returned home, the admiral, conscious that his active mind must have real occupation, proposed that he should be entered as a student of law at Lincoln's Inn.

Thus, too, he hoped to perfect the education of the son whom he expected to succeed him in the peerage which was already awaiting his acceptance under the title of Lord Weymouth.

To the study of law William earnestly applied his acute, comprehensive intellect for the following year. But then came a change. In 1665 the plague broke out. Like every one else who could remove, he left London. But in view of such sudden calls from life here to life hereafter, very solemn thoughts, and a religious sense of his responsibility to God for the right exercise of the talents that had been given him, took possession of his mind. His father marked the serious thoughtfulness which succeeded, and his manifest desire to withdraw from fashionable life. In remembrance of the past, he became alarmed, and forthwith resolved to send his son on a visit to his friend, the Duke of Ormond, then Lord Deputy in Ireland. After making acquaintance with the Ormond family, William was to proceed to the County of Cork, and undertake the management of the admiral's Shangarry estate. The viceregal court in Dublin at that period was said to be the purest in Europe, and remarkable for its refinement and mental cultivation. We are told it was to a great extent free from the vulgar excesses that prevailed in the gay dissipated society of the court of the second Charles. Hence it suited young Penn's tastes and tendencies, to a degree that the latter never could. He therefore remained in Dublin for a considerable time; and even joined the Earl of Arran, the Duke's second son, in a military expedition to quell an outbreak in the County of Antrim. The insurgents having fortified themselves in Carrickfergus castle, Arran accompanied by his youthful friend as a volunteer, undertook to dislodge them; and finally they restored peace to the district. His biographer says that young Penn behaved throughout with so much coolness and courage, as to extort general applause from experienced officers. The Duke of Ormond and Lord Arran were earnest in protesting that the ability he had displayed clearly pointed to the army as a profession for which his talents suited him in an eminent degree.

However well pleased the Admiral was with the duke's praise of his son's ability and military prowess, he did not wish him to become a soldier; and hence the last as well as the first military exploit of William Penn was in connection with the Castle of Carrickfergus. The first portrait for which he sat was painted in Dublin after his return, and in it he was represented in the armour which he wore on that occasion.*

But an important crisis was now at hand, which changed the whole current of his life. Another and a very different course of discipline was ere long assigned him by the Lord of all, preparing

---

* William Hepworth Dixon's *Life of William Penn*.

his heart and his hands to war in the cause of God and His righteousness—not with carnal weapons, but with the spiritual weapons of Divine truth, faith, and love.

Penn, on arriving at Shangarry Castle, found abundance of occupation. A great deal of work had to be got through, to bring the affairs connected with the estate into due order; but, finally, all was settled with so much dispatch and business-like ability that his father was rejoiced. William Hepworth Dixon depicts, with much graphic power, the events which succeeded :—

"The youth had not resided more than a few months at Shangarry Castle, before one of those incidents occurred which destroy in a day the most elaborate attempts to stifle the instincts of nature. Whilst the admiral in England was pluming himself on the triumphs of his worldly prudence, his son, on occasion of one of his frequent visits to Cork, heard by accident that Thomas Loe, his old Oxford acquaintance, was in the city and intended to preach that night. He thought of his boyish enthusiasm at college, and wondered how the preacher's eloquence would stand the censures of his riper judgment. Curiosity prompted him to stay and listen. The fervid orator took for his text the passage, 'There is a faith that overcomes the world, and there is a faith that is overcome by the world.' Possessed by strong religious feeling, but at the same time docile and affectionate, he had hitherto oscillated between two duties—duty to God, and duty to his father. The case was one in which the strongest minds might waver for a time. On the one side his filial affection, the example of his brilliant friends, the worldly ambition seldom quite a stranger to the soul of man—all pleaded powerfully in favour of his father's views. On the other there were only the low whisperings in his own heart. But that still voice would not be silenced. Often as he had escaped from thought into business or gay society, the moment of repose again brought back the old emotions. The crisis had come at last. Under Thomas Loe's influence they were restored to a permanent sway. From that night he was a Quaker in his heart."

Again and again he attended the meeting of the Friends in Cork; and always with the deep conviction that in their assemblies worship, "in spirit and in truth," was acceptably offered up to "the Father of mercies and the God of all comfort." The truthful, kind, unostentatious demeanour of these persecuted disciples of Christ with whom he now worshipped won his confidence; and he resolved, come what would, to cast in his lot with theirs. In their meetings he had experienced such heart-felt spiritual communion as he had never enjoyed elsewhere. He believed his spiritual eyes were now opened to see with some degree of clearness what was of God, and what was not.

But it was not long ere a circumstance occurred

which must have given him a foretaste of the trials which awaited him if, in defiance of paternal admonitions, he should identify himself with the persecuted Friends; for, on the 3rd of Ninth-month, 1667, their meeting in Cork, at which he was present, was broken up by a band of constables and soldiers; and all the men, eighteen in number, were made prisoners and taken before the mayor. Observing among them the young heir of Shangarry, the magistrate said it was not necessary that he should go to prison if he would give bail for his good behaviour. This Penn declined to do, and, boldly questioning the legality of the whole proceeding, was imprisoned with the rest. From the jail he wrote to his friend Lord Ossory, eldest son of the Duke of Ormond, and then holding the presidency of Munster. The following is an extract from the letter:—

William Penn to the Earl of Ossory, Lord President of Munster.

"The occasion may seem as strange as my cause is just, but your lordship will no less extend your charity in the one case than your justice in the other. Religion, which is at once my crime and mine innocence, makes me a prisoner for being in the assembly of the people called Quakers, when there came constables, backed with soldiers, rudely and arbitrarily requiring every man's appearance before the mayor; and amongst the others haled me before him. He charged me with being present at a riotous and tumultuous assembly, and unless I would give bond for my good behaviour, he would commit me. I asked for his authority. His answer was a proclamation in the year 1660, and new instructions to revive that dead, antiquated order. I leave your lordship to judge if that proclamation relates to this concernment—that which was only designed to suppress Fifth Monarchy murderers. And since the King's Lord Lieutenant and yourself are fully persuaded the intention of these called Quakers, by their meetings, was really the service of God, and that you have virtually repealed that other law by a long continuance of freedom, I hope your lordship will not now begin an unwonted severity by suffering any one to indulge so much malice with his nearest neighbours; but that there may be a speedy releasement of all, to attend their honest callings and the enjoyment of their families.

"Though to dissent from a national system imposed by authority renders men heretics in some eyes, yet I dare believe your lordship is better read in reason and theology than to subscribe a maxim so vulgar and untrue. It is not long since you were a solicitor for the liberty I now crave, when you concluded there was no way so effectual to improve this country as to dispense freedom in things relating to conscience. My humble supplication therefore to you is, that so malicious and injurious a practice towards innocent Englishmen may not receive any countenance from your lordship, for it would not resemble that clemency and English spirit that hath hitherto made you honourable."

Lord Ossory promptly interfered to have his young friend released. But the Earl was sorry to find him, on his liberation, in no way disposed to give up his connection with the persecuted Quakers. Ossory therefore lost no time in writing to inform the admiral respecting his son's imprisonment, release, and continued association with the Friends. The whole family was dismayed at the intelligence, and the young man was forthwith recalled by the disappointed father. He promptly obeyed the summons, presenting himself as soon as possible before his parents in London. At first, they were a little cheered on noticing no particular change in his manners or dress, except in not uncovering his head when he addressed them. He continued to wear the fashionable cavalier costume; the long curls, the plume, and the rapier were still in their wonted places, as were the rings and other gold ornaments. No thought had as yet been directed by him to these customary decorations; but in after times they were all laid aside for what was more simple, though not for any style of dress peculiarly distinguishing the Quakers from other strictly religious people of those times.

His father, remembering how he had been before won over, did not at first begin with him harshly.

The biographer who wrote the sketch of William Penn's life which accompanied the second edition of his works, published after his decease, dwells as follows on the scenes that ensued between father and son:—

"My pen is diffident of her ability to describe that most pathetic and moving contest. The father, actuated by natural love, aiming at his son's temporal honour; he, guided by a divine impulse, having chiefly in view the Truth of God and his own eternal welfare. His father grieved to see the well-accomplished son of his hopes, now ripe for worldly promotion, voluntarily turning his back on it; he no less afflicted to think that a compliance with his earthly father's pleasure was inconsistent with obedience to his Heavenly Father. The earthly parent pressing conformity to the fashions and customs of the times, earnestly entreating and beseeching him to yield to this desire; the son, of a loving and tender disposition, in an extreme agony of spirit to behold his father's trouble, modestly craving leave to refrain from what would hurt his conscience; and, when not granted, solemnly declaring that he could not yield; his father thereon threatening to disinherit him; he humbly resigning all things of that sort to his father's will, who perceiving that neither entreaty nor threats prevailed, turned his back on him in anger; and the son lifted up his heart to God for strength to sustain him in that time of bitter trial."

When all the admiral's endeavours proved ineffectual to shake William's religious resolutions, the disconcerted father, unable any longer to endure him in his sight, fairly turned him out of doors. But his mother, well knowing his deep feeling and devotedness, never suffered her heart to be hardened against her son. She saw him occasionally, and supplied him with the means of procuring the necessaries of life; whilst the Friends received him cordially in their midst as a brother beloved. In 1668, when in the twenty-fourth year of his age, he came forward amongst them as a minister of the Gospel. This circumstance is thus alluded to in the sketch of his life published with his works:—
"Being redeemed by the power of Christ, he was sent to call others from under the dominion of Satan into the glorious liberty of the sons of God, that they might receive remission of sins, and an inheritance among them that are sanctified through faith in Jesus Christ."

The same year in which he appeared as a minister he first came forward as a religious writer, his earliest work being *Truth Exalted*. Then followed a reply to an author who had published *A Guide to True Religion*, in which he had misstated Quaker doctrines. The reply was entitled *The Guide Mistaken*. His next work was *The Sandy Foundation Shaken*. This publication resulted from his and George Whitehead's having been unfairly prevented from orally replying to a Calvinistic preacher, who had grossly assailed the soundness of Friends' doctrines, and had in a most outrageous manner taken exception to them on three special points. He agreed, on being privately remonstrated with, publicly to make good his charges, and of course to hear what they had to say in reply. However, having spoken as long as he wished, he would not suffer the audience to listen to what the Friends had to say, but removed the lights, and broke up the meeting by force, whilst they were stating their views. *The Sandy Foundation Shaken* was written to prove that the doctrine of "One God subsisting in *three separate and distinct persons*" was not consistent with Holy Scripture; and that "the impossibility of God pardoning sinners without a plenary satisfaction," and "the justification of impure persons by an imputative righteousness," were liable to the same objection, as theological dogmas unwarranted by Holy Scripture.

The extreme difficulty of arguing on such questions, so as not to be misunderstood by persons accustomed to regard these dogmas as embodying established scriptural truth, may be easily imagined. And it is not improbable that there was some want of due caution on Penn's part. It is certain that his confining himself to the points laid down, without at the same time giving expression in that work to his own full faith in the scriptural truth of Christ's oneness with the Father, and his belief in the scriptural offices of the Holy Spirit, led to serious misunderstanding. As he did not dwell at all on these points of belief in *The Sandy Foundation Shaken*, his enemies declared that he did not hold them, and they assailed him accordingly.

The outcry which was thus raised soon stirred up the persecuting spirit in some of the heads of the Church which he had forsaken. They were not slow in procuring an order for his imprisonment in the Tower, on an accusation of blasphemy. None of his friends except his father, who was not likely to avail himself of the permission, was suffered to visit him there. His servant, who alone had free access to him, brought him word that the Bishop of London was resolved that he should either publicly recant, or die a prisoner. To this he replied, "Thou mayest tell my father, who I know will ask thee, that these are my words in answer, 'My prison shall be my grave before I will budge a jot, for I owe obedience of my conscience to no mortal man.' But I have no need to fear; God will make amends for all. They are mistaken in me; I value not their threats and resolutions. In me shall they behold a resolution that is above fear, conscience that is above cruelty, and a baffle put to their designs by the spirit of patience—the companion of all the tribulated flock of the blessed Jesus, who is the author and finisher of the faith that overcomes the world."

That "faith which overcomes the world" was

now his in truth; and its sustaining power kept up his spirit in the solitude to which he was condemned. And though he could not then go forth from place to place as a preacher of righteousness, his pen could send abroad his thoughts even more widely than his voice. Conscious of this, he used indefatigably in his Lord's service the talent he could command. Beside some rejoinders to the attacks of his enemies, which he sent forth from the Tower, he there and then wrote his great work, *No Cross, No Crown*. As coming from the pen of so young a man, this work, on account of the intimate knowledge of ecclesiastical history and the breadth of thought which it displays, was regarded as a marvellous composition, and passed through several editions during the author's lifetime.

Finding that many serious persons, who were not mere cavillers, were led by the representations put forward against him to think that he did not recognize the Deity of Christ the Saviour, because of its not being noticed in *The Sandy Foundation Shaken*, he wrote *Innocency with her Open Face*. In this work he gave a full exposition of his convictions on that important subject. His statements indicate so much careful examination and clearness of intellect, that I think it right in this connection to quote some of them. He says:—

"That which I am credibly informed to be the greatest reason for my imprisonment, and that noise about blasphemy which hath pierced so many ears of late, is my denying the divinity of Christ, which most busily hath been suggested as well to those in authority, as maliciously insinuated among the people. Wherefore, let me beseech you to be impartial and considerate in the perusal of this my vindication; which, being written in the fear of the Almighty God, and in the simplicity of Scripture dialect presented to you, I hope my innocency will appear beyond scruple.

"The prophets David and Isaiah speak thus, 'The Lord is my light and my salvation'—'I will give thee for a light unto the Gentiles'—and, speaking to the Church, 'For the Lord shall be thine everlasting light;' to which the evangelist adds concerning Christ, 'that was the true light which lighteth every man that cometh into the world'—'God is light, and in Him is no darkness at all.' From which I assert the unity of God and Christ, because though nominally distinguished, yet essentially the same divine light; for if Christ be that light, and that light be God, then is Christ God. Or if God be that light, and that light be Christ, then is God Christ. Again, in *Rev.* vi., 'And the city had no need of the sun, for the glory of God did lighten it, and the Lamb (Christ) is the light thereof;' by which the oneness of the nature of these lights plainly appears; for since God is not God without His own glory, and that His glory lightens (which it could never do if it were not light) and that the Lamb or Christ is that very same light, what can follow but that Christ the light and God the light are one pure eternal light?

"Next, from the word *Saviour* it is manifest, 'I, even I, am the Lord, and besides me there is no Saviour;' 'and thou shalt know no God but me, for there is no Saviour beside;' and Mary said, 'My spirit hath rejoiced in God my Saviour;' and the Samaritans said unto the woman, 'Now we know that this is indeed the Christ, the Saviour of the world.'—'Therefore we suffer reproach because we trust in the living God, who is the Saviour of all men.'—'To the only wise God our Saviour be glory.'

"All these prove Christ to be God; for if none can save, or be properly styled *the Saviour*, but God, and yet that Christ is declared to save, and be properly called the Saviour, it must needs follow that Christ the Saviour is God."

"He that is 'The everlasting wisdom;' 'The divine power;' 'The true light;' 'The only Saviour;' 'The creating Word,' and 'Upholder of all things by His own power,' is without contradiction God. All these qualifications and divine properties are by the concurrent testimonies of scripture ascribed to the Lord Jesus Christ; therefore, without a scruple I call Him and believe Him really to be the Mighty God."

After such a full solemn statement as this, of course no room was left for calling in question William Penn's entire belief in the divinity of the

Lord Jesus. But still there remained his unrecanted declarations of the unscriptural character of the scholastic terms, and the other teaching against which he wrote in *The Sandy Foundation Shaken*. From these he did not recede in the slightest degree, when writing *Innocency with her Open Face*. Instead of doing so, his remarks only went to confirm or reiterate his former statements. Thus he concludes:—

"However positively I may reject or deny my adversaries' unscriptural and imaginary doctrine of *satisfaction*, let all know this, that I pretend to know no other name by which remission, atonement, and salvation can be obtained, but Jesus Christ the Saviour, who is the power and wisdom of God. As for *justification by an imputed righteousness*, I still say that whosoever believes in Christ shall have remission and justification; but then it must be such belief, such faith as can no more live without works than a body without a spirit; wherefore I assert that true faith comprehends evangelical obedience. And herein Dr. Stillingfleet comes to my support by this plain assertion, viz. 'Such, who make no other condition of the gospel but *believing*, ought to have a care to keep their hearts sounder than their heads,' thereby intimating the great imperfection and danger of such a notion. God Almighty bears me record that my design was nothing less or more than to wrest those sin-pleasing principles out of the hands, heads, and hearts of the people, from the fond persuasion of being justified by the personal righteousness of another, without any relation to their own obedience to God—that they might not sin on upon such a trust, till irrecoverably overtaken by eternal punishment."

William Penn, still continuing a prisoner without being brought to trial, notwithstanding all he had written and published, at length addressed a long letter to Lord Arlington, Secretary of State, asking him to interfere. He showed how contrary it was to every principle of justice, and every legal idea, ancient or modern, to keep a man imprisoned for holding certain opinions which he really did not hold, without allowing him an opportunity of clearing himself on open trial; and he asked, even if he did hold all the opinions objected to, by what law could he be legally imprisoned for doing so; and, if they wished to convince him of error, could they hope to effect it by such means. He says in conclusion:—" I make no apology for my letter as a trouble; because I think the honour that will accrue to thee by being just, and releasing the oppressed, exceeds the advantage that can succeed to me. And I am well assured any kindness and justice it may please thee to employ on that account cannot miss a plentiful reward from God, and praise of all virtuous men."

This letter bears date the 1st of Fifth-month, 1669, and in little more than a month after it was written the writer was released, after about eight months' imprisonment. On the 24th of Eighth-month he sailed from Bristol for Cork, where he arrived on the 26th. By his father's express orders, he was again to undertake the management of the Shangarry estate.

From all that can be ascertained, it seems that it was early in the eventful year 1668 that William Penn first met with Gulielma Maria Springett. Doubtless, though they had not previously been personally acquainted, she had heard something of his history; and had been told of the great ability and Christian faithfulness manifested by the young convert, son to the celebrated Admiral Sir William Penn. We may easily imagine how such a mind as hers, and such a heart as his, would be attracted towards each other on their first acquaintance. We may well understand, too, how Thomas Ellwood's generous spirit could rejoice, in a certain sense, in seeing the dawn of mutual love which was not to be mistaken by his practised eye. He saw, without a word being spoken, that "he for whom she was reserved" had come at last; and then, but not till then, could he find in his heart to devote himself to any one else.

Meantime William Penn, however charmed by this good and beautiful girl, was in no position to make any manifestation of his feelings, or even to suffer himself to dwell with certainty on his ever being able to do so. He was still banished from his father's house, and the Admiral's threat to disinherit him had not been retracted. It does not even appear that on sending him to Ireland he had had any personal interview with his son. His mother met him, and sometimes he came home to see her in his father's absence. It is also probable that through her the arrangement was made about his returning to Shangarry.

The following pages were ready for the press, when an interesting manuscript document respecting William Penn was obligingly forwarded to me by a member of the Huntly family of High Wycombe, to whose collection of old MSS. it belongs. As it gives many incidents of Penn's early history which were related by himself to his friend Thomas Harvey, including some not mentioned in any of the memoirs of him which have hitherto appeared, I shall now lay its substance, with occasional extracts, before the reader. Among other things it mentions an earlier meeting with Thomas Loe than that which took place at Oxford, and gives additional particulars of Admiral Penn's efforts to withdraw his son from Quakerism, and of William's first interview with Gulielma Maria Springett.

As it is certain that Thomas Loe was in Ireland both in 1655 and 1657, William Penn's earliest knowledge of him, as stated in the paper in question, must have been in one of these years, whilst he was yet a mere youth. It was most probably in 1655, when the admiral, having lately lost favor with the Cromwellian government, by whom he was regarded with suspicion, removed with his family to Ireland. For the four or five succeeding years he resided in the neighbourhood of Cork, where William must have received the elements of his education, for it was not till 1659 he was sent to Oxford, being then about fifteen years of age.

The document I have referred to is dated 1727, and is headed as follows:—

"*An account of the convincement of William Penn, delivered by himself to Thomas Harvey about thirty years since, which Thomas Harvey related to me in the following brief manner:—*

"He said, while he was but a child living at Cork with his father, Thomas Loe came thither. When it was rumoured a Quaker was come from England, his father proposed to some others to be like the noble Bereans, to hear him before they judged him. He accordingly sent to Thomas Loe to come to his house, where he had a meeting in the family. Though William was very young, he observed what effect Thomas Loe's preaching had on the hearers. A black servant of his father's could not contain himself from weeping aloud; and, looking on his father, he saw the tears running down his cheeks also. He [little William] then thought within himself, 'What if they would all be Quakers?' This opportunity he never quite forgot—the remembrance of it still recurring at times. He afterwards went to Oxford, where he continued till he was expelled for writing a book which the priests and masters of the college did not like. Then he was sent to France, further to prosecute his learning, and after he returned he was sent to Ireland."

The manuscript goes on to say that, on his second coming to Cork, being the only one of the family there, and requiring some articles of clothing, he went to the shop of a woman-Friend in the city to procure them. He expected she would have known him, but she did not. He was too much altered from the days of his boyhood, when the Friend had seen him, to be now recognized by her. However, he told her who he was, and he spoke to her of Thomas Loe, and of the meeting at his father's house ten or eleven years before. The manuscript says, " She admired at his remembering, but he told her he should never forget it; also if he only knew where that person was, if 'twere a hundred miles off, he would go to hear him again. She said he need not go so far, for the Friend had lately come thither, and would be at meeting the next day. So he went to the meeting, and when Thomas Loe stood up to preach, he was exceedingly reached, and wept much.

"After meeting, some Friends took notice of

him, and he went to a Friend's house with Thomas Loe. In discourse T. L. having said he should want a horse, his own being not fit to travel, on which William Penn offered him his sumpter-horse which he had brought from France. Thomas Loe not being willing to take it, W. P. thought it was because he was not enough of a Friend to have his horse accepted. He continued to go to meeting; and one day a soldier came into the Friends' meeting and made great disturbance, on which William Penn goes to him, takes him by the collar, and would have thrown him down stairs, but for the interference of a Friend or two who requested William to let him alone, telling him the Friends were a peaceable people, and would not have any disturbance made. Then he became very much concerned that he had caused them to be uneasy by his roughness.

"The soldier whom William Penn had expelled went to the magistrates, and brought officers and men who broke up the meeting, and took several of them prisoners, and him among the rest. They were brought before the magistrate, who, knowing W. P., said he did not think he was a Quaker, so would not send him to jail. But William told him, whether he thought it or not, he was one, and if he sent his friends to prison he was willing to go with them. Then the magistrate said he should go with them."

The MS. goes on to tell of the interference of the Deputy-governor of Munster for William's liberation, and also mentions his writing to inform the admiral, who forthwith ordered his son home. "Which order he obeyed, and landed at Bristol, where he stayed some meetings to strengthen himself, knowing his father would not be very pleasant upon him. Josiah Coal went with him to London, also to his father's house, to see how he was likely to be entertained. His father kept his temper while J. C. was there, but before going to bed, observing him use *thee* or *thou*, he was very angry."

The conversation of the father and son on this point, the MS. tells us, resulted in the former saying "he might *thee* or *thou* who he pleased, except the King, the Duke of York, and himself; these he should not *thee* or *thou*." But still William would not give his father to expect that he could in conscience make any such exceptions. On parting from him for the night, the admiral, with evidence of much displeasure, told his son to be ready to go out with him in the coach next morning when called on. William could sleep none that night, his mind being disturbed by a suspicion that his father had determined to take him to Court at once, to see how far courtly surroundings would aid in driving away his Quaker prepossessions.

"When the morning came, they went in the coach together, without William knowing where they were going, till the coachman was ordered to drive into the Park. Thus he found his father's intent was to have private discourse with him. He commenced by asking him what he could think of himself, after being trained up in learning and courtly accomplishments, nothing being spared to fit him to take the position of an ambassador at foreign courts, or that of a minister at home, that he should now become a Quaker. William told him that it was in obedience to the manifestation of God's will in his conscience, but that it was a cross to his own nature. He also reminded him of that former meeting in Cork, and told him that he believed he was himself at that time convinced of the truth of the doctrine of the Quakers; only that the grandeur of the world had been felt to be a too great sacrifice to give up. After more discourse they turned homewards. They stopped at a tavern on the way, where Sir William ordered a glass of wine." On entering a room on this pretext, he immediately locked the door. Father and son were now face to face, under the influence of stern displeasure on the one hand, and on the other, prayerful feeling to God for strength rightly to withstand or bear what was coming. William, remembering his early experience on returning from Oxford, expected something desperate. The thought arose that the admiral was going to cane him. But, instead of that, the father, looking earnestly at him, and laying his hands down on the table, solemnly told him he was going to kneel down to pray to Almighty God that his son might not be a Quaker, and that he might never again go to a Quaker meeting. William, opening the casement, declared that before he would listen to his father putting up such a prayer to God, he would leap out of the window. At that time a nobleman was passing the tavern in his coach, and observing Sir William's at the door, he alighted. Being directed to the room in which father and son were together, his knock came in time to arrest the catastrophe. He had evidently heard of William's return, and of the admiral's high displeasure. After saluting the former, the MS. says that " he turned to the father, and told him he might think himself happy in having a son who could despise the grandeur of the world, and refrain from the vices which so many were running into."

They paid a visit before they returned home to another nobleman, and the discourse with him also turned on the change in William. Here again the father was congratulated and the son's resolution commended. These congratulations were cheering to the young convert, whatever they might have been to the admiral. It would seem that, for a longer time than is generally supposed, William remained under his father's roof after his return from Ireland; and that in fact he had commenced to preach in Friends' meetings, and had become known as a Quaker preacher, before his final expulsion from home took place. He had been engaged with another preacher in visiting Friends' meetings in the country, one of which had been broken up by a magistrate, who wrote to Sir William, telling him what tumult his son had been making, and the admiral immediately despatched a letter ordering him to come home. The Friend who had been travelling with him advised him to obey his father. William decided to do so, and on his return he came to London; but, before going to Wanstead, he attended a meeting in the city. After that meeting, happening to be in the house of a Friend who resided in the neighbourhood, Gulielma Maria Springett came in and was introduced to him; this was in the year 1668, and was the first time he ever saw his future wife.

The manuscript account continues:—" Returning home, his father told him he had heard what work he had been making in the country, and after some discourse bid him take his clothes and begone from his house, for he should not be there any longer. Also, that he should dispose of his estates to them that pleased him better. William gave him to understand how great a cross it was to him to disoblige his father, not because of the disposal of his estates, but from the filial affection he bore to him." Thus father and son parted, William declaring his deep sorrow, but his still deeper conviction that he must in the first place obey God. Kissing his mother and his sister Margaret, he left the house with their cries of distress sounding in his ears.

William Penn had a brother named Richard, of whom we hear very little. It is probable he was at school or college at this time, as he seems to have been several years younger than William.

Before his imprisonment, William Penn attended the deathbed of Thomas Loe. On that occasion he wrote the following account of the last hours of his beloved and venerated friend:—

William Penn to Isaac Penington.

"I understand through thy dear wife of thy desire to be informed concerning the sickness and death of dear Thomas Loe. It was thus. When George Whitehead, Thomas Loe, and myself, after thou left us, were at Wickham, at the Duke of Buckingham's [on the business] relative to Friends' liberty, he was taken suddenly ill, which necessitated him to leave us, and hasten to the house of a Friend who lived near, where, after three hours, we found him from excessive retching very feverish. Business called me to the city, so that I left them. That evening he was brought by coach to Anne Greenhill's, where he remained about a week, at times very ill. By reason of the continual noise her house was exposed to, we removed him to Edward Man's; where we all had hopes of his speedy recovery, inasmuch as the retirement of the chamber in which he lay occasioned great rest. But, being infirm and under extraordinary fever, the strength of his constitution could not long support it, and for some time before he left us we daily expected his departure. About four days before he died I fell sick myself; but, hearing at what point it was with dear Thomas, I could not long keep my bed, but got up and hastened to him. I found him in readiness to depart. Friends, much affected, stood around his bed. When I came in, and had set myself upon the bedside, so shook was he by the power of the Lord, and overcome by the ravishing glory of His presence, that it was wonderful to all the Friends. Taking me by the hand, he spoke thus:—'Dear heart, bear thy cross, stand faithful for God, and bear thy testimony in thy day and generation; and God will give thee an eternal crown of glory, that none shall ever take from thee. There is not another way. Bear thy cross. Stand faithful for God. This is the way the holy men of old walked in, and it shall prosper. God has brought immortality to light, and immortal life is felt in its blessedness. Glory, glory to Thee, for Thou art eternally worthy! My heart is full. What shall I say? His love overcomes me. My cup runs over, my cup runs over. Glory, glory to his name for ever! Friends, keep your testimonies. Live to God, and He will be with you. Be not troubled; the love of God overcomes my heart.' It effected more than all the outward potions given him, for it so enlivened his spirits and raised him, that he soon after got up and walked about, saying to us, 'Many times when I have seemed to be going, the Lord has shined upon my tabernacle, and raised it up.'

"But it was then the will of the Lord that, after all his labour, perils, and travels, he should there lay down the body amongst his ancient friends. After some little time so greatly did his distemper increase, and his life sink, that we all gave him up, death appearing in almost every part. He lay some short time speechless, his spirit being centered, and at last he went away with great stillness, having finished his testimony, and left many demonstrations of his service and much fruit of his diligent labour. My soul loved him while living, and now bemoans his loss when dead. The day following we laid the mortal part in the ground, it having done its Master's work.

"With my dear love to thyself, wife, and family, I remain in true love

"Thy sincere friend,
"WM. PENN.

"London, 17th of 8th Mo. 1668."

The above is taken by kind permission, from the manuscript collection of Penington letters in possession of John S. Robson of Saffron Walden.

CHAPTER VII.

1665–1671.

Further persecution of the Friends.—The plague in London.—John Milton removes to Chalfont.—Magisterial tyranny.—Penington and Ellwood imprisoned.—The latter, on being released, visits Milton.—The manuscript of *Paradise Lost* handed to him to read.—*Paradise Regained* suggested by Ellwood.—Earl of Bridgwater imprisons Isaac Penington.—Penington's letter to his wife from Aylesbury jail.—Penington writes from prison to the Earl of Bridgwater.—A respite.—Another letter to his wife.—Writes to the Amersham Friends from Aylesbury jail,—and to George Fox.—Penington's letter to his uncle—to his cousin.—Removed by Habeas Corpus to London.—Dismissed by proclamation.—Purchases Woodside.—Rebuilding of the old house.—Imprisonment of Isaac Penington in Reading jail.—Is released.—Christian influence in prison.

HAVING glanced at William Penn's history up to the autumn of 1669, attention must now be more exclusively given to that of the Peningtons.

In 1665, religious persecution again disturbed the quiet that had prevailed for the previous few years among the worshippers who weekly assembled in the Penington parlour. Before this disturbance commenced, an illustrious poet, well known to some of the family at the Grange, had determined to seek a retreat in their neighbourhood, from the pestilence which was depopulating the capital. This was the summer of the great plague of London. Every week the number of its victims was increasing, whilst death in its most alarming form was spreading terror all around. As many as could leave the doomed city, and were not bound by conscience or by feelings of self-sacrifice to watch over the sick and dying, sought refuge in the country. John Milton, dependent as he was at that time on the sight of others, requested his former pupil to find a house for him near his own home. Thus Ellwood relates the circumstance:—" I was desired by my quondam master, Milton, to take a house for him in the neighborhood where I dwelt, that he might go out of the city, for the safety of himself and his family, the pestilence then growing hot in London. I took a pretty box for him in Giles Chalfont, a mile from me, of which I gave him notice, and intended to wait on him, and see him well settled in it, but was prevented by that imprisonment."

" That imprisonment," will be explained by the following extract from Ellwood's autobiography:—

" Some time before this, a very severe law was made against the Quakers by name, particularly prohibiting our meetings under the sharpest penalties; five pounds for the first offence so called, ten pounds for the second, and banishment for the third; under pain of condemnation for felony if escaping or returning without license. This act was looked upon to have been procured by the bishops, in order to bring us to conform to their way of worship. No sooner was that cruel law made, than it was put in execution with great severity. And although the storm it raised fell with greater weight on some other parts, yet we were not in Buckinghamshire wholly exempted therefrom, as it reached us after a time. For a Friend of Amersham, Edward Perrot, departing this life, the Friends of the adjacent country resorted pretty generally to the burial; so that there was a fair appearance of Friends and neighbours, the deceased having been well beloved by both. After we had spent some time together in the house, Morgan Watkins, who at that time happened to be at Isaac Penington's, being with us, the coffin was taken up and borne on Friends' shoulders through the street towards the burying-ground, which was at the town's end, being part of an orchard which the deceased in his lifetime had given to Friends for that purpose.

"It so happened that one Ambrose Bennet, a barrister-at-law, and a justice of the peace for that county, riding through the town that morning on his way to Aylesbury, was informed that there was a Quaker to be buried there that day, and that most of the Quakers in the country were coming to the burial. Upon this, he set up his horses and stayed; and when we, not knowing of his design, went innocently forward to perform our Christian duty for the interment of our friend, he rushed out of the inn upon us, with constables, and a rabble of rude fellows whom he had gathered together. Having his drawn sword in hand, he struck one of the foremost of the bearers with it, commanding them to set down the coffin. But Thomas Dell, the Friend who had been struck, being more concerned for the safety of the dead body than for his own, held the coffin fast. The justice observing this, and being enraged that his word, how unjust soever, was not forthwith obeyed, with a forcible thrust threw the coffin from the bearers' shoulders, so that it fell to the ground in the midst of the street; and there we were forced to leave it, for immediately thereupon the justice gave command for apprehending us, and the constables with the rabble fell on us, and drew some, and drove others into the inn; giving thereby an opportunity to the rest to walk away.

"Of those thus taken, I was one and Isaac Penington another. Being with many more put into a room under a guard, we were kept there till another justice had been sent for to join the other in committing us. Being called forth severally before them, they picked out ten of us, whom they committed to Aylesbury jail, for what neither we nor they knew; for we were not convicted of having either done or said any thing which the law could take hold of." "Our great concern was for our friend Isaac Penington, because of the tenderness of his constitution; but he was so lively in spirit, and so cheerfully given up to suffer, that he rather encouraged us than needed any from us."

The ten Friends thus committed were kept in prison for a month; when that time had elapsed, the doors were opened and they were discharged. On his return, Ellwood without delay sought his friend Milton, which visit he thus notes, " Now, being released, I soon made a visit to him to welcome him to the country. After some common discourses had passed between us, he called for a manuscript of his; which being brought he delivered it to me, bidding me take it home and read it at my leisure; and when I had so done, return him with my judgment thereupon.

" When I came home, and had set myself to read it, I found it was that excellent poem which is entitled *Paradise Lost*. After I had with the best attention read it through, I made him another visit, and returned him his book, with due acknowledgment of the favour he had done me in communicating it to me. He asked me how I liked it, and what I thought of it, which I modestly but freely told him; and after some further discourse about it, I pleasantly said to him, 'Thou hast said much here of *Paradise Lost*, but what hast thou to say about *Paradise Found?*' He made me no answer, but sat some time in a muse, then broke off that discourse and fell upon another subject. After the sickness was over, and the city, well cleansed, had become safely habitable again, he returned thither; and when afterwards I went to wait on him there, which I seldom failed doing whenever my occasions drew me to London, he showed me his second poem, called *Paradise Regained*, and in a pleasant tone said to me, 'This is owing to you, for you put it into my head by the question you put to me at Chalfont, which before I had not thought of.'"

It is pleasant to hear even this much of Milton in those days of his outward darkness and seclusion, when, abjuring politics, he devoted his thoughts to poetry. But whilst we cordially thank Ellwood for relating these incidents, we would have felt very much more indebted to him, if he had told us all that he could have told about the great poet during his retirement at Chalfont, where he is supposed to have remained till the spring of 1666. And we would have been still further obliged if he had let us know what the ladies at the Grange thought of the "heavenly epic," or if he read it to them. The "pretty box" which Thomas Ellwood took for his quondam master, as he calls Milton, is still standing. Although a plain farmhouse, it is of course regarded as the most interesting object in the neighbourhood of Chalfont.

Only four weeks elapsed from the time of that visit of Ellwood to Milton when the manuscript was placed in his hands, till Isaac Penington was again imprisoned by order of William Palmer, deputy-lieutenant of the County of Bucks. At the time the order was issued and executed, Mary Penington had not left her room after the birth of one of her children; I believe her youngest son Edward. The mittimus made out by Palmer was to the effect that the jailor of Aylesbury prison "should receive and keep the body of Isaac Penington in safe custody, during the pleasure of the Earl of Bridgwater." This Earl of Bridgwater, as it appears, had conceived a bitter antipathy to Isaac Penington, because he would neither, when addressing him, use the phrase "My Lord," nor sign himself, in writing to him, "Your humble servant." Penington had conscientiously adopted the truthfulness of address advocated by the Friends, and could not call any man "his lord" who was not so; nor call himself the servant of any one to whom he owed no service. The Earl had declared he should "lie in prison till he would rot," if he would not apologize to him for the omission, and address him in the manner which he conceived due to his rank.

Isaac Penington's mind was meantime so deeply centred in devotion to the Lord, and in resignation to His holy will in all things, that the prison surroundings were very lightly regarded when compared with the happiness he felt in the assurance that the persecution he was enduring would bring honour and exaltation to the cause of Truth. In humble adoration before God his Saviour, every murmuring thought was hushed, as he wrote to her from whom he was so cruelly separated:—

To his wife.

"1st of 7th month, 1665.

"My dear true love,

"I have hardly freedom to take notice of what hath passed so much as in my own thoughts; but I am satisfied in my very heart that the Lord, who is good, hath ordered things thus, and will bring about what He pleaseth thereby. Why should the fleshly-wise, reasoning part murmur, or find fault.

"Oh! be silent before the Lord all flesh within me, and disturb not my soul in waiting on my God for to perceive what He is working in me and for me, and which He maketh these uncouth occurrences conduce into.

"One thing have I desired of the Lord, even that I may be His, perfectly disposed of by Him, know nothing but Him, enjoy nothing but in His life and leadings. Thus must I give up and part with even thee, my most dear and worthy love, or I cannot be happy in my own soul or enjoy thee as I desire.

"I find my heart deeply desiring and breathing after the pure power of the Lord to reign in me; yet dare I not choose, but beg to be taught to wait; and to be made willing to drink the residue of the cup of suffering, both inward and outward, until the Lord see good to take it from my lips.

"Oh, my dear! say little concerning me; plead

not my cause, but be still in thy own spirit, and await what the Lord will do for me; that all the prayers which in the tenderness of my soul I have often put up for thee may have their full effect upon thee. My dear, be my true yoke-fellow, helpful to draw my heart toward the Lord, and from every thing but what is sanctified by the presence and leadings of His life. I feel, and thou knowest that I am, very dearly thine.

"J. P."*

Notwithstanding the declaration of the Earl of Bridgwater, Isaac Penington's friends, being aware that he had broken no law, calculated on his release whenever the assizes came round. But the Earl, also aware of that fact, took means to prevent a trial. Therefore, when the term arrived, no such case appeared. Thus term after term passed away without any trial, or any notice whatever of Isaac Penington's incarceration. It became evident that the mittimus made out by the deputy-lieutenant of the county was being literally obeyed, and that the prisoner was really designed to remain imprisoned during the pleasure of the haughty earl.

The Penington family, as before stated, continued to occupy the Grange for some years after the confiscation of Alderman Penington's estates,

---

* The autograph original of the above letter belonged to the late James Midgley's collection of ancient MSS. and is now in possession of his daughter.

among which this at Chalfont which he had given to his eldest son was included. What the circumstances were under which the son's family was allowed to remain in possession have not been alluded to in any document I have seen; nor have I met with any statement relative to the bestowal of the confiscated property, save that which I have quoted, which says that Alderman Penington's estates were given by Charles the Second to the Duke of Grafton. But the temporary permission to occupy what had formerly been their own house and home was withdrawn, and they were ejected from the Grange soon after Isaac Penington was cast into prison. Whether the Bridgwater influence had anything to do with this harsh proceeding at such a juncture is not evident, though we may well surmise it had. Be that as it may, the family was broken up, and they made several movements before they could obtain a tolerably comfortable abode. Gulielma with her maid went to Bristol, as Ellwood tells us, on a visit to her former maid, who had been married to a Bristol merchant. Mary Penington herself, with her younger children, went to Aylesbury, to be near her husband. There she took a small house. The tutor had lodgings in the neighborhood.

Of the many religious letters still in existence which were written by Isaac Penington in the prison at Aylesbury, some were addressed to his implacable enemy the Earl of Bridgwater. They show very clearly and beautifully the loving and forgiving spirit which influenced the writer, and evince unswerving fidelity to his Divine Master. The two following have been copied from the Penington MSS. belonging to J. S. Robson of Saffron Walden.

Isaac Penington to the Earl of Bridgwater.

"God is higher than man, and His will and laws are to be obeyed in the first place; man's only in the second, and that in due subordination to the will and laws of God. Now, friend, apply this thyself; and do that which is right and noble; that which is justifiable in God's sight; that thou mayest give a comfortable account to Him when He shall call on thee. That which thou hast done to me hath not made me thy enemy; but, in the midst of the sense of it, I desire thy true welfare; and that thou mayest so carry thyself in thy place, as neither to provoke God against thee in this world, nor in the world to come.

"Hast thou not afflicted me without cause? Wouldst thou have me to bow to thee wherein the Lord hath not given me liberty? Oh! come down in thy spirit before the Lord. Honour Him in thy heart and ways, and seek for the true nobility and honour that cometh from Him. Thou hast but a time to be in the world, and then eternity begins;

and what thou hast sown here thou must then reap.

"I send thee the enclosed. O that thou wouldst read it in fear and humility, lifting up thy heart to the Lord who giveth understanding, that it may be a blessing to thee, for in true love was it writ.

"Though the Lord beholdeth, and will plead the cause of His innocent ones, and the more helpless they are the more they are considered, yet I do not desire that thou shouldst suffer either from man or from God, on my account, but that thou mightest be guided to, and preserve, in that which will bring sweet rest, peace, and safety to all who are sheltered by it, in the stormy hour in which the Lord will make man to feel his sin and misery.

"This is the sum of what I have at present to say, who have writ this in the stirrings of true love towards thee, and from a desire that thou mightest feel the power of God forming thy heart, setting it aright, and causing it to bring forth the fruits of righteousness in thee." "I am thy friend in these things, and have written as a true lover of thy soul.
"I. P.

"From Aylesbury Jail, 24th of vi. mo. 1666."

The next document, which was written, as the date indicates, two months before the preceding, was probably that which Isaac Penington speaks of having enclosed in the above letter. It was evidently addressed to those magistrates who had countenanced the proceedings of the Earl of Bridgwater, as well as to the earl himself.

Isaac Penington, on behalf of himself and his friends, to the magistrates who were striving to crush out Quakerism by persecution.

"Why do ye persecute and afflict a man who desireth to live in the love and peace of God towards you? Will nothing satisfy you unless I deny the Lord whom I have sought and been acquainted with from my childhood, and whose favour and presence I cannot but value above all things? God appeareth not in outward shapes or voices, but in His truth revealed in the hearts and consciences of them that fear Him and wait upon Him; and he that denieth subjection to any manifestation in the pure light revealed there denieth God, and shall be denied of Him; this I dare not run the hazard of, through fear of any man. Ye are men—great men, many of you—but I know God to be greater, and that His power and authority over me is greater than yours; and therefore I am not to be blamed for yielding subjection to Him in the first place.

"O! think what ye are doing. Oh! that ye would yet consider! Can poor worm man contend against his Maker, and prosper? Alas! what are we? But if the Lord our God hath appeared to us, and in us, and ye in that respect are offended, and make war with us, do ye not thus contend against God? What will be the end of these things? and what are ye bringing this poor nation and yourselves unto? For of a truth God is righteous, and what ye have sown in the day of your power that ye must reap in the day of His righteous judgment; all the sufferings, oppressions, and cries of the innocent will then come upon you in full weight and measure, unless ye repent and change your ways.

"I write this in love, tenderness, and good will as the Lord knoweth, however ye may interpret it; and, after all my sufferings from you, I could freely lay down my life for your sakes, if it were the will of God thus to do you good.

"I have been and still am a patient sufferer for well-doing, blessing the Lord who redeemeth and preserveth the souls of His children out of evildoing, and who bringeth His indignation and wrath, with great perplexity and misery, upon nations and upon persons who set themselves in opposition to Him. Read *Is.* xxiv. and *Rom.* ii. 2, 9; and fear before Him, for it is good for man to be abased, and to be found in true fear before his Maker.

"I. P.

"Aylesbury, 23rd 4th mo. 1666."

It will be observed that the above letters in no degree partake of the usual tone of a prisoner asking for release. Throughout, the writer considers himself as a Christian minister, commissioned by the Lord; and as such, in addressing evil doers, he is striving under feelings of Christian concern to draw their hearts to God. But we have no evidence of any thing he said having touched the feelings or the consciences of either the Earl of Bridgwater, or of Palmer the deputy-lieutenant, who were chiefly instrumental in putting him into prison and keeping him there. However, it is probable his words touched some less hardened hearts; as it appears the Earl of Ancram interposed, and either by persuasion or some other means induced the deputy-lieutenant to liberate Isaac Penington.

His wife and some of his children, with two servants, were then living in the small house in Aylesbury. Thomas Ellwood, with the elder children, were lodging in a farmhouse in the parish of St. Giles Chalfont.

Mary Penington, who at various times was a severe sufferer from internal pain, seems to have gone to London for medical advice, accompanied by her daughter Gulielma, when the following letter was written. It has been copied by kind permission from the original, now the property of Silvanus Thompson of York; on the back it is directed to William Penington, Merchant, for M. P.

To his wife.

"19th of First-month, 1667.

"My dear love, whom my heart is still with, and whose happiness and full content is my great desire and delight.

"Leaving thee in so doubtful a condition, and there being such an earnestness in my mind to hear how it was with thee, it was pretty hard to me to miss of a letter from thee on the Third-day. Thomas Ellwood had one from W. P. on the Fourth-day, wherein there was very good and welcome news concerning thy health.

"On Third-day night were called E. H., W. R., and G. S., not having been called at the assizes. They said the judge spake much against the Papists at the assizes, and also gave a short charge relating to the fanatics. And I heard by a Windsor friend that they were forward, and preparing to be very sharp at Windsor.

"Yesterday I saw thy boy Ned at [*name illegible*] looking very well and fresh, if not too well; I mean, too fat. Bill and all thy children are well. Bill expects thy coming home at night. I bid him write to thee to come home; but he said no, he would go to London to thee. I said, 'If thou canst not get quiet, father will get all thy love from thee;' for he was exceedingly loving to me this morning in bed. He said, 'No! no! must not get all the love from mother.' My natural love makes me express these things, yet not without some fear lest I should be instrumental to draw thy mind too much into that nature which I myself want to be daily further and further drawn out of.

"My dear love is to thee, and to my dear Guli, and to my dear S. W. Mind it also to S. H. and J. B. and W. and S. B., and brother Daniel and his wife, and to the Pagetts, if thou see them,—which perhaps it might be convenient so to do if thou hast opportunity; for it seems some have endeavoured to instil into them as if we were neglectful of them, and had not love for them answerable to theirs for us.

"My dear, that the Lord may lead us more and more into His precious life, and under His holy power, and into the grace of, and subjection to His pure truth, that therein we may live to Him, and feel the daily change more and more into His holy image!

"Thine in all dearness, truth, and love,
"I. P.

"P.S.—Thomas Ellwood desires me to mind his love to thee and Guli Springett.

"My soul hath been poured out, my dear, in prayer for thy health and ease, if the Lord might see good; and for His doing thee good by the pain wherewith thou art afflicted; and for thy growth and prosperity in His truth. I also desire of the Lord prudence and wisdom, to guide me towards my children."

The term of Isaac Penington's liberation, after the release procured for him by the Earl of Ancram, was of less than a month's duration. The two wicked tyrants, Palmer and Bridgwater, contrived at the end of three weeks to have this unresisting Christian gentleman again imprisoned. He was then confined in a most unhealthy incommodious apartment of Aylesbury jail, which so much debilitated his tender constitution, and brought on such a severe attack of illness, that for a considerable time it was thought he would not have recovered. But he did survive, and after recovery still remained incarcerated, whilst his meek patient spirit endured without repining all the evil thus heaped on him, believing, as he did, that his Heavenly Father would cause good to come out of it. Again he had recourse to his pen to convey words of comfort or Christian counsel to those towards whom his spirit was drawn. During his various imprisonments he wrote several religious works, and his correspondence was very extensive. To the Friends of the neighbouring meetings he occasionally wrote epistles, and very often he wrote privately to individuals both at home and abroad. From letters which were written about this time the following are selected:—

To Friends in Amersham.

"Aylesbury, 4th 3rd mo. 1667.

"Friends,

"Our (spiritual) life is love, and peace, and tenderness; bearing one with another, and forgiving one another, not laying accusations one against another, but praying one for another, and helping one another with a tender hand, if there has been any slip or fall; and waiting till the Lord gives sense and repentance, if sense and repentance in any be wanting. Oh! wait to feel this spirit, and to be guided in this spirit, that ye may enjoy the Lord, and walk meekly, tenderly, peaceably, and lovingly one with another. Then ye will be a praise to the Lord, and any thing that may be amiss ye will come over in the true dominion, even in the Lamb's dominion; and that which is contrary shall be trampled upon, as life rises and rules in you. So watch your hearts and ways; and watch one over another in that which is gentle and tender, and knows it can neither preserve itself, nor help another out of the snare; but the Lord must be waited on to do this in and for us all. So mind Truth, the service, enjoyment, and possession of it in your hearts, and so walk as may bring no disgrace upon it, but may be a good savour in the places where ye live—the meek, innocent, tender, righteous life reigning in you, governing over you, and shining through you.

"Your friend in the Truth, and a desirer of your welfare therein,

"I. P."

To George Fox.

"Aylesbury jail, 15th 5th mo., 1667.

"Dear G. F.

"I feel the tender mercy of the Lord, and some proportion of that brokenness, fear, and humility which I have long waited for, and breathed after. Oh! blessed be the Lord, who hath fitted and restored me, and brought up my life from the grave.

"I feel a high esteem and dear love to thee, whom the Lord hath chosen, anointed, and honoured; and, dear G. F., I beg thy love and entreat thy prayers, in faith and assurance that the Lord hears thee, that I may be yet more broken, that I may be yet more filled with the fear of the Lord, and may walk in perfect humility and tenderness of spirit before Him all my days.

"Dear George, thou mayest know my wants and desires more fully than my own heart. Be helpful to me in tender love, that I may feel settlement and stability in the Truth, and perfect separation from all that is contrary thereto.

"I. P.

"P. S.—I entreat thy prayers for my family, that

the name of the Lord may be exalted, and his Truth flourish therein. Dear G. F., indeed my soul longs for the pure, full, and undisturbed reign of (spiritual) life in me."

―――――――

To his uncle.

"19th 7th mo., 1668.

"Dear Uncle,

"There is true and tender love in my heart towards thee, and in that love I cannot but desire that it may be well with thee forever; and to that end that thou mayest be acquainted with the power and life of religion, feeling it quickening and redeeming thy mind, heart, and soul to the Lord. Many take up a religion, as they apprehend, from the letter of the Scriptures, and strive to conform their hearts and practices thereto, which they think will avail. But, dear uncle, whoever receives not the (divine) power into his heart, which is stronger than the power which causeth to sin, and which captivateth the mind from the Lord, he is not a true witness of salvation. The Lord hath revealed His precious living virtue, and His pure redeeming power in this our day; blessed forever be His name! Oh! that thou mightest partake thereof, and in it receive the seal of thy everlasting redemption.

"Oh, dear uncle! dost thou thirst after the living

waters? Dost thou feel in thy heart a cry to the Father of spirits daily? This is precious with the Lord, and this the Lord will answer and accept.

"But, indeed, many have a name to live, and think they live now to God, and shall live with Him forever, and yet are dead in His sight, being not in union with that which quickens, but only in a notion concerning it. Oh, dear uncle, cry to God night and day, thou mayest be of the number of the true sheep which hear and know the shepherd's voice, and in the certain leadings of His spirit follow Him, the Lamb, whithersoever he goes.

"In the truth of my love I have sent thee the enclosed, which may the Lord God of mercy, love, and power make serviceable to thee. I am thy truly affectionate nephew, sensible of thy love to me, and answering it in returns of unfeigned love to thee.

"I. P."

To his Cousin.

"Dear Cousin,

"Thou hast had many wanderings and outgoings, as well as others. Oh! return now with others to the Shepherd and Bishop of souls, and feel thy mind stayed upon Him, that thou mayest go out from Him no more. The path He hath now revealed is plain, so that he who runs may read, and a fool need not err therein. But there is a wisdom which cannot know it, and will not walk therein, which wisdom is near thee. O! take heed of it.

"The Jews had the Scriptures, and searched them which foretold of the coming of Christ in the flesh, and yet could not thereby know Him when He came. How then was He to be known? why, by the revelation of the spirit. So John the Baptist knew Him. For the same that sent John to baptize discovered Him to him. And so the disciples knew Him. 'Flesh and blood hath not revealed this to thee, but my Father.' And can any know his appearance in this day but by the revelation of the spirit? And can any be saved by Him but they that receive Him in spirit? Can any be saved from Satan's power but by the power of God working in the heart against it? It will not serve any to think to be saved by righteousness and cleanness being *imputed* to them, for they must also feel cleanness within. 'Create in me a clean heart, O God, and renew a right spirit within me,' said David.

"Dear cousin, I have prayed for thee many times, especially whilst in prison, and I have felt for thy sore distress. But there is no reaping benefit from my prayers, but as thou comest into the new way, and walkest with God in the new and living covenant. This is the plain despised path which the wisdom in all sorts of professors overlooks; and so they miss the one thing necessary, and get up a notion concerning Christ, instead of [coming to] Christ himself."

Isaac Penington had taken no legal steps to procure his own release; and from his letter to his wife of 7th month, 1665, it seems that he did not wish her to " plead his cause." Those who had procured his imprisonment seemed determined that he should remain in prison until he consented to apologise. Under these circumstances a relative of Mary Penington, whose name is unknown, took out a writ of Habeas Corpus early in 1668, which brought him to London for trial; and as it was then ascertained that there was no case whatever to try—no record against him—he was at once liberated. Most other men would have sued for false imprisonment those who had illegally caused them so much suffering: but not so Isaac Penington.

Some unprincipled men, who had observed his unresisting spirit, refused to pay him money which they owed him, and one of Mary Penington's relatives commenced a lawsuit to deprive her of one of her estates. The case was thrown into Chancery, and was lost, because neither she nor her husband would take an oath to verify their claims. Mary Penington herself tells us of these trials, adding, " Thus we were stripped of my husband's estate, and wronged of a great part of mine. After this, we were tossed up and down from place to place, to our great weariness and charge; seeing no place to abide in, in this country, near to meetings, which had formerly been held at our house at Chalfont. We were pressed in our spirits to stay amongst the Friends here, if any house could be found with conveniencies, though it were but ordinarily decent.

"We sought in many places within the compass of four or five miles from that meeting, but could find none. Yet having still such a sense of its being our right place, we had not freedom to settle anywhere else; so we boarded at Waltham-abbey during the summer, for our children's accommodation at the school there, and left our friends to enquire further for us. But in all that time of seeking it had never entered into our thoughts of buying a place. Nay, we rather endeavoured to have a state of disentanglement, and to procure a habitation without land. But, seeing no place like to fit us in the country near those people, I told my husband I was not willing to go from them into any other place, except it were to our own estate in Kent. This he liked not to do, taking exception against the air, and against the dirtiness of the place. This put me into a great strait. I could not bear, except to go to Kent, to leave those we had been instrumental in gathering to the Truth, and who had known our sufferings respecting our estate, and who compassionated us. We and they had suffered together, and had been comforted together. They had a sense of our former condition, and were compassionate of us; we being in their sight so stripped, they expected no great things, such as would answer to our rank in the world; but rather wondered we were able to live so decently, and to pay every one their own. Our submitting thus to mean things, which our present condition occasioned, was honorable before them, but strangers would have despised it, which would have been uneasy to us.

"Thus it was that the temper amongst our acquaintances and countrymen here helped us to bear the meanness and the great straitness, so much more than we had ever known before, having been born to and having lived in great plenty. One day, when we were about going to Waltham Abbey, R. T. coming to see us, and bewailing our going out of the country, and having no place near them to return to, said, 'Why will you not buy some little place near us?' I refused this with great neglect, saying our condition would not admit of such a thing, for we had not an hundred pounds beside our rents, and that we must sell some of my land if we do so. He told me he had an uncle who would sell a place that was about thirty pounds a year, which stood near the meeting-house at Amersham, and was in a healthy place, and that the house being trimmed might be made habitable. My husband was not there at that time; but soon after R. B. came, and I told him what R. T. had proposed; he seemed to encourage the thing, and said he had heard there were some rooms in the house that might serve.

"That night Thomas Ellwood came out of Kent, and told me he had much to do to come back without selling my farm at West Bur. I laid these things together, and said, 'I think this must be our way, if we can sell West Bur to buy this that R. T. has offered, and with the overplus money put the house in a condition to receive us.' Next day I took Anne Bull with me, and went on foot to Woodside, to John Humphries' house, to view it, and its situation. I came in by Hill's-lane through the orchard; but it looked so ruinous, and unlike what could be trimmed up for us, that I did not go into the house. So it quite fell through till we were going away, having been disappointed of a house at Beaconsfield, which my husband had been in treaty about. Upon this we pressed again to see the house, which I did, Thomas Ellwood and H. B. going with me; my husband having said he left the decision to me. So I went into the house, and they viewed the grounds; and in half an hour's time I had the form of the thing in my mind, what to sell, what to pull down, what to add, and cast how it would be done with the overplus money. So I gave up to have them to treat for it, and let us know at Waltham; which they did, and sent us word the title was clear, but they judged it £50 too dear. When I received that message, I had my mind much to the Lord in this thing; that if it were the place He gave us liberty to be in, He would order it for us. I had requested of my husband that, seeing he had lost all, and the children had no provision but my estate, and that we were so tossed about, and had no dwelling-place for ourselves or our children, I might build some little thing for them. My husband was averse to building; but I, weighing that could I part with some land, and buy the place with the money, and put it in condition for us and them, and he not to be troubled with the building, but that it should be made over to Friends for me and the children; then he, considering that the estate was mine, and that he had lost all of his, and that thus that suffering had been brought upon me, was willing that I should do what I would. And he added that he took delight that I should be answered in this, though it was contrary to his temper either to own a house or to build one.

"So I sent word to our friends that they should conclude for it; that I did not matter £50 if they thought well of it in other respects. Then it went on. I was often in prayer to the Lord that I might be preserved from entanglements and cumber, and that it might be such an habitation as would manifest that the Lord was again restoring us, and had a regard to us. When it was bought, I went industriously and cheerfully about the business, though I saw many unusual incumbrances present themselves before me; under which I still cried to the Lord that I might go through in His fear, and not cumber or darken my mind.

"After we had concluded for it, we met with a great interruption; the woman being advised to make prey upon us by an unreasonable demand for her consent. I earnestly desired of the Lord to make way for us to get clear of the whole matter, though with great loss, rather than that we should run into entanglements in the management of it, the dread of running into debt was so heavy on me. But I got over that, and went on to plant, and to make provision for building, till the surveyor put me out of my own way. He put us upon rearing from the ground a new part, and my husband falling in with his plan, I could not avoid it. It brought great trouble upon me; for I did not see my way clear as before. Having stepped from my own plan, and not knowing how to compass this charge, I took no pleasure in doing anything about it. At length I fell ill, and could not look after it, and great was my exercise; one while fearing the Lord did not approve of what I had done; another while saying within myself, I did not seek great things nor vain glory in wishing a fine habitation. For as I cast it at first, and did not intend to do more, it would have been very ordinary. After many close exercises and earnest prayers, I came to a clearness that I had an honest intent in what I did, the full expense being undiscerned. I then felt my mind stayed, and acted without disquiet;

and the building was afterwards managed by me rather in delight, through an assurance that the undertaking was a right one.

"Part of the house fell down from the new casting of it, and in the falling I was most remarkably preserved. This wrought in me a care how to compass what had to be done. After a time I felt an innocent enjoyment arise in my mind, and I went on very cheerfully, never looking out with apprehension; and when there was occasion for money to be paid, I found I still had it, having contracted my family expenses. My rents came in steadily, and by selling old houses, and bark, and several other things, the expenses of the building were met, and I then had pleasure instead of pain in laying out the money. Indeed my mind was so daily turned towards the Lord in conducting this affair, and so continually was I provided with money, that I often thought, and sometimes said, that if I had lived in the time when building of houses for the service or worship of the Lord was accepted and blessed, I could not have had in such work a sweeter, stiller, or pleasanter time.

"I set all things in order of a morning before I went to meeting, and so left them unthought of till I returned; rarely finding them so much as to rise in my mind when going to, or when at meetings. Thus was my mind kept sweet and savory; for I had nothing in all that affair that disquieted me, having no further anxiety than that nothing should be wasted; and this I perceived by eye, without disquieting care being administered that would produce anger or fretting. I lay down sweetly and very pleasantly at night, awaked with a sweet sense of the work before me in the morning, was employed all day thereat, but had no burden on my mind. This seasoned me, and kept me pleasant and in health, and now I am free to leave this account of it with my children.

"The building was completed in less than four years; I could have compassed it in much less time, but then I should have been straitened for money; doing it by degrees, it stole on undiscerned in point of charge. Now all is finished except the washhouse; and I have taken up one hundred pounds; and during that time we have not omitted being helpful to others in giving or lending in our places."

It appears that the rebuilding of Woodside House commenced early in 1669; and having been, as Mary Penington states, nearly four years in hands, it was probably finished about the close of 1672 or early in 1673. While in progress, the Peningtons occupied Berrie House near Amersham; and several of the children were then at school at Waltham-abbey. The rebuilding must have been done in a very substantial manner, for we find the house is still, after a lapse of nearly two centuries, a tenantable habitation. It is now a farmhouse, and well known in Amersham as the an. ient residence of the Peningtons.

Sad to relate, in 1672 Isaac Penington was again made a prisoner. On this occasion his imprisonment was in Reading jail, and arose out of a visit he paid to Friends who were there confined. It appears from Besse's account,* that a magistrate who was very bitter against the Friends, hearing from the jailer of Penington being there, sent for him, tendered to him the oath of allegiance, and then made his refusal to swear the ostensible reason for imprisonment. He continued a prisoner there for the space of twenty-one months, till Charles the Second released by letters patent such Friends as were imprisoned throughout the nation on suits of the Crown. Isaac Penington then left for the sixth and last time the confinement of a prison. A Friend, who was his fellow sufferer in several of his imprisonments, gives the following description of his conduct.

"Being made willing by the power of God to suffer with great patience, cheerfulness, contentedness and true nobility of spirit, he was a good example to me and others. I do not remember that ever I saw him cast down or dejected during the time of his close confinement; or ever heard him speak hardly of those that persecuted him; for he

---

* See p. 31, vol. i., of "*A Collection of the Sufferings of the People called Quakers for the Testimony of a good conscience, from the time of their being first distinguished by that name in the year 1650, to the time of the Act commonly called the Act of Toleration, granted to Protestant Dissenters in the first year of the reign of King William the Third and Queen Mary, in the year 1689,*" 2 vols. folio. Lond. 1753.

was of that temper to love enemies, and to do good to them that hated him; having received a measure of that virtue from Christ his master that taught him so to do. Indeed, I may truly say, in the prison he was a help to the weak, being made instrumental in the hand of the Lord for that end. Oh! the remembrance of the glory that did often overshadow us in the place of our confinement; so that indeed the prison was made by the Lord, who was powerfully with us, as a pleasant palace. I was often, with many more, by those streams of [spiritual] life that did many times flow through him as a vessel, greatly overcome with a sense of the pure presence and love of our God, that was plentifully spread abroad in our hearts." What a testimony to the heavenly mindedness and truly Christian experience of that good man!

During the period of Isaac Penington's imprisonment and his wife's building occupation, some other events occurred in the family which must be referred to in another chapter.

CHAPTER VIII.

1666–1669.

Quaker meeting at Hedgerly.—Ambrose Bennett, the magistrate, breaks it up.—Judith Parker, the doctor's wife, remonstrates.—Bennett again imprisons Friends.—Release from prison.—Solemn meeting of Friends for the restoration of those who had been drawn away by John Perrot.—Perrot's mission to the Pope.—His imprisonment in Rome.—Release and return home.—Extravagant proceedings.—Establishment of meetings for discipline by George Fox.—Ellwood's choice of a wife.—Details of his courtship.—Is accepted.—Adventurous journey with Gulielma M. Springett.—Ellwood's bravery.—Gulielma's return home.—Ellwood's marriage.—Isaac Penington's son lost at sea.—Ellwood's grief.—His poetical effusions.

WHILST Isaac Penington remained a prisoner at Aylesbury, Thomas Ellwood, as the tutor of his sons, had considerable care of the family affairs, and he sometimes gives us an interesting glimpse into their history as well as his own. He tells us that " There was in those times (1666) a meeting once a month in the house of George Salter, a Friend of Hedgerly, to which he sometimes went. Morgan Watkins being then with us, he and I, with Guli and her maid, and one Judith Parker, wife of Dr. Parker, one of the College of Physicians, London, with a daughter of theirs (neither of whom

233

were Quakers, but as acquaintances of Mary Penington were with her on a visit) walked over to that meeting.

"The place was about a mile from the house of Ambrose Bennett, the justice who the summer before had sent me and some other Friends to Aylesbury prison, from the burial of Edward Parrot of Amersham. He, by what means I know not, getting notice not only of the meeting, but, as we supposed, of our being there, came himself to it; and as he came, catched up a stackwood stick, big enough to knock any man down, and brought it with him hidden under his cloak. Being come to the house, he stood for a while without the door, out of sight, listening to hear what was said, for Morgan was then speaking in the meeting. But certainly he heard very imperfectly, if it was true what we heard he said afterwards among his companions, as an argument that Morgan was a Jesuit, viz: that in his preaching he trolled over Latin as fluently as ever he heard any one; whereas Morgan, good man! was better versed in Welsh than in Latin, which I suppose he had never learned: I am sure he did not understand it.

"When this martial justice, who at Amersham had with his drawn sword struck an unarmed man, who he knew would not strike again, had now stood some time abroad, on a sudden he rushed in among us, with the stackwood stick held up in his hand ready to strike, crying out, 'Make way there!'

and an ancient woman not getting soon enough out of his way, he struck her with the stick a shrewd blow over the breast. Then, pressing through the crowd to the place where Morgan stood, he plucked him from thence, and caused so great a disorder in the room that it broke the meeting up; yet would not the people go away, but tarried to see what the issue would be.

"Then, taking pen and paper, he sat down at the table among us, and asked several of us our names, which we gave, and he set them down in writing. Amongst others he asked Judith Parker, the doctor's wife, what her name was, which she readily told him. Thence taking occasion to discourse him, she so overmastered him by clear reason delivered in fine language, that he, glad to be rid of her, struck out her name and dismissed her; yet did not she remove, but kept her place amongst us. When he had taken what number of names he thought fit, he singled out half a dozen; whereof Morgan was one, I another, one man more, and three women, of which the woman of the house was one, although her husband then was, and for divers years before had been, a prisoner in the Fleet for tithes, and had no one to take care of his family and business but her, his wife.

"Us six he committed to Aylesbury jail: which when the doctor's wife heard him read to the constable, she attacked him again, and having put him in mind that it was a sickly time, and that the pestilence was reported to be in that place, she, in handsome terms, desired him to consider in time how he would answer the cry of our blood, if by his sending us to be shut up in an infected place we should lose our lives. This made him alter his purpose, and by a new mittimus he sent us to the house of correction at Wycombe. And although he committed us upon the act for banishment, which limited a certain time for imprisonment, yet he, in his mittimus, limited no time, but ordered us to be kept till we should be delivered by due course of law; so little regardful was he, though a lawyer, of keeping to the letter of the law.

"We were committed on the 13th day of the month called March, 1666, and were kept close prisoners there till the 7th day of the month called June, which was some days above twelve weeks, and much above what the act required. Then were we sent for to the justice's house, and the rest being released, Morgan Watkins and I were required to find sureties for our appearance at next assizes; Morgan being, in his second mittimus, represented as a notorious offender in preaching, and I as being upon the second conviction, in order to banishment. There we lay till the 25th day of the same month; and then, by the favour of the Earl of Ancram, being brought before him at his house, we were discharged from the prison, upon our promise to appear, if at liberty and in health, at the assizes;

which we did, and were there discharged by proclamation.

"After we had been discharged at the assizes, I returned to Isaac Penington's family at Bottrel's in Chalfont, and, as I remember, Morgan Watkins with me, leaving Isaac Penington a prisoner in Aylesbury jail. The lodging we had in this farmhouse proving too strait and inconvenient for the family, I took larger and better lodgings for them in Berrie House at Amersham.

"Some time after was that memorable meeting appointed to be holden at London, through a divine opening in that eminent servant of God, George Fox, for the restoring and bringing in again of those who had gone out from Truth, and from the holy unity of Friends, by the means and ministry of John Perrot. This man came pretty early among Friends, and too early took upon him the ministerial office; and being, though little in person, yet great in opinion of himself, nothing less would serve him than to go and convert the Pope. In order thereunto, having a better man than himself, John Luff, to accompany him, they travelled to Rome, where they had not been long ere they were taken up and clapped into prison. Luff was put into the Inquisition, and Perrot in their Bedlam for madmen. Luff died in prison, not without well grounded suspicion of being murdered there. But Perrot was kept in Rome for some time, and now and then sent over an epistle to be printed here, written in such an affected and fantastic style, as might have induced an indifferent reader to believe they in Rome had suited the place of his confinement to his condition."

Without going into all of Ellwood's details about this John Perrot, I may briefly state that Friends, through great efforts and interest, succeeded in procuring his release. But after his return home he went off into much eccentricity; so that those who had been his friends could not approve of his proceedings, and then he declared against them. The report of his great sufferings at Rome, and the assumption of great sanctity of manner and appearance gained him the compassion of many kind-hearted Friends, on whose feelings he wrought in declaring for extreme notions and observances, which more experienced, stable, religious minds could not unite with. But, so earnest was Perrot, and so persevering, that he got up a party which supported him. Thomas Ellwood says, although he never had any esteem for the man, either in regard to his natural parts or ministerial gift, yet he had sympathized in degree with those who had taken up his cause, till the Lord opened his understanding; which was some time prior to the calling of the meeting in question, of which he speaks thus:

" When that solemn meeting was appointed at London, for a travail of spirit on behalf of those who had thus gone out, that they might rightly return, and be sensibly received into the unity of the body again, my spirit rejoiced, and with gladness of heart I went to it, as did many others both of city and country. With great simplicity and humility of mind we did there acknowledge our error, and take shame to ourselves. And some that lived at too remote a distance in this nation, as well as beyond the seas, upon notice reaching them of that meeting, and the intended service of it, did the like by writing, in letters directed to and openly read in the meeting; which for that purpose was continued many days.

"Not long after this, George Fox was moved of the Lord to travel through the country, from county to county, to advise and encourage Friends to set up monthly and quarterly meetings, for the better ordering of the affairs of the church; in taking care of the poor; and for exercising true gospel discipline in dealing with any that might walk disorderly under our name; and to see that such as marry amongst us act fairly and clearly in that respect.

"When he came into this country, I was one of the many Friends that were with him at the meeting for that purpose. Afterwards I travelled with Guli and her maid into the West of England, to meet him there, and to visit Friends in those parts; and we went as far as Topsham in Devonshire before we found him. He had been in Cornwall, and was then returning, and came in unexpectedly to Topsham where we were. Had he not then come thither, we were to have left that day for Cornwall. But then we turned back, and went with him through Devonshire, Somersetshire, and Dorsetshire, having generally very good meetings; and the work he was chiefly concerned in went on very prosperously.

"By the time we got back from that journey, the summer was pretty far gone; and the following winter I spent with the children of the family as before, without any remarkable alteration in my circumstances until the next spring (1669), when I found in myself a disposition of mind to change my single life for a married state. The object of my affection was a Friend whose name was Mary Ellis, whom for divers years I had had an acquaintance with, in the way of common friendship only; and in whom I thought I saw those fair prints of truth and solid virtue which I afterwards found in her to a sublime degree. What her condition was in a worldly view as to estate, I was wholly a stranger to, nor did I desire to know. I had once, a year or two before, had an opportunity to do her a small piece of service in which she wanted some assistance; wherein I acted with all sincerity and freedom of mind, not expecting or desiring any advantage, but in the satisfaction of being able to serve a friend and help the helpless.

"That little intercourse of common kindness between us ended without the least thought (I am verily persuaded on her part, and well assured on my own) of any other relation than that of a free and fair friendship. Nor did it lead us into any closer conversation, or more intimate acquaintance one with the other, than had been before. But some time after, and that a good while, I found my heart secretly drawn towards her. Yet was I not hasty in proposing, but waited to feel a satisfactory settlement of mind therein, before I took any step thereto.

"After some time, I took an opportunity to open my mind therein unto my much honoured friends Isaac and Mary Penington; who then stood *parentum loco* (instead of parents) to me. They, having solemnly weighed the matter, expressed their unity therewith; and indeed their approbation was no small confirmation to me. Yet took I still further deliberation, often retiring in spirit to the Lord, and asking Him for direction before I addressed myself to her. At length, as I was sitting all alone waiting upon the Lord for counsel and guidance, I felt the words sweetly arise in me, as if I had heard a voice which said, 'Go, and prevail.' Faith springing up in my heart, I immediately arose and went, nothing doubting.

"When I came to her lodgings, which were about a mile from me, her maid told me she was in her chamber. Having been under some indisposition which had obliged her to keep her chamber, she had not yet left. I therefore desired the maid to acquaint her mistress that I was come to give her a visit; whereupon I was invited to go up to her. And after some little time spent in common conversation, feeling my spirit weightily concerned, I solemnly opened my mind unto her with respect to the particular business I came about; which I soon perceived was a great surprisal to her; for she had taken an apprehension, as others also had done, that mine eye had been fixed elsewhere, and nearer home.

"I used not many words to her; but I felt as if a divine power went along with the words, and fixed the matter expressed by them so fast in her breast, that, as she afterwards acknowledged to me, she could not shut it out. I made at that time but a short visit. Having told her I did not expect any answer from her then, but desired she would in the most solemn manner weigh the proposal made, and in due time give me such an answer thereunto as the Lord should give her, I took my departure, leaving the issue to the Lord.

"I had a journey then at hand, which I foresaw would take me up two weeks' time. Wherefore, the day before I was to set out, I went to visit her again, to acquaint her with my journey, and excuse my absence; not yet pressing her for an answer, but assuring her that I felt in myself an increase of affection to her, and hoped to receive a suitable return from her in the Lord's time; to whom in the meantime I committed both her, myself, and the concern between us. And indeed I found at my return that I could not have left it in a better hand; for the Lord had been my advocate in my absence, and had so far answered all her objections, that when I came to her again she rather acquainted me with them than urged them. From that time forwards we entertained each other with affectionate kindness, in order to marriage; which yet we did not hasten to, but went on deliberately.

" While this affair stood thus with me, I had occasion to take another journey into Kent and Sussex; which yet I would not mention here but for a particular accident which befel me on the way. The occasion of this journey was to accompany Mary Penington's daughter, Guli, to her uncle Springett's in Sussex, and from thence among her tenants. We tarried in London the first night, and set out next morning on the Tunbridge road. The Seven Oaks lying in our way, we put in there to bait; but truly we had much ado to get either provisions or room for ourselves or horses, the house was so full of guests, and those not of the better sort. For the Duke of York being, as we were told, on the road that day for the Wells, divers of his guards and some of the meaner sort of his retinue had nearly filled all the inns there. I left John Gigger, who waited on Guli in this journey, and was her menial servant, to take care for the horses, while I did the like as well as I could for her. When I got a little room to put her into, I went to see what relief the kitchen would afford us;

and with much ado, by praying hard and paying dear, I got a small joint of meat from the spit.

"After a short repast, being weary of our quarters, we quickly mounted and took the road again, willing to hasten from a place where we found nothing but rudeness. A knot of fellows followed us, designing, as we afterwards found, to make sport for themselves. We were on a spot of fine, smooth, sandy way, whereon the horses trod so softly that we heard them not till one of them was upon us. I was then riding abreast with Guli, and discoursing with her; when, on a sudden, hearing a little noise, and turning mine eye that way, I saw a horseman coming up on the further side of her horse, having his left arm stretched out, just ready to take her about the waist, and pluck her off backwards from her own horse, to lay her before him on his. I had but just time to thrust forth my whip between him and her, and bid him stand off. At the same time, reining my horse to let hers go before me, I thrust in between her and him, and, being better mounted than he, my horse run him off. But his horse, though weaker than mine, being nimble, he slipped by me, and got up to her on the near side, endeavouring to seize her; to prevent which I thrust in upon him again, and in our jostling we drove her quite out of the way, and almost into the next hedge.

"While we were thus contending, I heard a noise of loud laughter behind us, and, turning my head that way, I saw three or four horsemen more, who could scarcely sit their horses for laughing, to see the sport their companion made with us. From thence I saw it was a plot laid, and that this rude fellow was not to be dallied with, wherefore I admonished him to take warning in time, and to give over, lest he repented too late. He had in his hand a short thick truncheon, which he held up at me; laying hold on it with a strong gripe, I suddenly wrenched it out of his hand, and threw it at as great a distance behind me as I could.

"Whilst he rode back to fetch his truncheon, I called up honest John Gigger, who was indeed a right honest man, and of a temper so thoroughly peaceable that he had not hitherto put in at all. But now I roused him, and bid him ride so close up to his mistress's horse on the further side that no horse might thrust in between, and I would endeavour to guard the near side. But he, good man, not thinking perhaps that it was respectful enough for him to ride so near his mistress, left room enough for another to push in between. And, indeed, as soon as the brute had recovered his truncheon, he came up directly hither, and had thrust in, had not I by a nimble turn chopped in upon him, and kept him at bay. I then told him I had hitherto spared him, but I wished him not to provoke me further. This I said with such a tone as bespoke high resentment of the abuse put upon us, and withal I pressed so close upon him with my horse, that I suffered him not to come up any more to Guli.

"His companions, who kept an equal distance behind us, both heard and saw all this, and thereupon two of them advancing, came up to us. I then thought I was likely to have my hands full, but Providence turned it otherwise. For they, seeing the contest rise so high, and probably fearing it would rise higher, not knowing where it might stop, came in to part us; which they did by taking him away, one of them leading his horse by the bridle, and the other driving him on with his whip, and so carried him off.

"One of their company stayed behind, and it so happened that a great shower just then falling, we betook ourselves for shelter under a thick, well spread oak which stood hard by. Thither also came that other person whom I observed wore the Duke's livery. Whilst we put on our defensive garments against the weather, he took the opportunity to discourse with me about the man who had been so rude to us, endeavoring to excuse him by alleging that he had drunk a little too liberally. I let him know that one vice would not excuse another; that although but one of them was actually concerned in the abuse, yet he and the rest of them were abettors of it, and accessaries to it; that I was not ignorant whose livery they wore, and was well assured their lord would not maintain them in committing such outrages upon travellers on the road, to our injury and his dishonour; that I understood the Duke was coming down, and that they might expect to be called to an account for this rude proceeding. He begged hard that we would pass the offence, and make no complaint to their lord; for he said he knew the Duke would be very severe, and that it would be the utter ruin of the young man. When he had said what he could, he went off before us, without any ground given him to expect favour; and when we had fitted ourselves for the weather, we followed at our own pace.

"When we came to Tunbridge, I set John Gigger foremost, bidding him lead on briskly through the town, and, placing Guli in the middle, I came close up after her. We were expected, I perceived; for, though it rained very hard, the street was thronged with men who looked very earnestly on us, but did not offer any affront. We had a good way to ride beyond Tunbridge, and beyond the Wells, in byways among the woods, and were the later for the hindrance we had on the way; when, being come to Herbert Springett's house, Guli acquainted her uncle what danger and trouble she had met on the way, and he would have had the persons prosecuted, but since Providence had so well preserved her and delivered her from it, she chose to pass by the offence.

"When Guli had finished the business she went upon, we returned home, and I delivered her safe to her glad mother. From that time forward I continued my visits to my best beloved friend until we were married, which was on the 28th of the Eighth month (October), 1669. We took each other in a select meeting of the ancient and grave Friends, holden in a Friend's house, where, in those times, not only the monthly meeting for business but the public meeting for worship was sometimes kept. A very solemn meeting it was, and in a weighty frame of spirit we were, in which we sensibly felt the Lord was with us, and was joining us; the sense whereof remained with us all our lifetime, and was of good service, and very comfortable to us on all occasions.

"My next care was to secure my wife what money she had, and which with herself were bestowed on me. For I held that it would be an abominable crime in me, and would savour of the highest ingratitude, if I, though it were but through negligence, should leave any room for my father, in case I should be suddenly taken away, to break in upon her estate, and deprive her of any part of that which had been and ought to be her own. Wherefore, with the first opportunity (as I remember, the very next day, and before I knew particularly what she had) I made my will, and thereby secured to her whatever I was possessed of, as well as all that which she brought, with that little which I had before I married her.

"Towards the latter part of the summer following, I went into Kent again, and in my passage through London received the unwelcome news of the loss of a very hopeful youth, who had formerly been under my care for education. This was Isaac Penington, the second son of my worthy friends Isaac and Mary Penington, a boy of excellent parts, whose great abilities bespoke him likely to be a great man, had he lived to be a man. He was designed to be a merchant, and before he was thought ripe enough to be entered thereunto, his parents at somebody's request gave leave that he might go a voyage to Barbadoes; to spend a little time, see the place, and be somewhat acquainted with the sea. He went under the care and conduct of a choice Friend and sailor, John Grove of London, who was master of a vessel which traded to that island. He made the voyage thither very well, found the watery element agreeable, had his health there, liked the place, was much pleased with his entertainment there, and was returning home with a little cargo in return for goods he had taken out as ventures from his divers friends; when, on a sudden, through unwariness he dropped overboard, and the vessel being under sail with a brisk gale blowing he was irrecoverably lost.

"This unhappy accident took from the afflicted master all the pleasure of the voyage, and he moaned for the loss of this youth as if he had been his own, yea, only son; for, as he was in himself a man of worthy mind, so the boy by his witty and handsome behaviour in general, and courteous carriage towards him in particular, had very much wrought into his favour.

"As for me, I thought it was one of the sharpest strokes I had ever met with; for I had loved the child very well, and had conceived great hopes of general good from him; and it grieved me the deeper to think how deeply it would pierce his afflicted parents.

"Sorrow for this disaster was my companion on that journey, and I travelled the roads under great exercise of mind, revolving in my thoughts the manifold accidents which attend the life of man, and the great uncertainty of all human things. I could find no centre, no firm basis for the mind of man to rest upon, but the Divine Power and will of the Almighty. This consideration wrought in my spirit a sort of contempt of the supposed happiness and pleasure of this world, and raised my contemplation higher. This, as it ripened, came into some degree of digestion in the following lines, which I inclosed in a letter of condolence I sent by the first post into Buckinghamshire to my dear friends, the afflicted parents. Upon my return home, going to visit them, we sat down, and solemnly mixed our sorrows and tears together."

His " Solitary Thoughts."

SOLITARY THOUGHTS

ON THE UNCERTAINTY OF ALL HUMAN THINGS.

" Transibunt cito, quæ vos mansura putatis."

What ground, alas! has any man
  To set his heart on things below,
Which, when they seem most like to stand,
  Fly like an arrow from a bow?
    Things subject to exterior sense
    Are to mutation most prepense.

If stately houses we erect,
  And therein think to take delight,
On what a sudden are we checked,
  And all our hopes made groundless quite!
    One little spark in ashes lays
    What we were building half our days.

If on estates an eye we cast,
  And pleasure there expect to find,
A secret providential blast
  Brings disappointment to our mind.
    Who's now on top ere long may feel
    The circling motion of the wheel.

If we our tender babes embrace,
  And comfort hope in them to have,
Alas! in what a little space
  Is hope laid with them in the grave!
    What promiseth content
    Is in a moment from us rent.

But is there nothing, then, that's sure
  For man to fix his heart upon?
Nothing that always will endure
  When all these transient things are gone?

Sad state where man, with grief oppress'd,
Finds nought wherein his mind may rest.

Oh yes! there is a God above,
  Who unto men is also nigh,
On whose unalterable love
  We may with confidence rely.
    No disappointment can befall
    While trusting Him that's All in All.

In Him o'er all if we delight,
  And in His precepts pleasure take,
We shall be sure to do aright.
  'Tis not His nature to forsake.
    A proper object He alone
    For man to set his heart upon.
                    T. E.

Kent, 4th, 7th mo. 1670.

I add two hymns written by Thomas Ellwood about the same time, in consequence of mental trouble induced partly by the persecuting spirit abroad, and partly by his father's conduct towards him and his wife soon after their marriage. They have some poetical merit, and much pious feeling.

TO THE HOLY ONE.

Eternal God! Preserver of all those
  (Without respect of person or degree,)
Who in thy faithfulness their trust repose,
  And place their confidence alone in Thee,
Be Thou my succour; for thou know'st that I
On Thy protection, Lord, alone rely.

Surround me, Father, with thy mighty power;
    Support me daily by thine holy arm;
Preserve me faithful in the evil hour;
    Stretch forth thine hand to save me from all harm;
Be thou my helmet, breastplate, sword, and shield,
And make my foes before thy power to yield.

Teach me the spiritual battle so to fight
    That when the enemy shall me beset,
Armed cap-a-pie with armour of thy light,
    A perfect conquest o'er him I may get,
And with Thy battle-axe may cleave the head
Of him who bites that part whereon I tread.

Then, being from domestic foes set free,
    The cruelties of men I shall not fear,
But in Thy quarrel, Lord, undaunted be,
    And for Thy sake the loss of all things bear,
Yea, though in dungeons lock'd, with joy will sing
A song of praise to Thee, my God, my King.

                                  T. E.
Sussex, 11th mo. 1669.

A SONG OF PRAISE.

Thy love, dear Father! and thy tender care
    Have in my heart begot a strong desire
To celebrate thy name with praises rare,
    That others, too, thy goodness may admire,
    And learn to yield to what thou dost require.

Many have been the trials of my mind,
    My exercises great, great my distress;
Full oft my ruin hath my foe designed;
    My sorrows then my pen cannot express,
    Nor could the best of men afford redress.

When thus beset to Thee I lift mine eye,
  And with a mournful heart my moan do make,
How oft with eyes o'erflowing did I cry,
  My God, my God, oh do not me forsake,
  Regard my tears, some pity on me take!

And to the glory of thy holy Name,
  Eternal God! whom I both love and fear,
I hereby do declare I never came
  Before thy throne, and found thee loth to hear,
  But always ready with an open ear.

And though sometimes thou seem'st thy face to hide,
  As one that had withdrawn thy love from me,
'Tis that my faith may to the full be tried,
  And that I thereby may the better see
  How weak I am, when not upheld by thee.

For underneath thy holy arm I feel,
  Encompassing with strength as with a wall,
That if the enemy trip up my heel,
  Thou ready art to save me from a fall.
  To thee belong thanksgivings over all!

And for thy tender love, my God, my King,
  My heart shall magnify thee all my days;
My tongue of thy renown shall daily sing;
  My pen shall also grateful trophies raise,
  As monuments to thy eternal praise.

Thomas Ellwood was an industrious and voluminous writer. The History of his Life, written by himself, is a most interesting and characteristic piece of autobiography. It reached a second edition within the year after his death, and has since been frequently reprinted. His longest work is his *Sacred History of the Holy Scriptures of the Old and the New Testament; digested into due method with respect to order of time and place, with observations tending to illustrate some passages therein.* It is full of his own raciness and mother wit, is very pleasant reading, and reached a fourth edition in 1778. His other prose writings are nearly all on controversial subjects in defence of the doctrines of Friends, and have never been republished. The titles of some of them are characteristic of the age, and will sufficiently indicate their tenor:

> The Foundation of Tythes Shaken;
> An Antidote against the infection of W. Rogers' book;
> A Seasonable Disswasive from Persecution;
> A Fair Examination of a Foul Paper;
> Rogero-Mastix, a Rod for W. R.; etc.

His greatest poetical effort is his *Davideis*, the life of David, King of Israel, a sacred poem in five books, which, as the author in his preface informs us, was composed not with a view to publication, but for his "own diversion." It first appeared in 1712, during his lifetime, and reached its fourth and last edition in 1792. Many of his shorter pieces on serious subjects are interspersed through the autobiography, and generally owe more of their interest to the subjects than to the execution.

I have now before me an octavo volume of great

antiquarian and personal interest to all admirers of Ellwood. It contains about eighty leaves of strong paper tinted by age, is bound in green and gold, with gilt edges, and is in excellent preservation.* It contains Ellwood's shorter poems, written by his own hand, and severally signed with his initials. Most of them are serious or devotional; several are merely transcripts of those in the autobiography; but others are of a more secular character, such as

>A Satyrick Poem on the Wickham Play, its Actors and Abettors;
>A Prospect;
>A Direction to my Friend inquiring the way to my House;
>On an Envious Rayler;
>To my Courteous Friend, Edmond Waller, the Poet, etc.

Although Ellwood had Milton for his "master," and Waller for his "courteous friend" and neighbour at Beaconsfield, his own poems are not of a high order, but they evince a pious, kindly, playful disposition, a sense of humour, a love of nature and natural beauty, considerable taste and learning, and are always perfectly intelligible, which cannot be alleged of more eminent poets in times nearer to our own. Of all the pieces in this volume the

---

* For the inspection of this interesting MS. volume, and liberty to select from it, I am indebted to the kindness of my friend Anna Huntley of High Wycombe, into whose possession it came through her father, the late Joseph Steevens of that place.

following is the most remarkable. It was probably written shortly after Milton's death, which occurred in 1674, and evinces that,

> "though fallen on evil days,
> On evil days though fallen, and evil tongues,
> In darkness, and with dangers compassed round,
> And solitude,"

the great poet had in his Quaker pupil one who fully appreciated his sublime genius, and foresaw the grandeur of his future reputation.

UPON THE EXCELLENTLY LEARNED
JOHN MILTON.
An Epitaph.

Within this arch embalm'd doth lie
One whose high fame can never die;
MILTON, whose most ingenious pen
Obligéd has all learnéd men.

Great his undertakings were,
  (None greater of their kind,)
Which sufficiently declare
  The worth and greatness of his mind.

Mean adversaries he declin'd,
And battle with the chiefest join'd.

Not e'en the Royal Portraiture
  Proudly could before him stand,
    But fell and broke.
Not able, as it seems, t'endure
  The heavy stroke
    Of his *Iconoclastes* hand.

Thus the so-fam'd *Eikon Basilike*
Became the trophy of his victory.

On his triumphant chariot too did wait
One who had long the crown of learning wore,
And of renown had treasur'd up good store,
But never found an equal match before,
Which puff'd him up, and made him too elate.

This was the great SALMATIUS, he whose name
Had tower'd so high upon the wing of fame,
   And never knew till now
   What 'twas alas! to bow;
For many a gallant captive by the heel
Had he in triumph dragg'd at's chariot-wheel.
But now is fain to stoop, and see the bough
Torn from his own to deck another's brow.
This broke his heart; for, having lost his fame,
He died 'tis hard to say whether thro' grief or shame.
Thus great SALMATIUS, in his winding sheet,
Lies prostrate at far greater MILTON's feet—
MILTON in whom all brave endowments meet!

The majesty of Poesy he reviv'd,
   The common road forsaking,
   And unto Helicon a new track making,
To write in measures without rhyme contriv'd.

He knew the beauty of a verse well made
   Doth in a just and due proportion lie
   Of parts, true feet, right cadence, symphony,
(A thing by vulgar poets lightly weigh'd,)
   Not in the tinkling chime
   Of a harsh and far-fetch'd rhyme.

Two great examples of this kind he left,
  (The natural issue of his teeming brain);
One shows how man of Eden was bereft;
  In t'other man doth Paradise regain,
  So far as naked notion can attain.

Nature in him a large foundation laid,
  And he had also superbuilt thereon
A structure great, indeed, and fair enough,
Of well-prepar'd and finely-polish'd stuff,
  Admir'd by all but equalléd by none.

  So that of him it might be said
    (And that most truly too,)
      Nature and Art
      Had play'd their part,
  As if they had a wager laid
  Which of them most for him should do.

His natural abilities
Were doubtless of the largest size;
  And thereunto he surely had acquir'd
Learning as much as could be well desir'd.
More known his learning was not than admir'd.

  Profound his judgment was and clear;
    His apprehension of the highest strain;
His reason all before it down did bear,
  So forcible, demonstrative, and plain
    It did appear.

  Lofty fancy, deep conceit,
  Style concise and language great
  Render'd his discourse complete,
On whatsoever subject he did treat.
  Invention never higher rose
  In poetic strains or prose.

In tongues he so much skill had got,
He might be called *The Polyglott*.

Even they 'gainst whom he writ
Could not but admire his wit,
   And were forcéd to confess
(For indeed it was in vain
To deny a thing so plain,)
   That their parts than his were less.

Unto him the Muses sent,—
And that, too, not in compliment;
   For doubtless 'twas his due,
   As all that knew him knew—
The title of *Most Excellent*,
   Of which title may he rest
   Now and evermore possess'd!

                               T. E.

CHAPTER IX.

1670.

William Penn recalled from Ireland.—Reconciliation with his father.—Decline of the Admiral's health.—Conventicle Act.—William Penn a prisoner with William Meade.—His letter to his father from prison.—Penn and Meade at the bar.—Indicted for a riot.—The jury refuse to bring them in guilty.—The Recorder repeatedly insists that they must reconsider their verdict.—They persist in presenting the same.—Are confined to the juryroom for two nights and two days without food.—Ultimate triumph of jury, and liberation of the prisoners.—Jurymen and prisoners committed for pretended contempt of court.—Penn's letters from prison to his dying father.—Release from prison.—The jurymen bring an action against the Recorder for false imprisonment.—Triumph of the jury.—Death of Admiral Sir William Penn.—His last advice to his son.—The Admiral's monument.—William Penn's ability as a controversialist.

WILLIAM PENN had been about eight months in Ireland attending to the affairs of the Shangarry estate, when he was recalled in consequence of his father's declining health. The admiral by that time had fully realized the strength of his son's religious convictions. No longer hoping to influence them by worldly considerations, or to see them altered, he was anxious only for a reconciliation, which took place immediately on William's return. This was a great joy to his mother, and a comfort to both father and son, between whom mutual confidence was entirely restored. The admiral's health did not improve. Hard service and active energetic work of both body and mind, under many varieties of circumstance and climate, had done a work not to be undone. The hardy seaman, perceiving that inroads on his constitution had been made which could not be remedied except by total rest, gave up his public duties, and retired from the Navy Board. But the rest and retirement came too late; health did not follow. However, a great change in his religious views and feelings came over his mind, when his son could speak to him and act as he did with the freedom indicated by the events and letters which follow.

Doubtless, William's presence was then very comforting to the admiral. The remembrance of the part in life which his son had so early chosen, must have acted as a continual reminder that he himself had, in his worldly aspirations, been treading a very different path; that he had in fact been merely pursuing shadows which had fled before him, and which now neither in retrospect nor in hope could yield happiness. The honours of the gay world, on which he had once calculated so eagerly, had altogether lost their charm, a cloud had fallen on them, as the thoughts and prospect of death and eternity opened before him. From this point of view he was now disposed to commend William's unflinching adherence to his own convictions of truth, which had led to his imprisonment the previous year. No opposition whatever was now made to his frequenting the Friends' meetings in the city, at which William was not only a regular attender but at which he often preached. The admiral's family residence was then at Wanstead.

The spirit of religious persecution had at this juncture reached a great height in London, the Conventicle Act having been recently renewed, with additional clauses to render it more severe than ever against dissent from the Established Church. All dissenters except the Friends endeavoured to hide themselves or their meetings to avoid its penalties. But when the city authorities took upon them to nail up the doors and windows of the Friends' meeting-houses, they met in the yard, or, where no such space existed, assembled in the adjoining street. And thus it was on the First-day, the 14th of Seventh-month, 1670, that those who attended Gracechurch-street meeting, finding the meeting-house closed against them, assembled in the space in front, where William Penn addressed them at a considerable length. A band of musketeers came up to arrest him, and were making a great commotion to get to him, when William Meade interposed, and asked them to wait till he finished speaking, and that he would then engage him to be forthcoming. They, finding great difficulty to get through the crowd, waited accordingly, and then took both Penn and Meade to prison.

This arrest was made known next morning to Admiral Penn by the following letter.

William Penn to his Father.

"Second-day morning, 15th, 6th mo. 1670.

"My dear Father,

"This comes by the hand of one who can best allay the trouble it brings. As true as ever Paul said it, such as live godly in Christ Jesus shall suffer persecution. So, for no other reason, am I at present a sufferer. Yesterday I was taken by a band of soldiers, with one Captain Meade, and in the evening carried before the Mayor; he proceeded against me according to the ancient law; he told me I should have my hat pulled off, for all I was Admiral Penn's son. I told him I desired to be in common with others, and sought no refuge from the common usage. I discoursed with him about the hat; but he avoided it. Because I did not readily answer him as to my name, William, when he asked me in order to a mittimus, he bid his clerk write one for Bridewell, and there would he see me whipped himself, for all I was Penn's son that starved the seamen. Indeed these words grieved me, and they manifested his great malice to the whole company, about one hundred people. I told him I could very well bear his severe expressions concerning myself, but was sorry to hear him speak those abuses of my father that was not present; at which the assembly seemed to murmur. In short, he committed that person and me as rioters; and at present we are at the sign of the Black Dog in Newgate market.

"And now, dear father, be not displeased nor grieved. What if this be designed of the Lord for an exercise of our patience? Several Independents were taken from Sir J. Dethick's, and Baptists elsewhere. It is the effect of commotion in the spirits of some, which the Lord will rebuke: and I doubt not that I may be at liberty in a day or two to see thee. I am very well, and have no trouble upon my spirits besides my absence from thee at this juncture; otherwise I can say I was never better, and what they have to charge me with is harmless.

"Well, eternity, which is at the door (for He that shall come will come, and will not tarry)— *that* shall make amends for all. The Lord God everlasting consolate and support thee by His holy power, and preserve thee to eternal rest and glory. Amen.

"Thy faithful and obedient son,
"WILLIAM PENN.
"My duty to my mother.

"*For my dear father, Sir William Penn.*"

The Captain Meade who was Penn's companion in prison had recently joined the Friends. He had been a Cromwellian officer, and at one period of his life, as may be inferred from the indictment, was a linen-draper, but his position by inheritance was that of an Essex country gentleman, owning considerable landed property in that county. He was afterwards married to one of the Fells of Swarthmoor Hall. At the time of their arrest Penn and Meade appear to have had little previous acquaintance.

They were brought to trial on the 1st of September, sixteen days after their arrest. Ten justices were on the bench, including the Lord Mayor and the Recorder. The jury being impanelled, the indictment declared "that William Penn, gentleman, and William Meade, late of London, linen-draper, with divers other persons to the jury unknown, to the number of three hundred, the 15th day of August, in the twenty-second year of the King, about eleven of the clock in the forenoon of the same day, with force and arms, &c. in the parish of St. Bennet Gracechurch, in Bridge ward, London, in the street called Gracechurch-street, unlawfully and tumultuously did assemble and congregate themselves together, to the disturbance of the peace of the said lord the King. And the aforesaid William Penn and William Meade, together with other persons to the jury aforesaid unknown, then and there assembled and congregated together; the aforesaid William Penn, by agreement between him and William Meade before made, and by abetment of the aforesaid William Meade, then and

The indictment.

there in the open street did take upon himself to preach and speak, and then and there did preach and speak unto the aforesaid William Meade and other persons there in the street aforesaid, being assembled and congregated together; by reason whereof a great concourse and tumult of people in the street aforesaid then and there a long time did remain and continue, in contempt of the said lord the King and his law; to the great disturbance of his peace, to the great terror and disturbance of many of his liege people and subjects, to the ill example of all others in the like case offenders, and against the peace of the said lord the King, his crown and dignity."

There were many errors in the above indictment. The date was incorrect; none were armed; none had used force but the soldiers; there had been no agreement beforehand between the accused persons; William Meade did not speak to William Penn, not having been able to get near him; there was no tumult but what was made by the soldiers; and in the evidence for the prosecution no proof whatever was adduced that established, or went to establish, those statements. William Penn had preached; that is, the witnesses supposed it was preaching, but admitted they had not heard anything he said. However, it had been all in the open street, not in any conventicle; therefore the Conventicle Act did not reach the case. Notwithstanding all this, the bench determined it should be adjudged "an unlawful assembly, congregated together to disturb the peace of the King, and William Penn and William Meade conspiritors against his Majesty's royal crown and dignity." Every difficulty that could be suggested to prevent an open full defence was raised by the presiding magistrates.

When the case for the prosecution closed, William Penn having at length secured silence in the court, came forward himself to conduct the defence.

"*Penn.*—We confess ourselves to be so far from recanting, or declining to vindicate the assembling ourselves to preach, pray, or worship God, that we declare to all the world, that we do believe it to be our indispensable duty to meet incessantly upon so good an account; nor shall all the powers upon earth be able to divert us from thus reverencing and adoring our God who made us.

"*Sheriff Brown.*—You are not here for worshipping God, but for breaking the laws.

"*Penn.*—I affirm I have broken no law; nor am I guilty of the indictment that is laid to my charge; and to the end that the bench, the jury, myself, and those who hear us may have a more direct understanding of this procedure, I desire you would let me know by what law it is you prosecute me, and on what law you ground your indictment.

"*Recorder.*—Upon the common law.

"*Penn.*—Where is that common law?

"*Recorder.*—You must not think I am able to

sum up so many years and ever so many adjudged cases, which we call common law, to answer your curiosity.

"*Penn.*—This answer, I am sure, is very short of my question; for if it be *common*, it should not be so hard to produce.

"*Recorder.*—Sir, will you plead to your indictment?

"*Penn.*—Shall I plead to an indictment that hath no foundation in law? If it contains that law you say I have broken, why should you decline to produce that law, since it will be impossible for the jury to determine or agree to bring in their verdict, who hath not the law produced by which they should measure the truth of this indictment.

"*Recorder.*—You are a saucy fellow; speak to the indictment.

"*Penn.*—I say it is my place to speak to matter of law. I am arraigned a prisoner. My liberty, which is next to life itself, is now concerned. You are many against me, and it is hard if I must not make the best of my case. I say again, unless you show me and the people the law you ground your indictment upon, I shall take it for granted your proceedings are merely arbitrary."

On making this declaration, the magistrates unitedly set at the prisoner, and by dint of vehement vituperation tried to bear him down. He replied calmly and logically, till the Recorder, to stop the magisterial uproar, said, addressing the prisoner, " The question is, whether you are guilty of this indictment."

" *Penn.*—The question is not whether I am guilty of this indictment, but whether this indictment be legal. It is too general and imperfect an answer to say it is common law, unless we know both where and what it is; for where there is no law there is no transgression; and that law which is not in being, so far from being common law, is no law at all.

" *Recorder.*—You are an impertinent fellow. Will you teach the court what law is? It is *lex non scripta*—that which many have studied thirty or forty years to know—and would you have me tell you in a moment?

" *Penn.*—Certainly, if the common law be so hard to be understood, it is far from being very common; but if the Lord Coke in his *Institutes* be of any weight, he tells us that common law is common right, and common right is the Great Charter of privileges confirmed by 9 Henry III. c. 29; by 25 Edward I. c. 1; and by 2 Edward III. c. 8.

" *Recorder.*—Sir, you are a very troublesome fellow, and it is not for the honour of the court to allow you to go on.

" *Penn.*—I have asked but one question, and you have not answered me, though the rights and privileges of every Englishman are concerned in it.

" *Recorder.*—If I should suffer you to ask questions till to-morrow morning, you would be never the wiser.

"*Penn.*—That would depend upon the answers.

"*Recorder.*—Sir, we must not stand to hear you talk all night.

"*Penn.*—I design no affront to the court, but to be heard in my just plea. And I must plainly tell you, that if you deny me the oyer of that law which you suggest I have broken, you do at once deny me an acknowledged right, and evince to the whole world your resolution to sacrifice the privileges of Englishmen to your sinister and arbitrary designs.

"*Recorder.*—Take him away. (*To the Lord Mayor.*) My Lord, if you take not some course with this pestilent fellow, to stop his mouth, we shall not be able to do anything to-night.

"*Lord Mayor.*—Take him away; take him away; turn him into the dock.

"*Penn.*—These are but so many vain exclamations. Is this justice or true judgment? Must I be taken away because I plead for the fundamental laws of England? However (*addressing the jury*) this I leave upon your consciences; who are my sole judges, that if these ancient fundamental laws, which relate to liberty and property, and are not limited to particular persuasions in matters of religion, must not be indispensably maintained, who can say he has a right to the coat upon his back? If not, our liberties are open to be invaded, our families enslaved and led away in triumph, and our estates ruined. The Lord of Heaven and earth will be judge between us in this matter."

The bench would listen to nothing further from the prisoner, but had him forcibly dragged into the bale-dock—a deep place, like a well, at the farthest extremity of the courthouse, in which he could neither see nor be seen. Then William Meade came forward to speak to the indictment, and with outspoken plainness told them of the falsehoods with which it was filled. " Therein I am accused," said he, "that I met *vi et armis, illicitè et tumultuosè*. Time was when I had freedom to use a carnal weapon, and then I thought I feared no one; but now I fear the living God, and dare not make use thereof to hurt any man: nor do I know that I demeaned myself as a tumultuous person; for I am a peaceable man." Turning to the jury, the old soldier, now become a peace-loving Quaker, told them that if the Recorder would not inform them what constituted a riot, a rout, and an unlawful assembly, he would quote for them the opinions of Lord Coke. On doing which the Recorder made a scornful bow, and derisively thanked him for the information. Meade met this by a ready retort. The Lord Mayor declared he deserved to have his tongue cut out, and the bench decided that he also must be removed into the bale-dock.

The Recorder, then, in the prisoners' absence, delivered his charge to the jury, and they retired for consultation. Three hours having elapsed, the jury returned agreed in their verdict; and the prisoners having been placed at the bar, the names of the jurymen were called over.

"*Clerk.*—Look upon the prisoners at the bar; how say you? Is William Penn guilty of the matter whereof he stands indicted in manner and form, or not guilty?

"*Foreman.*—Guilty of speaking in Gracious-street.

"*Court.*—Is that all?

"*Foreman.*—That is all I have in commission.

"*Recorder.*—You had as good say nothing.

"*Lord Mayor.*—Was it not an unlawful assembly? You mean he was speaking to a tumult of people there?

"*Foreman.*—My Lord, this was all I had in commission."

Uproarious was the wrath of the Lord Mayor and of the whole bench. They tried to intimidate, they threatened, they vituperated, and refused to accept the verdict. Finally, they ordered the jury to be locked up till they brought forth another. They returned in half an hour with a written verdict which they had all signed, only differing from the first by declaring William Meade *Not guilty.* The magistrates were furious against the jury, and refused to accept what they presented. Penn, who was now present, appealed to them to hold to their rights—rights which were dear to every true Englishman. The Recorder's dictum was in the following words, "Gentlemen, you shall not be dismissed till we have a verdict the court will accept; and you shall be locked up without meat, drink, fire, or tobacco. We shall have a verdict by the help of God, or you shall starve for it."

The jury repeatedly said, "We are all agreed," and declared that therefore they could come no nearer to the wishes of the court.

"*Recorder*.—Gentlemen, you must be content with your hard fate; let your patience overcome it, for the court is resolved to have a verdict, and that before you can be dismissed."

Several persons were then sworn to see that the jury be kept all night without meat, fire, drink, or any other accommodation. The court then adjourned till the next morning, "Sunday, the 4th instant."

Seven o'clock on Sunday morning found the magistrates assembled, the prisoners at the bar, and the court-house filled to overflowing with anxious spectators, when the twelve jurymen appeared. Silence being proclaimed, and the jurymen's names called over, the clerk demanded, "Are you agreed upon your verdict?"

"*Jury*.—Yes.

"*Clerk*.—Who shall speak for you?

"*Jury*.—Our foreman.

"*Clerk*.—What say you? Look upon the prisoner at the bar. Is William Penn guilty of the matter whereof he stands indicted in manner and form as aforesaid, or not guilty?

"*Foreman.*—William Penn is guilty of speaking in Gracious-street.

"*Lord Mayor.*—To an unlawful assembly?

"*Edward Bushell.*—No, my lord; we give no other verdict than what we gave last night; we have no other verdict to give."

Then followed another scene of vehement pressure. The jury were again ordered to retire, and again on their return gave in the same verdict.

The Recorder, who regarded Edward Bushell as the main stay of the jury, called him a factious fellow, and threatened to set a mark upon him, and the Lord Mayor declared he would slit his nose.

"*Penn.*—It is intolerable that my jury should be thus menaced. Is this according to fundamental law? Are not they my proper judges by the Great Charter of England? What hope is there of ever having justice done when juries are threatened and their verdict rejected? I am grieved to see such arbitrary proceedings. Did not the Lieutenant of the Tower pronounce one of them worse than a felon? Do you not condemn for factious fellows those who do not answer your ends? Unhappy are those juries who are threatened to be fined, and starved, and ruined, if they give not in verdicts contrary to their consciences.

"*Recorder.*—My Lord, you must take a course with that same fellow.

"*Lord Mayor.*—Stop his mouth: jailer, bring fetters, and stake him to the ground.

"*Penn.*—Do your pleasure: I matter not your fetters.

"*Recorder.*—Till now I never understood the policy and prudence of the Spaniards in suffering the Inquisition among them; and certainly it will never be well with us till something of the Spanish Inquisition be in England."

The jury was again forced to return to the jury-room, and remain there for another day and night. Early next morning, the court having reassembled, the jury entered, and the usual questions being put, the same verdict was tendered, and again refused. Folding up the paper, the foreman, after a moment's consultation, declared he had in commission from the jury to return the verdict of *Not Guilty.*

"*Clerk.*—Then hearken to your verdict. You say that William Penn is not guilty in manner and form as he stands indicted; you say that William Meade is not guilty in manner and form as he stands indicted, and so you all say.

"*Jury.*—Yes, so we all say."

A burst of deep sympathetic congratulation filled the crowded court-house during the moments of confounded amazement that overspread the bench, which the Recorder checked by addressing the jury.

"*Recorder.*—I am sorry, gentlemen, you have followed your own judgments and opinions, rather than the good and wholesome advice given you.

God keep my life out of your hands; but for this the court fines you forty marks a man, and imprisonment till paid."

At this juncture, Penn stepped forward and said, " I demand my liberty, being freed by the verdict of the jury."

" *Lord Mayor.*—No, you are in for your fines.

" *Penn.*—Fines for what?

" *Lord Mayor.*—For contempt of court.

" *Penn.*—I ask if it be according to the fundamental laws of England that any Englishman should be fined or amerced but by the judgment of his peers or jury? Since it expressly contradicts the 14th and 29th chapters of the Great Charter of England, which says, 'No freeman ought to be amerced but by the oath of good and lawful men of the vicinage.'

" *Recorder.*—Take him away, take him away out of the court."

They then hurried the prisoners to the bale-dock, and from thence sent them to Newgate, for the non-payment of the imposed fines, and after them were sent the twelve jurymen, in consequence of refusing to pay the fines laid on them for not bringing in a verdict that pleased the bench.

As soon as the prisoners were back again in their Newgate quarters, William Penn lost no time in writing as follows, to relieve the suspense at Wanstead :

William Penn to his father.

"5th of 7th month, 1670.

"Dear Father,

"Because I cannot come, I write. These are to let thee know that this morning about seven we were remanded to the sessions. The jury, after two nights and two days being locked up, came down and offered their former verdict; but that being refused as not positive, they explained themselves [by pronouncing the prisoners] *Not guilty*. Upon this the bench were amazed, and the whole court so satisfied that they made a kind of hymn. But that the Mayor, Recorder, and Robinson might add to their malice, they fined us for not pulling off our hats, and have kept us prisoners for the money— an injurious trifle, which will blow over, as we shall bring it to the Common Pleas, because it was against law, and not sessed by a jury.

"How great a dissatisfaction their actions have begot may reasonably be conjectured by the bare mention of them. 1st.—That the jury was about six times rejected in their verdict; and, besides illegal menaces, were kept two days and two nights without bed, tobacco, provisions, &c. 2nd.—That a session should be held on the first day of the week. 3rd.—That the jury, the only judges by law, should be fined forty marks each [for the verdict they brought in,] and to be prisoners till they have paid it. However, their verdict for us is accepted, because they (the magistrates) dare not deny it.

"This is the substance. The particular circumstances I shall personally relate, if the Lord will. I am more concerned at thy distemper and the pains that attend it, than at my own mere imprisonment, which works for the best.

"I am, dear father,
"Thy obedient son,
"WILLIAM PENN."

Robinson, named in this letter, was, next to the Recorder and the Lord Mayor, the most active of the presiding magistrates. He was the infamous Sir John Robinson, Lieutenant of the Tower, whose cruelty and avarice are so strongly stigmatized by Lucy Hutchinson in connection with Colonel Hutchinson's imprisonment, and that of the others who were implicated in the trial of Charles the First.

Day by day William heard of his father, and wrote to him. The next letter was as follows:—

William Penn to his father, Admiral Penn.

"Newgate, 6th, 7th mo. 1670.

"Dear Father,
"I desire thee not to be troubled at my present confinement; I could scarce suffer on a better account, nor by a worse hand, and the will of God be done. It is more grievous and un-

easy to me that thou should be so heavily exercised, God Almighty knows, than any worldly concernment. I am cleared by the jury, and they are here in my place, and resolved to lie till they get out by law. Every six hours they demand their freedom, by advice of counsel.

"They (the court) have so overshot themselves, that the generality of people much detest them. I entreat thee not to purchase my liberty. They will repent them of their proceedings. I am now a prisoner notoriously against law. I desire in fervent prayer the Lord God to strengthen and support thee, and to anchor thy mind in thoughts of the immutable blessed state which is over all perishing concerns.

"I am, dear father,
"Thy obedient son,
"WILLIAM PENN."

Another day arrived, and again the imprisoned son wrote to Wanstead :—

William Penn to his father, Admiral Penn.

"Newgate, 7th September, 1670.

"Dear Father,
"I am truly grieved to hear of thy present illness.
"If God in His holy will did see meet that I should be freed, I could heartily embrace it; yet,

considering I cannot be free but upon such terms as strengthen their arbitrary and base proceedings, I rather choose to suffer any hardship, and I am persuaded some clearer way will suddenly be found to obtain my liberty; which is no way so desirable to me as on the account of being with thee.

"I am not without hope that the Lord will sanctify the endeavours of thy physician unto a cure, and then much of my solicitude will be at an end. My present restraint is so far from being humour, that I would rather perish than release myself by an indirect course, or to satiate their revengeful, avaricious appetites. The advantage of such freedom would fall very short of the trouble of accepting it. Solace thy mind in the thoughts of better things, dear father. Let not this wicked world disturb thy mind, and whatever shall come to pass, I hope in all conditions to approve myself thy obedient son,

"WILLIAM PENN."

The foregoing details of that extraordinary trial, taken in connection with these affectionate letters of the son to his father, place before us materials from which the tone, temper, courage, character, and feelings of William Penn may be clearly comprehended by the reader who chooses to study them. They will be found to stand the highest test of what is truly just, noble, dauntless, patriotic, and Christian.

The disposal of the case of fines on the jury for their verdict is detailed by Mr. Dixon, in his *Life of William Penn*, as follows.

"Up to this period the usage of the courts with regard to verdicts had never been reduced to a legal and positive form. From the days of the Tudors it had been the occasional practice of the bench to inflict fines on contumacious and inconvenient juries; for centuries it had practically remained an unsettled question of law, whether the jury had or had not a right so far to exercise its own discretion as to bring in a verdict contrary to the sense of the court. This great point was now to be decided. Bushell and his fellow jurors, at Penn's suggestion, brought an action against Sir Samuel Starling, and Sir John Howell, the Lord Mayor, and the Recorder of London, for unjust imprisonment. On the 5th of September they were committed to Newgate, counsel was engaged, and application immediately made to the Court of Common Pleas; but it was not until the 9th of November that a writ of Habeas Corpus was issued to the governor of the jail, to bring up the person of Edward Bushell. Newdegate, Size, Waller, and Broome appeared as counsel for the prisoners; Scroggs and Maynard for the King; that is, for Starling and Howell, the King's justices. Freeman has preserved the heads of this famous appeal.

"The defence was taken on the ground that the jury had brought in a verdict contrary to the laws of England, to manifest evidence, and to the direction of the court. Newdegate urged against this defence, that so far as the laws of England were concerned, the defence was bad, inasmuch as the question of law cannot occur until the facts are proved. Here the facts were not proved to the satisfaction of the men who were called upon by the constitution to investigate them; consequently, the laws not being invoked, they could not be violated. The second point of the defence Broome met by showing that it is the special function of the jury to judge of the evidence submitted to it, and that in the eye of the law that body is presumed to be a more competent judge of whether evidence is good or bad than the court. This argument also met the last point of the defence; the bench might be deceived in its opinion; the jury, being agreed amongst themselves, are presumed to be infallible. The bench therefore, though at liberty to offer suggestions to the jurymen for their consideration, may not lawfully coerce them.

"The Court of Common Pleas adopted these views. Sir John Vaughan summed up the argument on both sides, and gave a learned exposition of the question as a piece of historical law, ending with a verdict for Edward Bushell on behalf of himself and his fellow prisoners. They were consequently ordered to be set at liberty in open court. Ten of the other eleven judges agreed in the verdict given by Sir John Vaughan. Chief Baron

Turner merely abstained from giving an opinion on the point, as he had not been present in court to hear the argument of counsel. The verdict may therefore be considered as the unanimous expression of the twelve judges."

Thus the course adopted by the Lord Mayor and Recorder being condemned by the Court of Common Pleas, Bushell and his fellows left Newgate victorious. The fines imposed upon Penn and Meade appear to have been paid by some unknown friend the same day on which the last letter was written by Penn to his father.

All hopes of the recovery of the admiral soon passed from his son's mind after his return to Wanstead. The account of his dying father's advice to him, which he inserted in a subsequent edition of his *No Cross, No Crown*, is as follows:—

"Son William, I am weary of the world! I would not live over my days again if I could command it with a wish, for the snares of life appear greater than the fear of death.

"It troubles me that I have offended a gracious God. The thought of that has followed me to this day. Oh! have a care of sin! It is that which is the sting both of life and death.

"Three things I commend to you.

"*First*, let nothing in this world tempt you to wrong your conscience: so you will keep peace at home, which will be a feast to you in the day of trouble.

"*Secondly.*—Whatever you design to do, lay it justly, and time it seasonably.

"*Lastly.*—Be not troubled at disappointments, for if they may be recovered, do it; if they cannot, trouble is vain. If you could not have helped it, be content; there is often peace and profit in submitting to Providence, for afflictions make wise. If you could have helped it, let not your trouble exceed instruction for another time.

"These rules will carry you with firmness and comfort through this inconstant world."

At another time he inveighed against the profaneness and impiety of the age, and expressed his apprehension that divine judgments would fall upon England, on account of the wickedness of her nobility and gentry. Just before he died, looking with compassion at his son, he said, " Son William, if you and your Friends keep to your plain way of preaching, and to your plain way of living, you will make an end of the priests to the end of the world." He afterwards added: " Bury me by my mother. Live in love. Shun all manner of evil, and I pray God to bless you all; and He will bless you."

Thus having spoken, the spirit of this brave seaman left its earthly tenement.

His desire to be buried near his mother was carried out, and there, in the parish church of Redcliff in the city of Bristol, where his remains were laid, a monument was erected to his memory with the following inscription :—

Admiral Penn's epitaph.

To the just memory of
SIR WILLIAM PENN,
KNIGHT AND SOMETIMES GENERAL,
born at Bristol, Anno 1621,

Son of Captain Giles Penn, several years Consul for the English in the Mediterranean, of the Penns of Penlodge in the County of Wilts, and those Penns of Penn in the
County of Bucks;
and by his Mother from the Gilberts in the County of Somerset, originally from Yorkshire.

Addicted from his youth to maritime affairs,
he was made Captain at the years of 21,
Rear-Admiral of Ireland at 23,
Vice-Admiral of Ireland at 25,
Admiral of the Straights at 29,
Vice-Admiral of England at 31,
and General in the first Dutch War at 32;
whence returning, in Anno 1655, he was chosen
a Parliament-man for Weymouth;
1660 made Commissioner of the Admiralty and Navy,
Governor of the Town and Port of Kinsale,
Vice-Admiral of Munster, and a Member of the
Provincial Council;
And in Anno 1665 was chosen Great Captain Commander
under his Royal Highness, in that
signal and most successful Fight against the Dutch Fleet.

Then he took leave of the sea, his old element,
but continued still his other employs
till 1669, at which time, through bodily infirmities
contracted by the care and fatigue of public affairs,
he withdrew, prepared and made for his end;
and with a gentle and even gale, in much peace,
arrived and anchored in his last and best Port,
at Wanstead, in the County of Essex,
the 16th of September, 1676,
being then but 49 years and 4 months old.

To his Name and Memory
his surviving Lady hath erected this remembrance.

Admiral Penn, having provided for his wife, his son Richard (who survived him only three years) and his only daughter, Margaret Lowther, appointed William his executor and residuary legatee, a bequest which entitled him to estates in England and Ireland worth about £1500 a year, and to his father's claims on government for money lent to the state and arrears of salary amounting to nearly £15,000. And further, having anticipated that William would have much to endure from the intolerant spirit of the age, he had shortly before his death sent a message to the Duke of York, with his dying request that he would endeavour to protect him and would use his influence with the King to secure his protection also. The Duke gave his solemn promise to do so, and seems never to have forgotten it.

When his father's funeral was duly solemnized, and the immediate claims which devolved upon him as executor were settled, William Penn visited Buckinghamshire. Part of the family property lay there, and another treasure, far more precious to him, was also in that county. Of his visits to Gulielma Maria Springett, or to his other Amersham friends, during his sojourn in their neighbourhood on this occasion, neither letter nor narrative remains to tell us. We have abundant details, however, of a public controversy which he held at West Wycombe with a Baptist minister and his supporters; but into this or his numerous other discussions with disputants who assailed his religious tenets I have no thought of following him. The activity and compass of William Penn's mind were something wonderful, and it did a wonderful work in that day, when religious controversy was a necessity to a society whose principles were vehemently assailed on all sides.

This young champion of the Quaker faith seemed raised up by the Lord to continue the warfare, when others had been cut off by the pestilence and privations to which they had been consigned by their persecutors. He, recognizing the call of his Divine Master, and His guiding care in the position which thus devolved on him, embraced it cordially. He dwelt on his dying father's thoughts and advice with feelings overflowing with thankfulness to God. So changed were they from those of earlier days, so Christian-like were they, and so encouraging to him to pursue with unwavering course the religious path he had entered, that they now stimulated his zeal. Yes! pursue that path he must, with God's help, let come what would; nothing but physical inability should deter him from upholding the Truth as promulgated by the Lord Jesus, and now maintained in its integrity by the Friends. He preached, he wrote, he disputed, whenever calumny and opposition to the Truth presented themselves, whether from Episcopalian, Presbyterian, Independent, or Baptist. With reference to this period of his career, he has been aptly termed "The sword of the new sect, kept perpetually unsheathed to meet its enemies in battle."

Moses Amyrault, who has been before alluded to as William Penn's French preceptor at Saumur, with whom he had read the ancient Fathers, and studied early Church history, belonged to the Calvinistic section of Protestants. He had written many works on theology, several of which were read throughout Protestant Europe. His inquiring English pupil must, under such a master, have gone into all the reasoning and systematizing of the dogmatic theology of that day. It is clear that he fully understood the peculiar doctrines of the Calvinistic system, and the authorities to which it owed its origin and progress in the Christian church. Having seen, as he believed, much evil resulting from its adoption, William Penn earnestly withstood it, and he was all the better prepared by the training he had had under Amyrault, to meet the arguments of those who came forward in its defence.

CHAPTER X.

1672–1679.

Sir John Robinson again imprisons William Penn.—Sends him to Newgate.—State of that prison.—Penn's prison occupation.—Release. —Visits the Continent.—His marriage.—Settles at Ruscombe.—Visit of the Swarthmoor family.—Imprisonment of George Fox.—William Penn writes to his friend in prison.—Controversy between Penn and Baxter.—Penn as a controversialist.—As an arbitrator.—Quaker trusteeship in connection with New Jersey.—Purchase of land from the Indians.—Government of New Jersey.—The Penns settle at Worminghurst.—Family concerns.—Another Continental visit.—Penn's speeches before the Parliamentary Committee.—His address to Protestants.

Some of the magistrates who had been thwarted in their purpose respecting the two Quaker prisoners, and who were also smarting under the defeat experienced in the suit of the jury against them, were determined on revenge, and could not rest till they again tried some plan by which Penn, the chief aggressor, might be brought within their power. Of these, Sir John Robinson, Lieutenant of the Tower, was the leader. Cruel and unscrupulous, he was cunning as well as cruel; and to effect his purpose on this occasion, he set spies to watch Penn's movements after his return from

Buckinghamshire, in order to discover some pretext on which to apprehend him.

During the interim Penn had prepared a detailed account of his trial, in which he pointed out what was contrary to constitutional law and to the ancient charters in the late proceedings. This he published under the title of *The People's Ancient and Just Liberties Asserted*. The whole affair and the subsequent publication manifested so much legal ability and undaunted determination on the part of the writer, that the more cautious among the magistrates who had sat on the bench did not wish to interfere with him again. However, Sir John, who was a nephew of Archbishop Laud, and son to the Archdeacon of Nottingham, having vindictive feelings towards dissenters, and seeing that he could get Penn into his power by tendering the oath of allegiance in case of other failures, was determined to persevere in searching for an occasion. Having discovered that on a certain morning he intended to be at the Friends' meeting at Wheeler-street, a constable and guard of soldiers were stationed outside after the meeting assembled, till William Penn stood up to preach. The sergeant and constable then entered, and pulling him down, handed him over to the military guard, who conducted him forthwith to the Tower. He was kept there till evening, when Sir John Robinson, with the Lord Mayor, Sir Samuel Stirling, Sir John Sheldon, and some who were not on the bench on the previous occasion, arrived. Robinson took care this time that the trial should be of such a character as not to require a jury in order to obtain a conviction. The examination was conducted by himself, the public being excluded.

"*Sir John Robinson.*—What is this person's name?

"*Constable.*—Mr. Penn, sir.

"*Robinson.*—Is your name Penn?

"*Penn.*—Dost thou not know me?

"*Robinson.*—I don't know you. I don't desire to know such as you.

"*Penn.*—If not, why didst thou send for me hither?

"*Robinson.*—Is that your name, sir?

"*Penn.*—Yes, yes, my name is Penn. I am not ashamed of my name.

"*Robinson.*—Constable, where did you find him?

"*Constable.*—At Wheeler-street, at a meeting, speaking to the people.

"*Robinson.*—You mean he was speaking to an unlawful assembly.

"*Constable.*—I do not know indeed, sir; he was there, and he was speaking.

"*Robinson.*—Give them their oaths.

"*Penn.*—Hold; do not swear the man. I freely acknowledge I was at Wheeler-street, and that I spoke to an assembly of people there.

"*Robinson.*—No matter; give them the oaths. Mr. Penn, you know the law better than I can tell you, and you know these things are contrary to law.

"*Penn.*—If thou believest me to be better known in the law than thyself, hear me, for I know no law I have transgressed. Laws are to be construed strictly and literally, or more explanatorily and lenitively. In the first sense, the execution of many laws may be *extrema injuria*, the greatest wrong; in the latter way applied, wisdom and moderation. I would have thee choose the latter. Now, whereas I am probably to be tried by the late act against conventicles, I conceive it doth not reach me.

"*Robinson.*—No, sir, I shall not proceed upon that law.

"*Penn.*—What then? I am sure that law was intended for a standard on these occasions.

"*Robinson.*—The Oxford Act of six months.

"*Penn.*—That of all acts cannot concern me. I was never in orders, neither episcopally nor classically, and one of them is intended by the preamble of that act.

"*Robinson.*—No, no, any that speak in unlawful assemblies, and you spoke in an unlawful assembly."

William Penn proved to him the entire illegality of applying the provisions of that act to him. Baffled in his design of making the Oxford Act serve his purpose, Sir John had recourse to the old snare—tendering the oath of allegiance to a man who he knew nothing on earth would induce to swear, because he regarded all swearing as forbidden by Christ; and one who he knew would rather die than take up arms against the King or government. Penn showed him the injustice, the inapplicability, and the total perversion of the design for which the oath of allegiance was prepared, to tender it to a man whose allegiance was not and could not be doubted.

The Lieutenant of the Tower, driven from point to point, at length said, "You do nothing but stir up the people to sedition; and there was one of your friends told me you preached sedition, and meddled with the government.

"*Penn.*—We (Friends) have the unhappiness to be misrepresented. But bring me the man that will dare to justify this accusation to my face, and if I am not able to make it appear that it is both my practice and that of all the Friends to instil principles of peace on all occasions, (and war only against spiritual wickedness, that all men may be brought to fear God and work righteousness,) I shall contentedly undergo the severest punishment your laws can expose me to. As for the King, I make this offer, if any one living can make appear directly or indirectly, from the time I have been called a Quaker, (since it is from thence you date my sedition,) I have contrived or acted anything injurious to his person, or to the English government, I shall submit my person to your utmost cruelties. But it is hard that, being innocent, I should be reputed guilty.

"*Robinson.*—Well, I must send you to Newgate for six months; and when they are expired, you will come out.

"*Penn.*—Thou well knowest a larger imprisonment has not daunted me. Alas, you mistake your interests, and you will miss your aim. This is not the way to compass your ends.

"*Robinson.*—You bring yourself into trouble, heading parties and drawing people after you.

"*Penn.*—I would have thee and all men know I scorn that religion which is not worth suffering for, and which is not able to sustain those who are afflicted for it. Mine is; and whatever be my lot, I am resigned to the will of God. Thy religion persecutes, mine forgives, and I desire that God may forgive you all that are concerned in my commitment. I leave you, wishing you everlasting salvation.

"*Robinson.*—Send a corporal with a file of musqueteers with him.

"*Penn.*—No, no. Send thy lacquey; I know the way to Newgate."

As Sir John had not been able to get up any thing against him, that could bring into his own keeping in the Tower this " gentleman with a plentiful estate," as he termed him, from whom no doubt he had hoped to obtain extortions, he forthwith consigned him to Newgate. This was the second time within three months that he had been cast into that miserable prison, the state of which, and its bad management in that age, have already been exhibited through Thomas Ellwood's graphic detail. And from William Penn himself we know it was then much as it had been when Ellwood was one of its occupants. It is wonderful how, in such an abode, Penn was able to command the power of concentration indispensable for the composition of the works which he wrote there, and which from thence were scattered broadcast over England, Scotland, Ireland and America. It was then he wrote *The Great Case of Liberty of Conscience; Truth Rescued from Imposture; A Postscript to Truth Exalted;* and *An Apology for the Quakers*. The first and most considerable of these works, that *On Liberty of Conscience*, displays an enlarged charity, great research, and grasp of mind. Besides these, he wrote letters to a Roman Catholic who had taken offence at his *Caveat against Popery*, which was published before his imprisonment. He also wrote a dignified and temperate letter to the High Court of Parliament, explaining Quaker principles, and showing how unnecessarily and yet how severely their act against conventicles pressed on this loyal and peace-loving people. And he addressed a letter to the sheriffs of London on the state of Newgate prison, and the abuses practised by the jailors on such as either could not, or from scruples of conscience would not, purchase their favours. He and his friends had declined to do so on the latter ground. On looking at the great amount of important work accomplished during these six months, we may well rejoice in the consciousness of how our Heavenly Father can bring good results to His own cause out of the evil devices of wicked men. So it was then, and so it is now.

As soon as he was again clear of Newgate, and had paid a visit to his mother at Wanstead, William Penn lost no time till he saw his beloved Guli. But not even on this occasion did he tarry long in Buckinghamshire, believing it to be his duty to pay a missionary visit in gospel love to some Christian churches on the continent of Europe, he started for Holland, and visited those Dutch towns where, through the instrumentality of William Caton and others, the Friends' principles had made some way. He thence proceeded to Hanover, and in the free city of Emden he was the first who succeeded in obtaining an entrance for Quaker principles. A meeting was ultimately established there, which ever afterwards looked to William Penn as its founder. He afterwards visited other parts of Germany, made the acquaintance of Princess Elizabeth of the Rhine, and obtained some knowledge of her friends, the disciples of the famous De Labadie, originally a Jesuit, but then a Protestant of the strictest type.

As no family documents are forthcoming relative to the period which intervened between his return from the continent and the close of the year succeeding his settlement at Rickmansworth, I shall extract the bright picture given by his biographer William Hepworth Dixon:—

"After so long a separation, Penn was, not unreasonably, anxious to be near Guli Springett once, again. Calling to see his mother at Wanstead on his way to London, he made a short stay in the capital, visiting old friends, and reporting the results of his journey, and then posting down to Bucks, where he was received with open arms—by Miss Springett as her affianced husband, and by Ellwood and the Peningtons as the champion of their faith. In their society he seems to have passed a considerable time, dallying with the blissful days of courtship, and slowly making preparations for his marriage. He took a house in the first instance at Rickmansworth, about six miles from Chalfont, which being made ready for Guli's reception, the marriage rites were performed in the early spring of 1672, six or seven months after his liberation from Newgate, and husband and wife at once took up their residence in their new dwelling.

"Their honey-moon lasted long; the spring and summer came and went, but Penn still remained with his young and lovely wife at Rickmansworth; neither the flatteries of friends nor the attacks of foes could draw him away from his charming seclusion. During these summer months he neither wrote nor travelled; that very instinct of activity, and that restless and aggressive spirit, which were the sources of nearly all his usefulness, were, so to say, touched with the wand of the enchantress, and laid to rest. Since his expulsion from his father's house he had never known such repose of mind and body. Seeing him surrounded by all that makes domestic happiness complete—a charming home, a beautiful and loving wife, a plentiful estate, the prospect of a family, and a troop of attached and admiring friends,—those who knew him only at second hand imagined that the apostle of civil and religious liberty was now about to subside into the quiet country gentleman, more interested in cultivating his paternal acres, than with the progress of an unpopular doctrine and the general enlightenment of mankind. But those who reasoned so, knew little of William Penn, and perhaps still less of the lady who had now become his wife. Guli would herself have scorned the man who, through infirmity of purpose, could have allowed himself to sink into the mere sloth of the affections, and who, by his outward showing to the world, would have represented her alliance as bringing weakness to his character instead of strength. Penn was not that man. His interval of rest over, the preacher again resumed his work."

In the summer of 1673 they both went to Bristol, to meet George Fox and other Friends, who had just returned from a missionary visit to the West Indies and America. The family from Swarthmoor Hall were also there to receive them, and welcome their return. Before the autumn of that year closed, George Fox and his wife, with their son and daughter Thomas and Mary Lower, paid a visit to Rickmansworth, and from thence they proceeded into Worcestershire, holding meetings among the Friends as they moved along. To some of those meetings many others not Quakers came, and the clergy of the established Church, finding their congregations lessening, and ascertaining the cause, had Fox and Lower made prisoners, and sent to Worcester jail, because, as the mittimus expressed it, "They held meetings, upon the pretence of the exercise of religion, otherwise than is established by the laws of England."

Thomas Lower, who was brother to the Court physician Dr. Richard Lower, through interest made by his brother, was released, although he expostulated, and argued against being liberated, whilst, as he said, his father, whom he had accompanied throughout, taking a part in all his proceedings, was to be imprisoned. But it was all in vain. Fox was to be punished and Lower released on other grounds than those of justice. Meantime William Penn used all his skill and influence in aid of his imprisoned friend. He got his mother, Lady Penn, to write to Lord Windsor, who was lord-lieutenant of the county, and with whom she was intimately acquainted, entreating him to exert his influence not to allow the oath of allegiance to be tendered at the sessions to George Fox, which it was feared might be done in order to ensnare him, in case the other accusation was likely to be passed over. Lady Penn's letter was unavailing, and was perhaps forgotten by Lord Windsor, amid other interests which were crowding around him. Be that as it may, they did tender the oath, and then sent Fox back to prison, to be brought up on the next occasion as a disloyal subject, and, when condemned on the law of premunire, to be imprisoned for life and deprived of all his property.

As there were errors in the indictment, and various exceptions were taken by those engaged to defend the prisoner, this case was repeatedly argued both at Worcester and in London, before the sentence of premunire could be established against him. But at length it appeared to be confirmed. Margaret Fox then repaired to London, and waited on the King. Her husband says, " She laid before him my long and unjust imprisonment, and the justices' proceedings in tendering me the oath as a snare, whereby they had premunired me; so that I, being now his prisoner, it was in his power and at his pleasure to release me. The King spoke kindly to her, and referred her to the Lord-Keeper, to whom she went, but could not get what she desired; for he said the King could not release me but by a pardon, and I was not free to receive a pardon, knowing I had not done evil. I had rather have lain in prison all my days than have come out in any way dishonourable to Truth. Therefore I chose rather to have the validity of my indictment now tried before the judges of King's Bench." Thus the matter stood when the following letter was written.

William Penn to George Fox.

London, 1st 10th mo. 1674.

"Dear G. F.

"My fervent, upright love salutes thee. Thine per post and E. M. I have. For thy business it becomes me not to say [how much] I have endeavoured; but surely I have with much diligence attempted to get all done as I could desire; and I am yet resolved to make one push more about it; so that I cannot write a positive and conclusive account till next Seventh or Second day, by which time I hope to have an answer from this great man. His uncle died, and left him £3,000 per annum, and just married, which did divert the matter.

"I wrote concerning the writ of error that it must be received in open sessions, and the record of the judgment certified by the clerk up to judges of the King's Bench; and if then it appear that there is error to bear an Habeas Corpus, thou shalt have one. I have ever thought that was done in kindness. The King knows not that thou refused a pardon, only that we chose rather a more suitable way to thy innocency. I am, and shall stay in town to do my utmost. The Lord God knows that I could come in thy place to release thee: but the Lord's will be done.

"Dear George, things are pretty quiet, and meetings very full, and precious, and living, blessed be the Lord forever.

"J. Faldo's book twice answered by me is reprinted, or some think it is the remainder unsold bound up with an epistle in favour of it, subscribed by twenty-one priests, as Manton, Baxter, Bates, &c., but it shall be their burden. They will repent them when they know what they have done. As for the sufferings, I have spoken to G. W. &c. They say that there is not stock for such a work; that they have neither press nor materials for such a considerable work, and that £1500 will scarcely do it.

"My wife is well, and child; only teeth, she has one cut.

"The name of the everlasting Lord God be blessed and praised for His goodness and mercy, saith my soul. He is our blessed Rock; the life and joy of our days; the blessed portion of them that believe and obey. My unchangeable love flows to thee, dear George, and in it I salute thee, thy dear wife, T. L., and S. F.

"I am thy true and respectful friend,

"WILLIAM PENN."

The foregoing letter is addressed thus:—

"To Edward Barne,
"Physician in
"Worcester.[*]
"G. F."

It was upwards of two months after the date of the foregoing letter that the case was opened in the Court of King's Bench before Sir Matthew Hale, Lord Chief Justice of England, and three other judges, by whose decision George Fox was released by proclamation. He says:—"Thus, after I had suffered imprisonment for a year and almost two months for nothing, I was fairly set at liberty upon a trial of the errors of my indictment, without receiving any pardon, or coming under any engagement at all."

In the above letter where William Penn tells his friend of his child being well, "only teeth, she has one cut," we are in a very simple but certain way furnished with a fact not before known to those who have written about William and Guli Penn's children, viz., that Springett Penn was not, as is generally stated, their first child. It is evident that the baby who, in Tenth-month, 1674, had cut her first tooth, came before him, for Springett was not born till 1675. The fact is that this baby daughter was Margaret, who was so named for her grand-

---

[*] From the original in the possession of Silvanus Thompson, York.

mother, Lady Penn. She was their third child; the two elder ones, Gulielma Maria and William, died before the date of that letter—the little girl only a few weeks after her birth, and William when about a year old.

It does not appear what was the nature of the controversy alluded to in the letter to Fox, in which Faldos and Penn were engaged. The remark which follows, that Richard Baxter was one among other *priests* who had taken part with Faldos, and that they would repent it when they knew what they had done, gives no clue to the circumstance, though it leads us to infer that William Penn thought they sided with his antagonist through some misapprehension of the case.

In that controversial age, two such earnest men as Baxter and Penn could hardly come near together without some collision. A private discussion of their differences did not satisfy the Presbyterian champion. Therefore, when passing through Rickmansworth, he demanded a public opportunity of proving the errors of Quakerism. Penn was not slow in accepting the challenge, or in doing his utmost to provide accommodation for those who collected from all the surrounding country to witness the discussion. The controversy lasted for seven hours, from ten in the morning till five in the afternoon, and when it terminated each party was so well satisfied with the arguments of its representative, that both sides claimed the victory!

Such occurrences are among the peculiar features which marked the religious world in that age. The spirit of controversy was rife in all the sects, and the Quakers were among the most earnest and persevering of them all.

Into the religious disputations which drew forth the active powers of William Penn in vindicating the principles of " The Friends of Truth," I cannot think of entering; indeed I apprehend they would be tiresome to the reader as well as to the writer in these days, when our enjoyment of, and need for, such keen controversy has subsided. But then it was a necessity resulting from the spirit of the times; and as Penn in those days never shrank from a defence of the Truth when an enemy gave battle, he was seldom out of controversial harness.

But now a great absorbing interest took hold of his mind. This was to procure an asylum for Friends, and others who might choose to join them, in the New World, where perfect liberty of conscience, and just administration of laws founded on and regulated by christian morals, should prevail. But in order to have power to legislate for the internal government of a colony, possession, differing materially from that of ordinary settlers, must be obtained. Land-ownership might exist without any legislative power. In process of time, however, a providential hand placed all the requisite conditions within the reach of Penn and his co-religionists.

In the year 1675 the ownership of one half the tract of country called New Jersey, came by purchase from Lord Berkley, into the possession of Edward Bylling and John Fenwick, both Quakers; and as they had a dispute about its division, the matter was referred to William Penn for arbitration. On the dispute being adjusted by his kind offices, Fenwick sailed for the new country, accompanied by several other Friends, to enter on possession of the portion which had been assigned him. Meantime Bylling's affairs having become embarrassed, he assigned for the payment of his creditors whatever could be realized by the sale of the land he had purchased from Lord Berkley. At his earnest request, William Penn united with two of his creditors as trustees to see the matter fairly carried out. From the trusteeship thus commenced, in which the three Quakers were concerned, resulted the ultimate proprietorship and government of the province by the Quakers.

The trustees drew up a description of the country and its products, which they circulated throughout the kingdom, inviting Friends and others to emigrate thither; but earnestly recommending that "whosoever hath a desire to be concerned in this intended plantation should weigh the thing well before the Lord, and not headily or rashly conclude on any such remove; nor should they offer violence to the tender love of their near kindred, but soberly and conscientiously endeavour to obtain their good-will, and the unity of Friends where they live."

Among the first purchasers were two companies of Quakers, one from Yorkshire, the other from London, each of which contracted for a large tract of land. In the years 1677 and 1678 five vessels sailed for the province of West New Jersey, with eight hundred emigrants, most of whom were members of the Society of Friends. Commissioners were chosen by the proprietors from the London and Yorkshire companies, and sent out to inspect the settlement of the emigrants, and to see that the just rights of any who had previously settled there, as some Dutch and Swedes had done, should not be infringed; and with instructions to treat with the Indians, recognizing their native rights to those regions as hunting grounds, and to give them such compensation as should be mutually agreed on for allowing that section of the country to be differently appropriated.

The nature of the articles offered or demanded for the Indian goodwill of the land may seem to us comparatively small; but whatever it was that the Quaker commissioners gave them, it was very much more than any others gave in those days for similar lands; for none others fully recognized the native rights. Smith tells us in his history that, for the tract of country extending twenty miles on the Delaware river, and lying between Oldman's creek and Timber creek, which was treated for by those commissioners in the year 1677, they gave the Indians as follows:—thirty match coats, twenty guns, thirty kettles, one great kettle, thirty pair of hose, twenty fathoms of duffles, thirty petticoats, thirty narrow hoes, thirty bars of lead, fifteen small barrels of powder, seventy knives, thirty Indian axes, seventy combs, sixty pair of tobacco tongs, sixty pair of scissors, sixty tinshaw looking-glasses, one hundred and twenty awl blades, one hundred and twenty fish-hooks, two grasps of red point, one hundred and twenty needles, sixty tobacco boxes, one hundred and twenty pipes, two hundred bells, one hundred Jew's harps, and six anchors of rum. The last named item, six anchors of rum, was conceded by the Quaker commissioners without due experience as to the evil effect of ardent spirits on these natives of the forest. Some years after this transaction, when its fearfully demoralizing influence became manifest, the Friends endeavoured to establish total abstinence societies among them—which of course were not known by that name, although they embraced the principle which it now represents. At one of those meetings we are told eight Indian kings were present, one of whom made the following speech:—

"The strong liquor was first sold us by the Dutch; they were blind; they had no eyes; they did not see it was for our hurt. The next people that came among us were the Swedes, who continued the sale of the strong liquor to us; they also were blind; they had no eyes; they did not see it to be hurtful to us; but if people will sell it to us, we are so in love with it that we cannot forbear it. When we drink it, it makes us mad; we do not know what we do; we then abuse one another; we throw each other into the fire; seven score of our people have been killed by reason of drinking it, since the time it was first sold to us. These people that sell it have no eyes. But now there is a people come to live among us that have eyes; they see it to be for our hurt; they are willing to deny themselves the profit of it for our good. These people have eyes; we are glad such a people are come among us. We must put it down by mutual consent; the cask must be sealed up; it must be made fast; it must not leak by day or by night; and we give you these four belts of wampum, which we would have you lay up safe by you, to be witnesses of this agreement; and we would have you tell your children that these four belts of wampum are given you to be witnesses betwixt us and you of this agreement."

The Quaker commissioners recommended the adoption of various fundamental laws, which they sent home for the approval of the trustees. Among these a prominent one was, that "No person is to be molested for worshipping God according to his conscience." The rights of conscience and of religious as well as civil freedom were strictly maintained.

"The colony of West New Jersey," says Janney, "continued to prosper under the management of Penn and his associates. Colonists arrived in considerable numbers, good order and harmony prevailed, the country proved to be productive, the air was salubrious, and the Indians, being treated kindly and dealt with justly, were found to be excellent neighbours. The Friends, who had been persecuted with relentless severity in their native land, found a peaceful and happy asylum in the forests of the New World, among a people who had hitherto been reputed as ruthless savages. In the same province, ten years before, Carteret and Berkley required each colonist to provide himself with a good musket, powder and ball; but now the Friends came among their red brethren armed only with the weapons of Christian warfare—integrity, benevolence, and truth—and they met them without fear or suspicion."

The Friends from that day to this have never altered in their Christian interest for the Indians, and have never withdrawn their care and efforts to keep them from indulging in the use of spirituous stimulants; consequently the Red men up to the present time regard the American Quakers as their best and surest friends.

About the time Penn undertook the trusteeship, he removed his family from Rickmansworth to the Springett estate at Worminghurst in Sussex, which property came to him with his wife. Soon after he had got the American affairs into order and the Quaker emigration thither fairly started, he joined George Fox, Robert Barclay, and a few other Friends in a religious visit to the continent of Europe. Whilst on that missionary tour, he kept a journal. If he kept one on any other occasion it has not reached us, and therefore we may hold this to be an exceptional instance. In it he inserted various letters which passed between some persons of eminence and himself, in connection with religious interests in Holland, Germany, and Poland. This journal was ultimately published, and after going through many editions, was republished in 1835 as one of the volumes in Barclay's *Select Series of Narratives of the Early Friends*. It is consequently so accessible to most readers that I shall not pause over its details, but shall merely quote the opening and closing paragraphs :—

" On the 22nd of the Fifth-month, 1677, being the first day of the week, I left my dear wife and family at Worminghurst in Sussex, in the fear and love of God, and came well to London that night. The next day I employed myself on Friends' behalf that were in suffering (as prisoners), till the evening; and then went to my own mother's in Essex. On the 24th I took my journey to Colchester," and there he met the Friends who started with him for Rotterdam.

On the 2nd of Ninth-month, after an absence

His return home. 313

of a little more than three months, he again arrived at Worminghurst. He says: "I found my dear wife, child, and family all well, blessed be the name of the Lord God of all the families of the earth! I had that evening a sweet meeting among them, in which God's blessed power made us glad together; and I can say, truly blessed are they who can cheerfully give up to serve the Lord; great shall be the increase and growth of their treasure, which shall never end.

"To Him that was, and is, and is to come, the eternal, blessed, righteous, powerful, and faithful One, be glory, honour, and dominion for ever and ever! Amen.
"WILLIAM PENN."

Another family sorrow is dimly but certainly shadowed forth in the above words, "My dear wife and child." Little Margaret is not therein recognized; Springett is undoubtedly the dear child alluded to as being well. He was then nearly two years old. The daughter who is mentioned in Penn's letter to a friend, written in 1674, had during the interim been taken hence to join her sister and brother in Heaven.

The journal of William Penn's travels on the Continent in 1677 was written, as he tells us in the preface, for his own satisfaction and the information of some particular relatives and friends. Hence it was not designed for publication, nor was it sent to the press till 1694, seventeen years after its date. It was then brought to light through a copy that had been given to the Countess of Conway, probably by Guli or her mother, that lady being a close friend of the Peningtons. After the death of the Countess the copy in question was found among her papers by a gentleman who had access to them, and who forthwith applied to William Penn for permission to publish it. On a re-examination of its contents, the author gave the desired permission. At that time the Princess Elizabeth of the Rhine, several of whose letters to Penn, with his answers, enrich the pages of the journal, was dead; and so probably were some other ladies whose religious history it mentions; therefore, as a private record of religious feeling, the chief objection to its publicity at an earlier period no longer existed.

That which appeared to be the original manuscript of that journal, which William Penn himself wrote in 1677 for the information of his personal friends, came into my hands since I commenced the compilation of this work. It is in perfect preservation and is well written, but has the antiquated abbreviations which prevailed at that time, and which render old manuscripts so difficult to be read by those who are unaccustomed to them. But as I have since heard of the existence of another manuscript copy, with similar claims, it may be doubted whether William Penn himself wrote both.

The English people and their representatives in

parliament becoming more and more alarmed by the evident favour shown to Romanism by the King and his brother, a loud national call was heard for the revival of severe acts which had formerly been made against Papists. In conformity with this feeling, the parliament was proceeding to re-enact some persecuting laws against them which had fallen into disuse, when William Penn came forward to present petitions from the Society of Friends asking for discrimination in the laws between a conscientious objection against taking any oath whatever, and a disinclination to promise allegiance to the government and abjuration of the Papacy. The subject was referred to a committee, and William Penn, on the 22nd of March, 1678, was summoned for examination before it. He made a speech, explaining the great hardships the Friends had endured in consequence of their scruple against swearing, and concluded as follows:—

"It is hard that we must thus bear the stripes of another interest, and be their proxy in punishment, but it is worse that some men can be pleased with such administration. But mark: I would not be mistaken. I am far from thinking it fit, because I exclaim against the injustice of whipping Quakers for Papists, that Papists should be whipped for their consciences. No: though the hand, pretended to be lifted up against them, hath, I know not by what discretion, lighted heavily upon us, and we complain, yet we do not mean that any should take a fresh aim at them, or that they should come in our room; for we must give the liberty we ask, and cannot be false to our principles, though it were to relieve ourselves. And I humbly beg leave to add, that those methods against persons so qualified do not seem to me to be convincing, or, indeed, adequate to the reason of mankind; but this I submit to your consideration. To conclude: I hope we shall be held excused by the men of that profession (the Roman Catholic) in giving this distinguishing declaration, since it is not with design to expose them, but first to pay that regard we owe to the inquiry of this committee, and in the next place to relieve ourselves from the daily spoil and ruin which now attend and threaten many hundreds of families in the execution of laws which we humbly conceive were never made against us."

Notwithstanding the prevalent excitement, that speech, marked as it was by a spirit of Christian justice, was received with attention and favourable consideration by the committee. They could not but respect the noble independence and the tolerant, truthful spirit of the speaker, who ventured thus openly to express himself against the wild current of popular persecution of Roman Catholics. However, the members of committee wished to have another interview with him; some of them, who had known him in early life, felt certain of his candour and truthfulness, but others found it hard to renounce the idea that he was a Jesuit in disguise.

On his second appearance he thus addressed them. "The candid hearing our sufferings have received from you oblige me to add whatever can increase your satisfaction about us. I hope you do not believe I would tell you a lie. I thank God it is too late in the day for that. There are some here who have known me formerly, and I believe they will say I was never that man. It would be strange if, after a voluntary neglect of the advantages of this world, I should sit down in my retirement short of common truth." He then proceeded to explain his own position thus. "I was bred a Protestant, and that strictly too. Reading, travel, and observation for years made the religion of my education the religion of my judgment; and though the posture I am now in may seem strange to you, yet I am conscientious. I do tell you again, and solemnly declare in the presence of Almighty God, and before you all. that the profession I now make, and the society I now adhere to, have been so far from altering that Protestant judgment I had, that I am not conscious of having receded from an iota of any one principle maintained by those first Protestant reformers of Germany, and our own martyrs at home, against the see of Rome. On the contrary, I do with great truth assure you that we (the Friends) are of the same negative faith with the ancient Protestant church; and upon fitting occasion shall be ready, by God's assistance, to make it appear we are of the same belief as to the most fundamental, positive articles of her creed, too. And therefore it is that we think it hard, though we deny in common with her, those doctrines of Rome so zealously protested against, yet that we should be so unhappy as to suffer, and that with extreme severity, by those very laws on purpose made against the maintainers of those doctrines which we do so deny. We choose no suffering; for God knows what we have already suffered, and how many sufficient and trading families are reduced to great poverty by it. We think ourselves an useful people; we are sure we are a peaceable people; and if we must still suffer, let us not suffer as Popish recusants, but as Protestant dissenters.

"But I would obviate another objection that hath been made against us, namely, that we are enemies of government in general, and particularly disaffected to that which we live under. I think it not amiss, yea, it is my duty, now to declare to you in the sight of Almighty God, first that we believe government to be God's ordinance, and, next, that this present government is established by the providence of God and the law of the land, and that it is our Christian duty readily to obey it in all its just laws; and wherein we cannot comply through tenderness of conscience, in no such case to revile or conspire against the government, but with Christian humility and patience tire out all mistakes about us; and wait the better information of those who do as undeservedly as severely treat us. I know not what greater securities can be given by any people."

The committee, and finally the House of Commons, being at length satisfied that conscientious scruples against swearing alone prevented the Friends from taking the oaths, inserted a clause in the bill designed to relieve them from suffering the penalties enacted against disloyalty; and thus it was sent up to the House of Lords. But before it had gone through the Upper House, a sudden prorogation of parliament prevented its becoming law.

The summer of 1679 was not over when the pretended Popish plot, concocted by Titus Oates, threw the nation into the greatest ferment, and the stories of this abandoned impostor about what the Roman Catholics had done, and what they still resolved to do, aroused the utmost indignation of the people. Even the Parliament was stupefied with credulity and horror, so that all consideration for the Friends was lost sight of in consternation about the Popish plot. Savage persecution again resumed its work with intensified bitterness. Many Roman Catholics were accused, tried, and executed. The storm also came down unrelentingly on the heads of the innocent Quakers, who refused to take the required oaths or to discontinue or conceal their religious meetings. Any accusations of participation in the plot which were brought against them were easily refuted.

Whilst matters stood thus, William Penn, then in his country home at Worminghurst, wrote his *Address to Protestants*. A copy of the first edition of that work, published in the year 1679, during the season of the public fast and humiliation ordered in view of the plot, by Parliament, is now before me. It is in two parts. The first animadverts on the prevalent immoralities of the age, and the general disregard of God's laws throughout the nation, pointing especially to the responsibility of those in power, and the criminality of not using such power for the suppression of vice. The second part of the address takes a review of the religious errors prevailing among English Protestants, in matters of opinion, faith, and practice. This portion exhibits so clearly the religious principles of William Penn, that I would gladly give copious extracts from it if space permitted.

CHAPTER XI.

1673–1682.

Cessation of Isaac Penington's religious persecution.—Penington's letters —to his brother Arthur, a Roman Catholic—to Joseph Wright respecting his brother—to his sister Judith—to the Countess of Conway.—Peace and happiness at Woodside.—Isaac and Mary Penington visit their property in Kent.—Isaac Penington's death.—Mary Penington's memorial of her husband.—She anticipates her own decease. —Arranges her outward affairs and makes her will.—Takes her sons to school at Edmonton.—Her illness there.—Returns home.—Continued illness.—Her resignation, patience, and peace of mind.—She visits Worminghurst, and dies there.—Thomas Ellwood's lines on the death of his friends Isaac and Mary Penington.

AFTER the settlement of Isaac Penington at Woodside he suffered no further religious persecution. His constitution had been greatly impaired by the treatment he had previously endured, but the latter years of his life passed on peacefully, his affectionate wife watching carefully over his declining health. Their children grew up around them with indications of piety which made their parents' hearts thankful, and hopeful in view of the future. William and Gulielma Penn were near enough to ensure occasional intercourse between the two families; and we may imagine how happy the intercourse must have been between such cultivated religious minds, bound together as they were by the closest ties of love and relationship.

Isaac Penington had a brother Arthur, who had not only joined the Roman Catholics, but had entered into orders, and become a priest. Of his history beyond what may be drawn from two of Isaac's letters, no traces can be discovered. One of these letters was addressed to Arthur, the other to a mutual friend.

Isaac Penington to his brother Arthur.

"20th 7th mo. 1676.

" Dear brother,

" How can I hold my peace, and not testify of the love, mercy, and good-will of the Lord towards me, and invite others to the redeeming power of which the Lord in his goodness hath made me a partaker?

"And now, brother, a few words respecting thy return to what I sent thee—not for contention's sake, (the Lord knows my dwelling is in that life and peace which shuts it out,) but in the tender love and care of my heart concerning the eternal welfare of thy soul. All may agree in notions about the regenerating power, but all do not receive the regenerating power [into their hearts], nor are all truly regenerated in the sight of God; nor come to witness the head of the serpent crushed, and his works destroyed, and kingdom laid waste inwardly by this power; which must be witnessed if a man be translated out of the kingdom of darkness into the kingdom of the dear Son.

"But that the work of regeneration is only begun in this life, and not finished till the other life, is a great mistake. For the Scriptures testify that salvation is to be wrought out here, and not hereafter. Christ had all power in heaven and earth, and He sent forth His Spirit to carry out the work here, and His sanctifying power is able to sanctify thought, soul, body, and spirit. Holiness is not only to be begun here, but perfected in the fear of God. The whole armour of God is able to defend the whole man from all the assaults of the wicked one, for greater is He in the saints that preserves from sin, than he that tempts to sin.

"There is a holy hill of God, a spiritual Zion, a mountain whereupon His house is built, which the wing of the Almighty overshadows; and His sheep that are gathered by the great Shepherd and Bishop of the soul feed there, and none can make them afraid. The flesh will be rebelling against the Spirit until it be destroyed by the cross of our Lord Jesus Christ. But when a man is dead to sin, sin hath no more power over him. And this is true blessedness, begun by the pure power of the Word of Life in the heart.

"Blessed be the Lord, who hath brought many wanderers and distressed ones to the sight of the True Church, and to delightful obedience to her whose voice is not different to Christ's, but one with it; and such are in fellowship with the Father and Son, and with the saints who dwell in the light. These are clothed with the Lamb's innocency and righteousness, and do not dwell in darkness nor in sin; having crucified the old man with his affections and lusts, and put off the body of the sins of the flesh by the circumcision of Christ, and put on the new man created in Christ Jesus in the righteousness and holiness of Truth. They that are here dwell not in fancies, nor feed on fancies, but on eternal life, in the pure pastures of life, where the Shepherd of the inward spiritual Israel feeds his holy flock day by day.

"As for the Romish church, or any other church built up in the apostacy, the Lord has given me to see through them to that which was before them, and will be after them. And, oh! dear brother, if thou couldst but rightly wait for and meet with the holy, regenerating, purifying power which in tender love I have testified to thee of, it would lead thee to that which is the True Church indeed, which hath been persecuted by the dragon and the false church.

"The Lord hath made me thy brother in the line of nature. Oh! that thou wert my brother in that Truth which lives and abides for ever! Oh! that thou knew the church of the first-born—the Jerusalem which is above, which is free, which is the mother of all who are born of the regenerating virtue and power!

"I. P."

There is no evidence of the time which may have elapsed between the writing of the preceding letter and the undated letter which follows.

To Joseph Wright.

"I entreat thy son to acquaint my brother Arthur that I took very kindly and was glad of his affectionate expressions towards me; having been somewhat jealous that though *my* religion had enlarged my love towards him, yet *his* religion might have diminished his to me. I bless the Lord on his behalf, that he enjoys his health so well; and for myself, though formerly exceedingly weakly, yet the inward life and comfort which the Lord daily pleaseth to administer to me, increaseth the health and strength of my natural man beyond my expectation. Blessed be my tender and merciful Father, who hath visited one so distressed and miserable as I was for so many years.

"And whereas he saith he is like me in speech, but most unlike me in opinion, pray tell him from me that my religion doth not lie in opinions. I was weary and sick at heart of opinions, and, had not the Lord brought that to my hand which my soul wanted, I had never meddled with religion. But as I had felt in my heart that which was evil, and which was not of God, so the Lord God of my life pointed me to that of Him in my heart which was of another nature, teaching me to wait for and know His appearance there; in subjection I have experienced Him stronger than the strong man that was there before. And now truly I feel union with Him, and His blessed presence every day. What this is unto me my tongue cannot utter.

"I could be glad, if the Lord saw good, that I might see my brother before I die; and if I did see him, I should not be quarrelling with him about his religion, but embrace him in brotherly love. As for his being a papist, or an arch-papist, that doth not damp my tender affection to him. If he be a papist, I had rather have him a serious than a loose papist. If he hath met with anything of that which brings forth an holy conversation in him, he hath so far met with somewhat of my religion, which teacheth to order the conversation aright, in the light and by the spirit and power of the Lord Jesus.

"My religion is not a new thing, though more fully revealed now than in many foregoing ages. It consists in that which was long before popery was, and will be when popery shall be no more. He that would rightly know the True Church must know the living stones whereof the True Church is built, against which the gates of hell cannot possibly prevail. Oh! the daily joy of my heart in feeling my living membership in this church, where the true "gold," the "white raiment," the pure "eyesalve" (with which the eye, being anointed, sees aright) is received by such as the world knows not. Blessed be the name of the Lord!

"I desire my sincere, entire affection, as in God's sight, may be remembered to my dear brother.

"I. P."

No further traces of intercourse between these brothers have come to light. They had a sister Judith, to whom her elder brother occasionally wrote. Two of his letters to her, one written in 1678, the other without date, are in the manuscript collection of Penington letters in the Devonshire House. The following, without date, is selected for insertion.

Isaac Penington to his sister Judith.

"Dear sister,

"Is thy soul in unity with God, or art thou separated from Him? Whither art thou travelling? Oh, whither art thou travelling? Is it towards the eternal rest and peace of thy soul, or from thy soul's life towards spiritual death? Every day thou art sowing somewhat which thou must hereafter reap. What art thou daily sowing? Will the crop at last be comfortable to thee? Oh! dear sister, if thou art not able to bear the pains of the earthly body, should the Lord therein set his hand upon thee, how wilt thou be able to bear the misery which is prepared for souls that go out of this world unrenewed in nature, and unreconciled to God. And, indeed, my sister, to repent, and to believe, and be united to Christ, and grow up in the nature of another spirit, that there may be a reaping of what is spiritually sown, are things of great weight, fully as necessary as the Scripture expresseth. Now is thy time of being gathered to the Lord. If the time the Lord hath given thee be lost, what will become of thy soul? The enemy will do all he can to keep thee asleep; but the Lord hath not been wanting in sometimes awakening thee. If ever thou enter into the eternal rest, thou must hearken to the voice, and walk in the path that leads to that rest.

"Dear sister, I lay not stress on the outward forms of religion; but this I am sure of, every one that is saved must feel the power of spiritual life, and know of the secret rebukes of the Lord in heart, and be subject to Him therein. Take heed what thy heart chooseth, for that will be thy portion forever. If the spirit of this world prevail, and thou choose this world, thou art undone. If, under the awakening of God, thy soul chooses life, and His fear be planted in thy heart, His wisdom will teach thee to take up the cross daily to the nature and spirit in thee which are not of Him.

"I have writ this in the pity and love of God unto thee, who herein is seeking thy soul.

"Thy truly loving brother,   I. P."

to the Countess of Conway.

The Countess of Conway, to whom a manuscript copy of William Penn's travels in Holland was presented, as has been mentioned in the last chapter, was a correspondent of Isaac Penington. Several of his letters to her are extant. I select the following for insertion here.

Isaac Penington to the Countess of Conway.

"Dear Friend,

"As I was lately retired in spirit and waiting upon the Lord, having a sense in me of thy long, sore, and deep affliction and distress, there arose a scripture in my heart to lay before thee, namely, *Heb.* xii. 5, 6, 7, which I entreat thee to call for a Bible and hear read, before thou proceedest to what follows.

"Oh! my friend, after it hath pleased the Lord in tender mercy to visit us, and turn our minds from the world and from ourselves towards Him, and to beget and nourish that which is pure and living and of Himself in us, yet, notwithstanding this, there remains somewhat at first, and perhaps for a long time, which is to be searched out by the light of the Lord, and brought down and subdued by His afflicting hand. When there is somewhat of an holy will formed in the day of God's power; and the soul is in some measure brought to live to God, yet all the earthly will and wisdom is not thereby presently removed; hidden things of the old nature and spirit still remain perhaps, though they appear not, but sink into their root that they may save their life. And these man cannot possibly find out in his own heart, but as the Lord reveals them to him. But how doth the Lord point them out to us? Oh! consider this. By His casting into the furnace of affliction, the fire searcheth. Deep, sore, distressing affliction finds out both the seed and the chaff, purifying the pure gold and consuming the dross. Then at length the quiet state is witnessed, and the quiet fruit of righteousness brought forth by the searching and consuming operation of the fire. Oh! that thy soul may be brought to victory over all which is not of the pure life in thee, and that thou mayest feel healing, refreshment, support, and comfort from the God of thy life. May the Lord guide thee daily, and keep thy mind to Him. Help, pity, salvation will arise in His due time; (but not from anything thou canst do;) and faith will spring up, and patience be given, and hope in the tender Father of mercy, and a meek and quiet spirit be witnessed. Look not at thy pain as sorrow, how great soever. Look from them, beyond them, to the Deliverer whose tender spirit is able to do thee good by them.

"Oh! that the Lord may lead thee, day by day, in the right way, and keep thy mind stayed upon Him in whatever befalls thee, that the belief in His love, and hope and trust in His mercy, when thou art at the lowest ebb, may keep thy head above the billows.

"The Lord God of my life be with thee, preserving and ordering thy heart for the great day of His love and mercy, which will come in the appointed season, when thy heart is fitted by the Lord for it."

Isaac Penington's religious letters are numerous; some are in print and many still in manuscript. Judgment is required in selecting from them what may be interesting to readers in general of the present day. They are of a peculiar cast, corresponding of course with the mind from which they emanated; and that mind was by no means of a common order. In some of them his individual religious experience may have been sometimes made to an undue extent the standard by which the genuineness of the religious feelings of other minds was tested. It is common for persons of earnest religious minds not duly to recognise that which the Apostle tells us of the diversities of operation through the same Spirit. We are all more or less liable to be thus influenced; but some are conscious of the danger, and others are not. The latter will often, even when sincerely desiring to judge charitably and rightly, come to positively erroneous conclusions respecting the religious feelings of those who cannot see as they do.

It is pleasant to know that in life's evening the

family at Woodside were suffered to enjoy without molestation the peace and comfort of their humble home. It was not on what they lost of this world's wealth that the father and mother were then disposed to dwell, but on what they had gained in the sense of Divine approval, and the assurance of the Lord's presence being with them and their children. This added far more to their happiness than all the wealth the world could bestow. In true thankfulness and contentedness they could praise their Heavenly Father's care, which had circled around them amid fierce persecution, and now filled their hearts with love and devout trust in Him.

In the autumn of 1679 both husband and wife went into Kent to Mary Penington's native place; and, after visiting the tenants on her estate there, they remained a short time at one of the farms called Goodenstone Court. Just at the time they had fixed to return to Woodside, Isaac Penington took ill. His disease was one of acute suffering, and in a few days the closing scene of earthly life arrived. His soul ascended to its home on high, and his wife tells us her spirit was suffered at that moment to join his, and rejoicingly to see the Heavenly mansion prepared for him.

His remains were interred in the burial-ground belonging to his beloved friends of Chalfont at Jordans, where a small white headstone now marks the spot with the name and date, "*Isaac Penington*, 1679." His age was sixty-three.

Many testimonies were published respecting the Christian life and worth of this good man. I would gladly insert those from his wife, his son John, and William Penn, if space permitted. But as this is not the case, and as his devotion to God, his meekness of spirit, and his Christian character may be gathered from what has been already written, I shall confine myself to an extract from that of Mary Penington:—

"Whilst I keep silent touching thee, oh! thou blessed of the Lord and His people, my heart burneth within me. I must make mention of thee, for thou wast a most pleasant plant of renown, planted by the right hand of the Lord; 'and thou tookest deep root downwards, and sprangest upwards.' The dew of heaven fell on thee, and made thee fruitful, and thy fruit was fragrant and most delightful.

"Oh, where shall I begin to recount the Lord's remarkable dealings with thee! He set His love on thee, oh! thou who wert one of the Lord's peculiar choice. Thy very babyish days declared of what stock and lineage thou wert. Thou desiredst 'the sincere milk of the word as a new-born babe,' even in the bud of thy age; and who can declare how thou hadst travelled towards the Holy Land in the very infancy of thy days? Who can tell what thy soul felt in thy travel? Oh the heavenly, bright, living openings that were given thee! God's light shone round about thee. Such a state as I have never known of in any other, have I heard thee declare of. But this it did please the Lord to withdraw, and leave thee desolate and mourning—weary of the night and of the day—naked and poor in spirit—distressed and bowed down. Thou refusedst to be comforted, because thou couldst not feed on that which was not bread from heaven.

"In that state I married thee; my love was drawn to thee, because I found thou sawest the deceit of all notions. Thou didst remain as one who refused to be comforted by anything that had only the *appearance* of religion, till 'He came to His temple who is Truth and no lie.' For all those shows of religion were very manifest to thee, so that thou wert sick and weary of them all.

"This little testimony to thy hidden life, my dear and precious one, in a day when none of the Lord's gathered people knew thy face, nor were in any measure acquainted with thy many sorrows, have I stammered out, that it might not be forgotten. But now that the day hath broken forth, and that thou wert so eminently gathered into it, and a faithful publisher of it, I leave this other state of thine to be declared by the sons of the morning, who have witnessed the rising of the bright star of righteousness in thee, and its guiding thee to the Saviour, even Jesus, the First and the Last. They,

I say, who are strong, and have overcome the evil one. and are fathers in Israel, have declared of thy life in God, and have published it in many testimonies."

"Ah me! he is gone! he that none exceeded in kindness, in tenderness, in love inexpressible to the relation of a wife. Next to the love of God in Christ Jesus to my soul, was his love precious and delightful to me. My bosom one! my guide and counsellor! my pleasant companion! my tender, sympathizing friend! as near to the sense of my pain, sorrow, grief, and trouble, as it was possible! Yes, this great help and benefit is gone; and I, a poor worm, a very little one to him, compassed about with many infirmities, through mercy was enabled to let him go without an unadvised word of discontent or inordinate grief. Nay, further, such was the great kindness the Lord showed me in that hour, that my spirit ascended with him that very moment the spirit left his body, and I saw him safe in his own mansion, and rejoiced with him there. From this sight my spirit returned again, to perform my duty to his outward tabernacle.

"This testimony to Isaac Penington is from the greatest loser of all who had a share in his life,
"MARY PENINGTON."

"Written at my house at Woodside, the 27th of 2nd month, 1680, between Twelve and One at night, whilst watching by my sick child."

About four months after the foregoing date Mary Penington took William and Edward, her two youngest sons, to place them at school at Edmonton. Before leaving home she made her will, and arranged her family affairs, under the impression that her life was not likely to be of long duration. She also wrote a letter during that interval to her grandson Springett Penn, to be given to him after her death, when he had attained an age able to understand it. The letter in question is that from which I have obtained most of the information respecting Sir William Springett which is contained in the earlier pages of this work. It commences as follows :—

"Dear child,

"Thou bearing the name of thy worthy grandfather Springett, I felt one day the thing I desired was answered, which was the keeping up his name and memory. He dying before thy mother was born, thou couldst not have the opportunity of her putting thee in remembrance of him. So I am inclined to mention this good man to thee, that thou mayest preserve his memory in thy mind, and have it for a pattern; that, following him as he followed Christ, thou mayest not only continue his name in the family, but, walking in his footsteps, partake of his renown, by being the virtuous offspring of this truly great man."

During the interval in question she added the following record to her own personal narrative:—

"Now the Lord hath seen good to make me a widow, and leave me in a desolate condition as to my guide and companion; but He hath mercifully disentangled me, and I am in a very easy state as to my outward being. I have often desired of the Lord to make way for me, waiting on Him without distraction. Living a life free from cumber, I most thankfully and humbly, in deep sense of His gracious kind dealings, receive the disposing of my lands as from Him. I have cleared great part of the mortgage, and paid most of my bond debts, and I can compass very easily the ground in my hands.

"In this Fourth-month, 1680, I have made my will, and disposed of my estate, and have no considerable debt on it, and leave a handsome provision for J. P. and M. P., and the younger ones, to fit them for a decent calling. I have also left provision for my debts and legacies. I call it a comely provision for my children, considering they are provided for out of my lands of inheritance, having nothing of their father's. Though mourning for the loss of my worthy companion, and exercised with the sickness and weakness of my children, in my outward condition and habitation I am to my heart's content. No great family to cumber me; living private, with time to apply my heart to wisdom in the numbering of my days; believing them to be but few, I stand ready to die. Still I feel that death is the king of fear; and that strength to triumph over him must be given me in the needful time. The Lord must then stand by me, to resist that evil one who is often busy when the tabernacle is dissolving.

"Oh! Lord, what quiet, safety, or ease is there in any state but in feeling thy living power? All happiness is in this, and nothing but amazement, sorrow, perplexity and woe out of it. Oh! let me be kept by that power, and in it walk with God in His pure fear; and then I matter not how unseen I am, or how little friendship I have in the world. Oh Lord! thou knowest what I have yet to go through, but my hope is in thy mercy to guide and support me; and then I need not be doubtful, nor in concern about what is to come upon me.

"The foregoing I writ before I went to Edmonton, which was in Sixth-month, 1680. And as if I were to go thither on purpose to be proved by the Lord, according to what I had before written, and to be exercised by Him in all things that were in my view when I set my house in order, it pleased the Lord, in a week's time after my going there, to visit me with a violent burning fever, beyond what I ever felt. Indeed, it was very tedious. I made my moan in these words, 'Distress! distress!' feeling as if that comprehended sickness, uneasiness, want of rest and comfortable accommodation; it being a school, and so unquiet, with but little attendance, and away from my own home, where I could have had every thing I needed.

"I had scarcely any time in all that illness, that I could have taken even so much as a quarter of an hour for the settling of my affairs. The kindness and mercy of the Lord having put into my heart to consider that it might be as it was with my dear husband, that I should never return home again. These memorable dealings of the Lord with me I now recount this 3rd day of the Second month, 1681, in a thankful humble sense of His mercy, being in my bed still unrecovered of that forementioned illness, which commenced eight months since.

"Now it is upon me, in the holy fear of the Lord, to declare to you, my dear children, of what great service it was to me in my sickness, that I had nothing to do but to die when the Lord visited me. The Lord was pleased to assure me I should have a mansion, according to His good pleasure, in His holy habitation. Through this knowledge I was left in a quiet state, out of any feelings of the sting of death; not having the least desire to live, though I did not witness any measure of triumph and joy. I could often say it is enough that I am in peace, and have not a thought day nor night of anything that is to be done in preparation for my going hence.

"After having been fourteen days ill at Edmonton, my fever greatly abated, and in a month's time from that I came from thence to London in some degree of strength. After being seven weeks there, the Lord brought me home again to my own house. But that night I was smitten again with sickness, of which I remain weak and low to this day.

27th of 4th mo. 1681.—As I was waiting this morning on the Lord with some of my family, I found an inclination in my mind to mention the continuance of my illness to this day, which from the time of being first visited wants not many weeks of a year. In all that time, such has been the goodness of the Lord to me, that, as was said of Job, 'in all this he sinned not, nor charged God foolishly,' so may I say that, through the presence of God's power with me, I have not had a murmuring thought or a complaining mind. This has been my constant frame. It is well I have had no grievous thing to undergo, except these late sore fits of pain so full of anguish. The Lord hath graciously stopped my desires after every pleasant thing. I have not found in my heart to ask of Him to restore me to my former health and strength; that I might have the pleasantness of my natural sleep, or be able to walk about the house, or go abroad in the air, to take a view of the beautiful creation. All that I have desired during this long exercise in reference to my condition hath been some ease in my fits of pain. For this I have earnestly cried to the Lord for directions to some means of help, that I might have the pain removed. But, save in these fits of suffering, I have not asked anything of the Lord concerning life or health. I have waited upon Him with less distraction than when in health, and have many times said within myself, Oh! this is very sweet and easy. He makes my bed in my sickness, and holds my eyes waking to converse with Him.

"Death hath been many times before me, on which occasions I have rather embraced it than shrunk from it; having for the most part found a kind of yielding in my spirit to die. I had all my days a great sense of death, and subjection to the fear of it, till I came to be settled in the Truth; but now the fear of death, that is, the state after death, is removed. Yet there remaineth still a deep sense of the passage; how strait, hard, and difficult it is; even in some cases to those over whom the second death hath no power."

No further records have been discovered respecting Mary Penington, who died on the 18th of Seventh-month, 1682, at Worminghurst, where she was staying with her daughter Gulielma Penn. From thence her remains were taken for interment to Jordans, where they were laid beside those of her husband.

In the autograph volume of Thomas Ellwood's poetical pieces described in last chapter, I find the following heretofore unpublished lines, which refer in terms touchingly descriptive to Mary Penington's lingering illness after her husband's decease.

ON HIS DEAR DECEASED FRIENDS ISAAC AND MARY PENINGTON

Since first made one as one they lived together,
  In heart and mind, in life and spirit one,
Till death in part this unity did sever,
  By taking him, and leaving her alone,
  In silent grief his absence to bemoan.

He being gone, she could not long survive
  But daily from his death began to die,
And rather seemed to be, than was, alive,
  Joyless till by his side she came to lie,
  Her spirit joined to his again on high.

CHAPTER XII.

1681–1684.

William Penn applies to Charles II. for a grant of land in America.—Obtains a charter for Pennsylvania.—Penn's motives in this undertaking.—His code of laws.—His coadjutors in the work.—Algernon Sidney.—Penn's letter to Sidney.—Hepworth Dixon on the early Quakers.—Death of Lady Penn.—Penn's farewell letters on leaving England.—Emigration to Pennsylvania.—His treaty of peace with the Indians.—Purchases of land from them.—Gulielma. Penn in her husband's absence.—Poetical address by Thomas Ellwood to his friend in America.—Letter from Gulielma Penn to Margaret Fox.—William Penn's return.—His letter to Margaret Fox.

WILLIAM PENN's publication of his *Address to Protestants* in the year 1679 was succeeded by a period of electioneering politics, in consequence of his earnest desire that his friend Algernon Sidney should be returned as representative to parliament for Guilford. The high opinion he entertained of Sidney's integrity and legislative ability induced him to make all the honourable efforts he could for his return. But they were unavailing; for though he had a majority of votes, court influence was so strong in favour of his opponent, that Sidney was set aside by political manœuvres.

In consequence of his connection with New Jersey, Penn's thoughts had previously been directed to America as a grand theatre for the manifestation of what just legislation and good government could effect. The recent defeat of his friend Sidney increasingly disgusted him with what he saw at home. The unpaid debt which the King still owed to him as Admiral Penn's heir, was therefore now regarded as a providential opening through which another free colony might be established beyond the Atlantic. His heart and hopes became intensely fixed on the realization of this project, which he thought would enable him to prove, in the face of an unbelieving world, that national government may be successfully conducted on the strict basis of Christian morality. With the high and holy enthusiam of an enlightened mind, and all the religious earnestness of an unflinching persecuted Christian, he entered into the subject, and petitioned the King to sanction his project. It was opposed on various sides by intolerant men both in church and state; but still Penn persevered. Those who were open to conviction he succeeded in convincing, and those who were not, sunk into a minority when it became evident that the royal inclination leaned towards the request; and as the King felt it would be an easy way of getting clear of a debt which he could not repudiate, he became increasingly favourable to Penn's proposal. At length the deed of proprietorship was prepared, and the King's signature attached to it under the date 4th of March, 1681. On that occasion the following letter was written:—

*William Penn to his friend Robert Turner,
a Dublin merchant.*

"Dear Friend,

"After many waitings, watchings, solicitings, and disputes in council, this day my province was confirmed to me under the great seal of England, with large powers and privileges, by the name of Pennsylvania, a name the King would give it in honour of my father. I proposed New Wales, but the Secretary, a Welshman, refused to have it called New Wales Sylvania. Then, instead of Wales, they added *Penn* to it. Though I much opposed it, and went to the King to have it altered, he said it was past, and he would not take it upon him; nor could twenty guineas more to the Under-Secretary vary the name. I feared lest it should be looked on as vanity in me, and not respect, as it truly was, in the King to my father, whom he often mentions with praise."

In another letter to Robert Turner, Penn says that he never had his mind so exercised to the Lord about any outward substance, adding, "Let the Lord now guide me by His wisdom, and preserve me to honour His name, and serve His Truth and people, that an example and standard may be set up to the nations. There may be room to set it up *there*, though none here."

Throughout we may see that the mainspring of William Penn's project was a desire to promote the

Glory of God on earth, and the establishment of justice, peace, and good-will among men. These were his governing motives, and they are equally conspicuous in his legislation, and in the administration of his provincial government so far as he could control it. But if such good desires had not been aided by a comprehensive mind, a talent for organization, and great capacity for business, they would have utterly failed in setting up the standard which he wished to erect. A less active mind with such views would have been overwhelmed by the crowd of business, and the varied responsibilities which pressed upon him, after the deed of proprietorship was placed in his hands. He had at that time a wide acquaintance with the leading members of the Society of Friends, several of whom had been associated with him in the legislation for, and management of Eastern New Jersey. He knew those who were capable of aiding him in his object, and he availed himself of their assistance.

"It must not be supposed," says Janney, "that the admirable constitution and code of laws which have shed so much lustre on William Penn's name, were the unaided result of his single genius. Although there was probably no man then living whose mind was so free from prejudice, and so fully enlightened on the subject of government, yet there were among his friends, concerned with him in the enterprise, several persons of enlarged minds and liberal ideas, who performed an important though subordinate share, in the work. They had frequent conferences together, and the code they adopted was the result of their united labours.

"It must also be considered that the doctrines and discipline of the Society of Friends, which were first promulgated by George Fox, had a controlling influence on the mind of Penn, and furnished him with views and principles, which, being engrafted into his constitution and laws, gave rise to their most salutary and remarkable features." Janney then proceeds to compare and contrast the laws of Penn with those drafted for the Carolinas by John Locke, his great contemporary, and adds, "How shall we account for the remarkable disparity? Both men were possessed of talents and virtues of the highest order, combined with humane and tolerant feelings. Is not the superiority of Penn's frame of government to be attributed to the peculiar influence of his religious associations? He was united in fellowship with a people whose principles and practice were essentially democratic; they acknowledged no priestly distinction of clergy and laity; they placed a low estimate on hereditary rank, and they laid the foundation of their church discipline on the supremacy of that divine principle in man which leads to universal fraternity."

Assuredly Penn's American biographer is right. His social and religious surroundings, after he had joined the Friends, had trained William Penn's mind in a direction opposite to that which leads to class legislation. When he established just laws for all, without special privileges for any class, and liberty of conscience on its broadest religious basis; and declared that no armed soldiery was to be employed by the government in its concerns, or to be raised or recognized within the province; and that no oaths whatever were to be required of witnesses in the courts of justice; he was only bringing into national operation what his Quaker feelings and principles had previously caused him to regard as Christian morals.

In relation to crime and its suppression the great feature of his code was the substitution of *prevention* and *reformation* for legal vengeance. All the prisons were to be workhouses, in which the reformation of prisoners was to be aimed at. The means of education were to be placed within the reach of all, and men of every colour were to be equally protected by the laws. Then and for ages after the penal code of England awarded death as the punishment of a great variety of crimes. Penn at one bold stroke exempted from the punishment of death about two hundred offences which were then capital in England. Wilful murder was the only crime for which death was awarded in Pennsylvania. Its retention even in that case appears to have resulted from a conviction that if it were abolished, the government at home would have interposed to re-enact it. Such laws were but the national embodiment of these that have been upheld in the Society of Friends from its first organization.

Locke's frame of government for Carolina rested on the assumption that privileged classes are necessary in a state. What these privileges were to be both in church and state was elaborately defined. Dixon says that the Earl of Shaftesbury united with Locke in the work, and that "These two liberal and enlightened men had drawn up a form of government which England received as the perfection of wisdom." Yet their constitution and code proved an utter failure. He adds, "To understand how much Penn was wiser than his age, more imbued with the principles which have found their nobler utterances in our own, he must be measured not only against the fanatics of his sect, and unlettered men like Fox, but against the highest types of learning and liberality which it afforded. Between John Locke and William Penn there is a gulf like that which separates the seventeenth from the nineteenth century. Locke never escaped from the thraldom of local ideas; the one hundred and seventy years which have passed away since Penn founded the state which bears his name, seem only to have carried Europe so much nearer to the source from which his inspiration flowed."

It is not evident that W. Hepworth Dixon himself very clearly perceived the source from which Penn's inspiration flowed. Most certainly he has not traced it, if he did; nor has he done justice to

Penn's friends and co-workers in their great undertaking. Janney understood them and their history better, and he has brought forward the real circumstances of the case; showing the Quaker influences which had prepared Penn for the work, and the assistance he received from some of his fellow professors, who cordially aided without equalling him in sustaining and developing the new experiment.

Dixon introduces Algernon Sidney as if he were Penn's chief counsellor and only coadjutor; "so that it is quite impossible," he says, "to separate the exact share of one legislator from the other, so intricate and continuous was their mutual aid," in framing the constitution and preparing the laws for the government of Pennsylvania. This statement does not appear to have any other foundation than the writer's own deductions,—and, as appears to some of us, utterly unwarranted deductions—from a single letter written by Penn to Sidney. Dixon refers to that letter as his authority, and he gives the date as 13th of October, 1681, but does not quote from it. The reader will find it below.*

---

* *William Penn to Algernon Sidney.*

"13th October, 1681.

"There are many things make a man's life uneasy in the world, which are great abates to the pleasure of living, but scarcely one equal to that of the unkindness or injustice of friends.

"I have been asked by several since I came last to town if Colonel Sidney and I were fallen out, and when I denied it and laughed at it,

I must here say a few words for George Fox and the early Quakers in general, " whose fanaticism," and " grotesque follies," as Dixon terms them, have been placed before his readers in glowing colours. It is true he admits the fanaticism was shared at that time by the rest of the religious world, and that what was grand and genuine in their enthusiasm belonged to the Quakers themselves. Notwithstanding this admission, his reference to the

---

they told me I was mistaken, and, to convince me, stated that he had used me very ill to several persons if not companies, saying, 'I had a good country, but the basest laws in the world, not to be endured or lived under; and that the Turk was not more absolute than I.' This made me remember the discourse we had together at my house about me drawing constitutions, not as proposals, but as if fixed to the hand; and as my act to which the rest were to comply, if they would be concerned with me. I could not but call to mind that the objections were presently complied with, both by *my verbal denial of all such constructions as the words might bear, as if they were imposed and not yet free for debate.* And also that I took my pen and immediately altered the terms, so that they correspond (and, I truly thought, more properly) with thy sense. Upon this thou didst draw a draft as to the frame of government, gave it to me to read, and we discoursed it with considerable argument. It was afterwards called for back by thee to finish and polish; and I suspended proceedings in the business ever since.

"I met with this sort of language in the mouths of several: I shall not believe it; 'twere not well in me to an enemy, less so to a friend. But if it be true, I shall be sorry we ever were so well acquainted, or that I have given so much occasion to them that hate us, to laugh at me for more true friendship and steady kindness that I have been guilty of to any man I know living. It becomes not my pretensions to the things of another life to be much in pain about the uncertainties of this. Be it as it will, I am yet worthy of a line.

" Thy real friend,
" WILLIAM PENN."

Friends as fanatics is repeated. And he describes their proceedings in a style which leaves the impression that they well deserved the title. But his pictures, drawn from the statement of their enemies, are not correct; and, being distorted by their coloring, they do great injustice to a most devoted, persecuted, Christian people. It is quite true, however, that their enemies ascribed to them every grotesque folly which Penn's biographer recapitulates. But who would think of taking any man's history from the report of his bitter enemies? Such untested statements are unworthy of a historian, and unwarrantable in a history having any pretension to fidelity.

The whole reminds us of that which Isaac Penington said in one of his letters to his father, and which will be found at page 96 of this volume, respecting the extravagant stories then afloat about the Quakers. He tells him "if he takes things by the report of the enemies both to God and them, he shall be sure to hear and believe bad enough" of them. It is clear that Penn's biographer has founded the false character he gives George Fox and the early Friends upon the report of their enemies.

The poet Whittier has beautifully portrayed the true Quaker of the olden time in the following stanzas :—

Stanzas by Whittier.

The Quaker of the olden time!
  So calm, and firm, and true,
Unspotted by its wrong and crime,
  He walked the dark earth through.
The lust of power, the love of gain,
  The thousand lures of sin
Around him had no power to stain
  The purity within.

With that deep insight which detects
  All great things in the small,
And knows how each man's life affects
  The spiritual life of all,
He walked by faith and not by sight,
  By love and not by law;
The presence of the wrong or right
  He rather felt than saw.

He felt that wrong with wrong partakes;
  That nothing stands alone;
That whoso gives the motive makes
  His brother's sin his own.
And, pausing not for doubtful choice
  Of evils great or small,
He listened to that inward voice
  Which calls away from all.

Oh! spirit of that early day,
  So pure and strong and true,
Be with us in the narrow way
  Our faithful fathers knew.
Give strength the evil to forsake,
  The cross of Truth to bear,
And love and reverent fear to make
  Our daily lives a prayer!

William Penn's mother lived to see her son's experiment shadowed forth, but not to witness its consummation. She died early in 1682. This bereavement cast so deep a sorrow over his feelings, that for some time his health was affected. In writing to a friend he says, "Both thy letters came in a few days one of the other. My sickness on my mother's death, who was last Seventh-day interred, permitted me not to answer thee so soon as I desired." Lady Penn appears to have continued to live chiefly at Wanstead, from the time the family returned there, in 1659 or 1660, on leaving Ireland. Her remains were laid beside those of her son Richard in Walthamstow church.

The pressing calls on Penn's attention which his approaching departure for America occasioned, soon drew him into active life. Beside royal charters, and provincial laws, and his plans for the new city, and municipal regulations, he had a vast deal of other work to do for the infant colony. At length all was ready, and he embarked at Deal on board the ship *Welcome*, in company with about one hundred passengers, who were mostly Friends from Sussex, and weighed anchor on the first of Seventh month, 1682. To trace his movements thenceforward through the wide-spread duties that devolved on him as Governor of Pennsylvania, cannot be attempted in a sketch like this. He had many difficulties to cope with, many wants to provide for, and many sacrifices to make. He made these sacrifices without hesitation, and met all difficulties with energy, perseverance, and patience. These circumstances are associated with the early history of Pennsylvania; but his feelings on leaving his wife and children, and his religious aspirations for them and his friends, are not equally known. It is therefore to them that we shall more especially direct our attention.

William Penn left home with so strong a sense of the danger and uncertainty attendant on the path which lay before him, that he made provision for his family as if he was never to see them again. On this occasion he addressed a long letter to his wife, in which he states his views respecting the education of their children; whilst to them he speaks of their duties in early life as well as in mature age. He especially enjoins early devotion to God, and earnestness in serving Him on earth, adding, "Love and fear the Lord, keep close to meetings, and delight to wait on the Lord God of your father and mother among His despised people, as we have done. Count it your honour to be members of that society, and heirs of that living fellowship which is enjoyed among them, and for the experience of which your father's soul blesseth the Lord for ever.

"Next, be obedient to your dear mother, a woman whose virtue and good name is an honour to you. She hath been exceeded by none in her time for her plainness, integrity, industry, humanity, virtue, and good understanding—qualifications not usual among women of her condition and quality. Therefore honour and obey her, my dear children, as your mother; and as your father's love and delight. She loved your father with a deep and upright love, choosing him before all her many suitors. Though she be of a delicate constitution and noble spirit, yet she descended to the utmost care and tenderness for you in your infancy as a mother and as a nurse, performing for you the most painful acts of service. I charge you before the Lord to honour and obey, love and cherish your dear mother."

The following extract from the letter to his wife shows how highly he appreciated her, and that his ideas respecting the training of children were far in advance of the age in which he lived:—

" My dear wife,

"Remember thou wast the love of my youth, and much the joy of my life—the most beloved as well as the most worthy of all my earthly comforts; and the reason of that love was more thy inward than thy outward excellencies, which yet were many. God knows and thou knowest I can say it was a match of His making; and God's image in us both was the first thing, and the most amiable and engaging ornament in our eyes. Now I am to leave thee, and that without knowing whether I shall ever see thee more in this world. Take my counsel into thy bosom, and let it dwell with thee in my stead while thou livest.

"*Firstly.*—Let the fear of the Lord and zeal and love for His glory dwell richly in thy heart, and thou wilt watch for good over thyself and thy dear children and family.

"*Secondly.*—Be diligent in meetings for worship and business; stir up thyself and others therein; it is thy duty and place. Let meetings be kept once a day in the family, to wait upon the Lord who has given us so much time for ourselves. And, my dearest, to make thy family matters easy, divide thy time and be regular. Grieve not thyself with careless servants; rather pay them and let them go, if they will not be better by admonition.

"*Thirdly.*—Cast up thy income, and see what it daily amounts to, by which thou mayest have it in thy sight to keep within compass. I beseech thee to live low and sparingly till my debts are paid; and then enlarge as thou seest convenient. Remember thy mother's example, when thy father's public-spiritedness had worsted his estate, which is my case. I know thou art averse to the pomps of the world—a nobility natural to thee. I write not as doubtful, but to quicken thee for my sake, knowing that God will bless thy care. I need not bid thee to be humble, for thou art so; nor meek and patient, for it is thy natural disposition: but I pray thee be oft in retirement with the Lord, and guard against encroaching friendships [of the world]; keep them at arm's end.

"*Fourthly.*—And now, my dearest, let me commend to thy care my dear children; abundantly beloved by me, as the Lord's blessings, and the sweet pledges of our mutual and endeared affection. Above all things, endeavour to bring them up in the love of virtue, and in that holy plain way of it which we have lived in, that the world in no part of it get into my family. I had rather they were homely than finely bred as to outward behaviour; yet I love sweetness mixed with gravity, and cheerfulness tempered with sobriety. Religion in the heart leads into true civility, teaching men and women to be mild and courteous in their behaviour.

"*Fifthly.*—Bring them up in love of one another. Tell them it is the charge I left behind me, and that it is the way to have the love and blessing of God to rest upon them. Sometimes separate them, but not long; and allow them to give and send each other small things, to endear one another with. Once more I say, tell them how it was my counsel that they should be tender and affectionate one to another. For their learning be liberal. Spare no cost—for by such parsimony all is lost that is saved—but let it be useful knowledge they are taught, such as is consistent with truth and godliness. The exercise of ingenuity mixed with industry is good for the body and mind too. I recommend the useful parts of mathematics, building houses or ships, measuring, surveying, dialling, and navigation. But agriculture is especially in my eye. Rather keep an ingenious person in the house to teach them than send them to schools. Be sure to observe their genius, and do not cross it; let them not dwell too long on one thing, but make an agreeable change before they become weary. Let all their diversions have some little bodily labour in them."

The above letter was dated Worminghurst, 4th of Sixth-month, 1682.

The following is addressed to Margaret Fox of Swarthmoor Hall, wife to his friend George Fox, who was then at Enfield near London. The original is in the possession of Silvanus Thompson, York.

William Penn to Margaret Fox.

"Very dearly honoured and beloved M. F.

"In the precious love of God I salute thee, that by which He hath made us who were once strangers to the Lord and to one another, very near and very dear; and most sweet is our fellowship. Oh! that the nations knew it well! They shall yet know it, and rejoice in the salvation that is come to us.

"Dear Margaret, I am a-going. Remember me

in the Father's love, and may God be with thee, and bless thee and thine, with His temporal and His eternal blessings. This day I have had a precious meeting with the Friends of this city; many public Friends being there. Oh! the dissolving love of God!—all tender, meek, and loving. May God be with us all forever, staying or going! To thee, dear Margaret, and dear Thomas Lower and yours, this is my tender farewell in the Lord. (I pray Him to) let all things be and prosper with me, as mine eye is to be of service to the Lord in this thing. Some have been unkind, but my soul breathes for them and forgives them; and truly n peace flows as a river. Oh! dear Margaret, n..y the Lord be with us, and keep us in our several places, and do us good forever. Dear George I left yesterday at Enfield, much better. My soul loves him beyond [expression], and his dear love and care and counsel are in my heart. A sweet parting we had. So, dear Margaret and dear Thomas Lower, let me hear from you, that I may rejoice in your love. I have nought else to add but my wife's dear love, who is sweetly consenting and satisfied.

"Thy very loving friend and brother,

"WM. PENN.

"London, 14th of 6th mo. 1682.

"Thy daughter and son Rous are well. She and daughter went and came with us to and from Enfield. Salute me to dear Leonard Fell and Robert Withers, and friends thereaway."

He published three other letters under the title of *William Penn's Last Farewell to England*. They were dated from on board the *Welcome*, whilst lying in the Downs, 30th of Sixth-month, 1682. The first is *A Salutation to the Faithful;* the second, *A Reproof to the Unfaithful;* and the third, *A Visitation to the Inquiring*. All three manifest earnest religious feeling, and contain exhortation and advice suited to the various states addressed. Under the same date, which was the day before the *Welcome* weighed anchor, he also wrote to his friend Stephen Crisp. One passage of that letter is as follows :—

"Dear Stephen,
            We know one another. I need not say much to thee; but this I will say, that thy parting dwells with me, or rather thy love at my parting. How innocent, how tender, how like the little child that has no guile! The Lord will bless that ground (Philadelphia). I have also had a letter from thee which comforted me; for many are my trials, yet not more than my supplies from my Heavenly Father, whose glory I seek. And surely, Stephen, there is work enough to be done, and room to work in. Surely God will come in for a share in this planting-work, and that leaven shall

leaven the lump in time. I do no not believe the Lord's providence had run this way towards me, but that He has an heavenly end and service in it. So with Him I leave all, and myself, and thee, and His dear people."

Thus committing all to God, and strong in faith and hope, the Governor of Pennsylvania bade farewell to his family and friends, as the *Welcome* bore him from the shores of his native land.

The voyage was made in about eight weeks, which was then considered a good passage. But, whilst crossing the Atlantic, thirty of the emigrants who had sailed from the Downs died of the small-pox. The survivors, as long as they lived, had many a tale to tell of that sad passage, of William Penn's care and tenderness towards the sick, and his comforting exhortations and prayers with those who died on board.

Business cares and studies soon gathered around him, into which he entered with that administrative capacity and dispatch for which he was remarkable. Amid all these, the grand features of nature in the New World failed not to impress his imagination, and draw forth lively descriptions in his letters home. The woods, the flowers, the shrubs, and the native fruits of Pennsylvania were most charming to him. The site of his new city was a continual source of interest and occupation, whilst emigrants from Great Britain, Ireland, and Germany, were flocking to Pennsylvania as to a land of promised freedom and plenty.

From *Watson's Annals* we learn that the assembly to which Penn's frame of government and laws were submitted was held at Chester, three weeks after his arrival; and the first provincial assembly which was convened at Philadelphia, and was composed of seventy-two members, met in the Friends' meeting-house on the 10th of First-month, 1683. The representatives were elected by ballot. Watson says that "the only law added to the provincial code on that occasion was one enacted to prevent law-suits, by the institution of three ' Peace-makers,' after the manner of ordinary arbitration, to be chosen by each county court, that they might hear and end all differences." This, like many others in the Pennsylvania code, was merely enacting as a law that which was an established rule of Quaker discipline; for law-suits are discouraged among the Friends, arbitration being the substitute.

But it was William Penn's treaty of peace and brotherhood with the Indians which especially marked his first visit to America; and, beyond any other event in his career, has attracted the attention of the civilized world. Yet neither he nor the Friends associated with him were conscious of doing anything more than what simple Christian morality and human brotherhood suggested. They had ignored all war and bloodshed

for the settlement of disputes, as contrary to the
gospel of Christ. Therefore they went among
the Indians unarmed. They were not satisfied
with merely paying them for specified portions of
the country which they desired to occupy, but
they felt that these sons of the forest should be
told why they came among them unlike the other
colonists,—without weapons of war.

The title of the Indians and their right to compensation had been repeatedly recognized from the time of the first settlement of the Friends in New Jersey—that therefore was not new. Nor was it, as many suppose, the design of William Penn at the time of the famous treaty to pay them all off hand, then and there, for their lands. On the contrary, there were various separate purchases made at different times and from different tribes who occupied different localities. It does not appear that there was any purchase whatever in connection with the great treaty. Presents were given and speeches made on both sides, which embodied clearly defined promises of justice and peace, to the exclusion of all violence. In case of differences arising at any time, they were to be settled by arbitration; the arbitrators, twelve in number, to be fairly chosen by the parties concerned—half to be Englishmen and half Indians. Although the Indians made stately and eloquent speeches in answer to William Penn, of their replies little seems to have been preserved except their pledge " to live in love with Onas [Penn] and his children as long as the sun and moon shall endure."

When the account of this treaty reached Europe most of her politicians awaited with sneering smiles the consummation they expected to follow. " Going among the cruel Indian savages without arms, and pledging themselves never to use violence towards them! What folly! What madness!" But they waited and watched long, and still no violence or bloodshed ensued. Whilst the surrounding colonists were ever and anon at war with the Indians, and the scalping-knife and tomahawk brought death and terror to many a hearth, the Quakers of Pennsylvania and all their possessions remained uninjured—

> Safe that quiet Eden lay,
>   When the war whoop stirred the land ;
> Thence the Indian turned away
>   From their homes his bloody hand.

" He remembered the treaty with the sons of Onas, and kept it inviolate." The Friends of Pennsylvania on their side acted truthfully and honestly towards the Redmen; and the Indian people, even when at war with other English colonies, and when the original parties to the treaty had died off, regarded the lives and property of the children of Onas as sacred. Such was the treaty of peace and amity on which Voltaire remarked, that "it was the only one ever made without an oath, and the only one that never was broken."

We are told of two purchases of land from the Indians in 1683, whilst William Penn remained in the province. They lay in different directions. As regards one of these, the extent of country paid for was to run as far back as a man could walk in three days. It is stated that Penn himself, with several of his friends and a number of the Indian chiefs, began to walk over this land at the mouth of the Neshaminy, and walked up the Delaware. They are described as having, in a day and a half, got to a spruce-tree near the mouth of Baker's Creek, when the Governor decided that this would include as much land as would be wanted at present. A line was then run, and marked from that spruce-tree to Neshaminy, and the remainder left to be walked out when it should be wanted for settlement. It is said they walked leisurely after the Indian manner, sitting down sometimes to smoke their pipes, to eat biscuit and cheese, and drink a bottle of wine. It is certain they arrived at the spruce-tree in a day and a half, the whole distance being rather less than thirty miles.

Two years afterwards, when William Penn had returned to England, a purchase was made in another direction. A copy of the deed drawn up on this occasion is now before me, and I shall give it verbatim.

Deed of purchase.

Copy of a Deed of Purchase between William Penn and the Indians in 1685.

This Indenture witnesseth that we, Packenah, Jarkham, Sikalls, Partquesott, Jervis, Essepenauk, Felktroy, Hekeloppaw, Ecomer, Mackloha, Mettheonga, Wissa, Powey, Indian kings, Sachemakers, right owners of all lands from Quing Quingus, called Duck Creek, unto Uplands, called Chester Creek, all along by the west side of Delaware River, and so between the said creeks backwards as far as a man can ride in two days with a horse, for and in consideration of these following goods to us in hand paid and secured, to be paid by William Penn, proprietary and governor of the province of Pennsylvania, and territory thereof, viz.

20 guns, 20 fathoms match-coat, 20 fathoms strong water, 20 blankets, 20 kettles, 20 pounds powder, 100 bars of lead, 40 tomahawks, 100 knives, 40 pairs of stockings, 1 barrel of beer, 20 pounds red lead, 100 fathoms of wampan, 30 glass bottles, 30 pewter spoons, 100 awl blades, 300 tobacco pipes, 100 kinds of tobacco, tobacco tongs, 20 steels, 300 flints, 30 pairs scissors, 30 combs, 60 looking-glasses, 200 needles, 1 skipper of salt, 30 pounds of sugar, 5 gallons of molasses, 20 tobacco boxes, 100 jewsharps, 20 hoes, 30 gimlets, 30 wooden screw boxes, 100 strings of beads.

Do hereby acknowledge, etc.

Given under our hands at Newcastle 2nd day of 8th month, 1685.

[The above is a true copy taken from the original by Ephraim Morton,* of Washington County, Pennsylvania, formerly a clerk in the Land Office.]

---

* I am indebted for this document to a Friend in Rochdale, in whose family it has been for upwards of fifty years.

The Indians as well as the colonists were at liberty still to hunt over all the lands which were sold to the Governor, so long as they were not inclosed with fences or walls that would keep out the deer.

It has been already stated that Mary Penington visited her daughter at Worminghurst, and died there two weeks after William Penn sailed for America. We next hear of Gulielma Penn through her friend Thomas Ellwood, who in 1683 was brought into some difficulty about a book he had published. The work got into the hands of Sir Benjamin Tichbourne of Rickmansworth, who on reading it inferred that the author had some covert designs to serve, and made it a matter of serious examination. Another magistrate, Justice Fotherly, uniting with Tichbourne, demanded a searching investigation, and appointed a day when the author was bound to appear.

In the mean time, before that day arrived, an announcement reached Thomas Ellwood from Worminghurst, that his friend Guli Penn was very ill, and wished to see him. He hastened first to Justice Fotherly, and explained to him that it would greatly oblige him if the examination of his book could be proceeded with that morning, so as to permit him to go into Sussex to see his friend William Penn's wife. At the same time he stated that she was dangerously ill, and had sent an express requesting that he would lose no time in going to her; as he had been her intimate friend from childhood.

Ellwood says, "While I thus delivered myself, I observed a sensible alteration in the justice; and when I had done speaking, he first said he was very sorry for Madam Penn's illness, of whose virtues and worth he spoke very highly, but not more than was her due. Then he told me that for her sake he would do what he could to further my visit to her. "But," said he, "I am only one, and of myself can do nothing in it. Therefore you must go to Sir Benjamin Tichbourne, and see if you can prevail with him to meet me now." He did so, and explained the occasion of his visit. Both he and his lady, who was present, expressed great concern for Guli Penn's illness. Ultimately the justices allowed him to go, desiring him "to give their hearty respects and service to Madam Penn, with good wishes for a good journey." Having reached Worminghurst pretty early next morning, he found his friend in a hopeful state and daily improving, so that after a little time he returned home.

In the Wycombe manuscript collection of Ellwood's poems are the following unpublished lines, dated Fifth month, 1683, which were written about this time.

TO MY FRIEND IN AMERICA.

I envy not nor grudge the sweet content
  I hope thou takest under thy shady tree,
Where many an hour is innocently spent,
  From vexing cares, from noise, and tumult free,
    Where godly meetings are not riots made,
    Nor innocents by stratagems betrayed.

But, for mine own part, I expect not yet
  Such peaceful days—such quiet times to see;
My station in a troublous world is set,
  And daily trials still encompass me;
    This is my comfort, that my God is near
    To give me courage, and my spirit cheer.

The blustering winds blow hard, the foaming seas
  Raise their proud waves, the surging billows swell;
No human art this tempest can appease;
  He's only safe who with the Lord doth dwell.
    Though storms and violence should yet increase,
    In Him there is security and peace.

The following letter is from Gulielma Penn :—

To Margaret Fox.

Worminghurst, 2nd 6th mo. 1684.

"Dear friend M. F.

In a sense of that love and life by which we are united to God and made near one unto another, I salute thee. And, dear Margaret, I cannot express the sense I have of thy love and regard to me and my dear husband; but it is often before me with very great returns of love and affection, and desires for thy prosperity and preservation among God's people. I should be exceedingly glad if it were my lot once more to see thy face, but at present I see little likelihood. Yet methinks, if thou foundest a clearness, it would be happier if thou wert nearer thy dear husband and children, but I leave it to the Lord's ordering and thy freedom.

"There have been great reports of my husband coming with J. Purvis, A. Parker's brother-in-law; but he has returned without him, and brought letters. My husband was then very well on the 8th of the Fourth-month, and has some thoughts of coming, but when he did not mention. This puts a stop at present to my going; but with the Lord I desire to leave it, and commit him and myself to His holy ordering.

"I truly rejoice to hear thou art so well, and thy daughters, and their children, and that Thomas Lower had a little time to see them. I perceive they are bad about you, and that thy sufferings are large; but the Lord can, and I believe will, make it up. In Him is thy great reward for thy manifold exercises. They begin to be troublesome in this country also. They have not yet been here, but threaten it, they say.

"I desire my very dear love to thy son and daughter Lower, and to thy son and daughter

Abraham. We are all pretty well, I bless the Lord.

"Thy truly loving and affectionate friend,
"GULI PENN."

While Guli was writing the above, her husband was crossing the ocean on his return home. His arrival in England was announced to their venerated friend at Swarthmoor Hall in the following letter:—

William Penn to Margaret Fox.

"London, 22nd, 8th mo. 1684.

"Dear M. Fox,

"Whom my heart loveth and honoureth in the Lord, remembering thee in the ancient love and path of life which is most glorious in mine eyes; yea, excellent above all visible things. Dear Margaret, herein it is I enjoy the fellowship of thy spirit above time and distance, floods, and many waters.

"It is now a few days above three weeks since I arrived well in my native land. It was within seven miles of my own house that we landed. I found my dear wife and her children well, to the overcoming of my heart because of the mercies of the Lord to us. I have not missed a meal's meat or a night's rest since I went out of the country, and wonderfully hath the Lord preserved me through many troubles in the settlements I have made, both as to the government and the soil. I find many wrong stories let in of me, even by some I love; but, blessed be the Lord, they are the effects of envy, for things are sweetly well with Friends there, and many grow in wisdom. And in the outward things they increase finely. The love of divers Friends, especially those of Lancashire and Cheshire, was to thee. Our meetings are blessed, and I think there are eighteen in number in the province. Poor C. Hurst and brother died soon after arrival. Fixing on a low marshy place, for the river's sake, (though a dry bank was not a stone's cast from them,) they had agues and fevers, but no seasoning in any other settlement.

"My dear wife relates thy great love to her in my absence, and so she also wrote me word, which affected my heart and soul. I return thee my tender acknowledgment. My salutation is to thy dear children, and to Thomas Camm, Leonard Fell, and other faithful brethren.

"I have seen the King and the Duke. They and their nobles were very kind to me, and I hope the Lord will make way for me in their hearts, in order to serve His suffering people as well as my own interest.

"I shall be glad to hear of thy well being, and am with much affection thy faithful friend and brother in the Truth.

"WILLIAM PENN."*

* The originals of the two foregoing letters are in the Thirnbeck collections of old MSS., Bristol.

CHAPTER XIII.

1684-1693.

William Penn's difficulties about the boundary line of his province.—His outlay without due return.—His influence with James II.—Is accused of being a Jesuit.—His correspondence with Dr. Tilotson.—William Penn at Chester during the King's progress.—King James driven from the Throne.—The Prince and Princess of Orange invited to assume the Crown.—William Penn suspected of treasonable correspondence with the exiled James II.—Letter from Gulielma Maria Penn to Margaret Fox.—Death of George Fox.—William Penn arrested.—Examined before the King and Privy Council.—Is imprisoned.—His writings during his seclusion.—His province sequestrated.—Confiscation of his Irish estates.—Is restored to liberty.—Death of Gulielma Penn.

WHEN William Penn left Pennsylvania in the autumn of 1684, he expected to return with his wife and family, as soon as he could secure from the King and those concerned a definite settlement of the boundary line between his province and that of Lord Baltimore. But, in the winter of that year Charles II. died. Nothing had been effectually settled on the matter in question before that event, and hence the Governor of Pennsylvania was compelled to remain and watch for an opportunity to obtain a decision.

It will be seen by the letter in last chapter from

Gulielma Penn to Margaret Fox, that the thought of her going to her husband in America had been before them, and she seemed most anxious to carry out his wishes. To live in Philadelphia, his own city, the birthplace and home of religious freedom, the beau ideal of his own creation, the spot on earth of all others in which his brightest hopes were centred, was from first to last the desire of William Penn. He says, in a letter to Thomas Lloyd, dated 16th of First-month, 1685, " Keep up the people's hearts and love. I hope to be with them next fall, if the Lord prevent not. I long to be with you; no temptations prevail to fix me here." Certainly, there was nothing to fix him, but much to delay him. The fall came and passed away, but no settlement of the boundary was obtained. Again, when writing to Pennsylvania, he says, " We are all well through the Lord's mercy, and long to be with you, especially the children."

William Penn and his wife had systematically contracted their family expenditure, so as to allow as much as possible of their private income being applied to the expenses incident to the planting of a new colony, and the establishment of a new city. Most of the colonists were able working people; others took considerable property with them; so that the Governor did not calculate that the demand on his purse would be so long continued as it eventually was. His nature was so generous, so unselfish, that whilst his attention was absorbed in plans for the accommodation and prosperity of the settlers, he was liable to forget that much of what he laid out would never be returned to him. The sense of justice of corporate bodies, composed of settlers of every creed and class, was not in his absence always to be relied upon, and of this he was sometimes made painfully conscious. He remonstrated when each returning vessel brought call after call for money, bill after bill to be paid by the Governor. At length, in 1686, he peremptorily ordered that he be not drawn on for another penny; being then, as he stated, £5,000 in debt on their behalf; and no supplies, no quit rents, coming to him to help to clear it off. Writing to his agent he says, "If I cannot be supplied, I resolve to turn over a new leaf. There is nothing my soul breathes more for in this world, next to my dear family's life, than that I may see poor Pennsylvania again, and my wife has given up to go."

But it was long before the boundary question was even partially adjusted. Lord Baltimore, himself a Roman Catholic, with many friends at court, was determined not to yield to William Penn's suggestions, whilst the latter was too sensible of the importance of a settlement to the peace of the colonies to leave it undefined. In the mean time there were other affairs of great interest which claimed his attention. When the late King died, there were fourteen hundred Quakers lying in the prisons of England for conscience sake. To obtain their freedom he exerted himself to the utmost. But a full year elapsed before they were released; then, by the King's proclamation, the prison doors were opened, and all who were confined on account of their religion were allowed to walk forth as free men. It was not merely for those of his own society that Penn interposed to have such grievances removed as it was in the power of the King to prevent. The removal of every oppressive measure was an absolute pleasure as well as a matter of conscience to him. whoever were the sufferers. Possessing more of King James's confidence than any one else outside the Romish pale, and more than most of those within it, he obtained mercy or justice for many a suppliant by his intercession.

It was against this part of Penn's career that the late Lord Macaulay directed those calumnies which have been so ably refuted by Paget, Forster, Dixon, Janney, and others. A clue to the paltry motive which inspired them will be found in a remarkable anecdote, related at page 108 of William Tallack's *Friendly Sketches of America*. The poet Whittier refers to this subject with his wonted magnanimity in the following lines:—

How vainly he laboured to sully with blame
The white bust of Penn in the niche of his fame!
Self-will is self-wounding, perversity blind,
On himself fell the stain for the Quaker designed!
For the sake of his true-hearted father before him,
For the sake of the dear Quaker mother that bore him,

For the sake of his gifts and the works that outlive him,
And his brave words for freedom, we freely forgive him!

Gerard Croese says that " William Penn was the Quakers' sole patron at court, and on whom the hateful eyes of his enemies were intent. The King loved him as a singular and entire friend, and often honoured him with his company in private, and that not for one but many hours together, delaying to hear the best of his peers at the same time waiting for an audience." This friendship for Penn was the brightest feature in the life of that unfortunate monarch. But of course such favour brought to the subject of it the inveterate envy of courtiers. As the King's measures and his religion became more and more odious to the nation, the ears of the people were open to every evil rumor that could be invented against those whom he favoured. It was declared that Penn was not merely a Papist, but a Jesuit in disguise. Conscious of innocence, the victim of these calumnies was slow to regard them in any other light than as absurd slanders, which nobody who wished to know the truth would believe. But when at length he was told that even Dr. Tillotson, afterwards Archbishop of Canterbury, who knew him and had regarded him as a friend, had been instrumental in circulating the report, he felt that he should no longer keep silent, and the following correspondence ensued :—

William Penn to Dr. Tillotson.

"Charing-cross, 22d 11th mo. 1685.

"Worthy Friend,

"Being told that Dr. Tillotson suspected me, and so reported me a Papist,—I think a Jesuit,—and being closely prest, I take the liberty to ask thee if any such reflection fell from thee? If it did, I am sorry one I esteemed ever the first of his robe should so undeservedly stain me, for so I call it. And if the story be false, I am sorry they should so abuse Dr. Tillotson as well as myself, without cause. I add no more but that I abhor two principles in religion, and pity those that own them. The first is *obedience upon authority without conviction;* and the other, *the destroying them that differ from me for God's sake.* Such religion is without judgment, though not without teeth. Union is best, if right; else charity: and, as Hooker said, the time will come when a few words spoken with meekness, humility, and love, shall be more acceptable than volumes of controversies, which commonly destroy charity, the very best part of true religion. I mean not a charity that can change with all, but bear all, as I can Dr. Tillotson in what he dissents from me; and in this reflection, too, if said; which is not yet believed by thy Christian and true friend,

"WILLIAM PENN."

Dr. Tillotson to William Penn.

"Honoured Sir,

"The demand of your letter is very just and reasonable, and the manner of it very kind : therefore, in answer to it, be pleased to take the following account.

."The last time you did me the favour to see me at my house, I did, according to the freedom I always use where I profess any friendship, acquaint you with something I had heard of a correspondence you held with some at Rome, and particularly with some of the Jesuits there. At which you seemed a little surprised; and, after some general discourse about it, you said you would call on me some other time, and speak further of it. Since that time I never saw you but by accident and in passage, when I thought you always declined me, particularly at Sir William Jones's chamber, which was the last time I think I saw you; upon which occasion I took notice to him of your strangeness to me, and told what I thought might be the reason of it, and that I was sorry for it, because I had a particular esteem of your parts and temper. The same I believe I have said to some others, but to whom I do not so particularly remember. Since your going to Pennsylvania I never thought more of it, till lately, being in some company, one of them pressed me to declare whether I had not heard something of you which had satisfied me that you were a Papist. I answered, 'No! by no means.' I told him what I had heard, and what I had said to you, and of the strangeness that ensued upon it; but that this never went further with me than to make me suspect there was more in that report which I heard than I was at first willing to believe; and that if any made more of it, I should look upon him as very injurious both to Mr. Penn and myself.

"This is the truth of that matter; and whenever you will satisfy me that my suspicion of the truth of that report I had heard was groundless, I will heartily beg your pardon for it. I do fully concur with you *in abhorrence of the two principles* you mention, and in your approbation of that excellent saying of Mr. Hooker, for which I shall ever highly esteem him. I have endeavoured to make it one of the governing principles of my life, never to abate anything of humanity or charity to any man for his difference from me in opinion, and particularly to those of your persuasion, as several of them have had experience. I have been ready on all occasions to do them offices of kindness, being truly sorry to see them so hardly used; and though I thought them mistaken, yet in the main I believed them to be very honest. I thank you for your letter, and have a just esteem of the Christian temper of it, and rest your faithful friend,

"JOHN TILLOTSON."

William Penn to Dr. Tillotson.

"Charing-cross, 27th 2nd month, 1686.

"Worthy Friend,

"Having a much less opinion of my own memory than of Dr. Tillotson's truth, I will allow the fact, though not the jealousy: for, besides that I cannot look strange when I am well used, I have ever treated the name of Dr. Tillotson with regard. I might be grave and full of my own business; but my nature is not harsh, my education less, and my principles least of all. It was the opinion I had of the doctor's moderation, simplicity, and integrity, rather than his parts or post, that always made me set a value on his friendship; of them perhaps I am a better judge, leaving the others to men of deeper talents. I blame him nothing, but leave it to his own better thoughts, if in my affair his jealousy was not too nimble for his charity. I should hardly have endured the same thought of Dr. Tillotson on the like occasion, and less to speak of it.

"For the Roman correspondence I come freely to confession. I have not only no such thing with any Jesuit at Rome (though Protestants may have without offence) but I hold none with any Jesuit priest or regular in the world of that communion. And I know not one any where, and yet I am a Catholic, though not a Roman. I have feeling for mankind, and dare not deny others what I crave for myself, I mean liberty for the exercise of my religion; thinking faith, piety, and providence better security than force.

"Dr. Tillotson may be confident I am no Roman Catholic, but a Christian whose creed is the Scriptures of Truth, of which I hold a nobler evidence than the best church authority in the world." [Penn goes on to recommend Dr. Tillotson, in order clearly to understand his views, to read his *Address to Protestants*, from page 133 to the end; and to the first four chapters of his *No cross, No crown*. These he thought should convince him how far away he was from papacy] "to say nothing of *our most unceremonious and unworldly way of worship, and their pompous cult;*" adding, "Here I shall leave the business, with all due acknowledgments of thy friendly temper, and assurance of the sincere good wishes and respects of thy affectionate and real friend,

"WILLIAM PENN."

After the receipt of the above letter, Dr. Tillotson appears to have waited on William Penn to apologise, and to express his entire conviction of Penn's views having been misrepresented. However, that did not prevent the public from continuing to say that the doctor believed him to be a Papist, and a letter had even been placed in his hand reiterating the statement. This he forwarded to the Doctor, requesting him to state in writing the substance of what he had said verbally, which produced the following reply.

Dr. Tillotson to William Penn.

"April 29th, 1686

"Sir,

"I am very sorry that the suspicion I had entertained concerning you, of which I gave you the true account in my former letter, hath occasioned so much trouble and inconvenience to you; and I do now declare with great joy that I am fully satisfied there was no just ground for that suspicion, and therefore do heartily beg your pardon for it. And ever since you were pleased to give me that satisfaction, I have taken all occasions to vindicate you in this matter; and shall be ready to do it to the person that sent you the enclosed, whenever he will please to come to me. I will take the first opportunity to visit you at Charing-cross and renew our acquaintance, in which I took great pleasure.

"I rest your faithful friend,

"JOHN TILLOTSON."

When such a man as Tillotson could be so far misled by popular gossip as to suspect William Penn of being a Roman Catholic, or favorable to their doctrines, and to repeat that apprehension, we need not wonder that shallow thinkers and jealous courtiers would go still further. It is evident, however, that when Tillotson was questioned on the subject he was candid, and honourably and gladly acknowledged his error when the matter was clearly explained. But William Penn was more than candid: his was the conduct of the true Christian, who "suffereth long and is kind;"—"is not easily provoked, thinketh no evil, rejoiceth not in iniquity, but rejoiceth in the truth."

In the letter to James Harrison, his steward at Pennsbury, in 1687, he says, "As yet I cannot get clear, for besides that I am not in my private affairs fit to remove for a stay as that I intend when I come there, I am engaged in the public business of the nation; and Friends and others in authority would have me see the establishment of the liberty that I was a small instrument to begin in this land. The Lord has given me great entrance with the King, though not so much as 'tis said, and I confess I should rejoice to see poor England fixt and the penal laws repealed that are now suspended; and if it goes well with England, it cannot go ill with Pennsylvania. Unkindly used as I am, no poor slave in Turkey desires more earnestly I believe for deliverance, than I do to be with you; therefore be contented for a while, and God in his time will bring us together."

Again he writes, " 8th of Seventh-month, 1687. I am straitened for time, being just come home from the King's progress through Berkshire, Gloucestershire, Shropshire, Cheshire, Hampshire, and so home. I had two meetings on a First-day at Chester in the tennis court, where were about a thousand people, while the King was there."

This is the King's visit to Chester, and William Penn's meeting mentioned in the diary of Dr. Cartwright, Bishop of Chester, recently published by the Camden Society, wherein he says of King James, "He went to his devotions in the shire hall, and Mr. Penn held forth in the tennis-court, and I preached in the cathedral." William Penn held large meetings in various places, as he moved along with the royal party, as at Bristol; and at Chew in Somersetshire, where the people assembled in the open air, there being no building sufficient to contain the crowds.

In the spring of the year 1688 King James put forth his Declaration for universal liberty of conscience, and the suspension of the test act. Together with this was published an order of council, requiring the clergy to read the declaration in their churches. This order was extremely offensive to those of the Established Church. "They disapproved of the measure, as being in their view calculated to subvert the Protestant religion; but the chief ground on which they opposed it, was the unpopular prerogative claimed by the King to dispense with or suspend at his pleasure the laws of the realm." The Archbishop of Canterbury and six other bishops addressed him, respectfully explaining to him the reasons for which they could not comply with his command, and they were forthwith sent to the Tower. On that occasion William Penn exerted all his influence and power of persuasion to induce the King to liberate them, but he utterly failed. However, they were soon brought to trial, and triumphantly acquitted.

It was well known that Penn was opposed to the tests which excluded all dissenters from parliament. He had written against them in a work entitled *Good Advice to the Church of England*. Though printed anonymously, the authorship was known, and he suffered public odium accordingly. The national indignation was aroused, and was not again to be appeased by King James. In the autumn of 1688 the throne was declared vacant, and the Prince and Princess of Orange were invited to take possession of it.

William Penn might then have returned to Pennsylvania had he chosen to do so; but he well knew that such a step would be interpreted unfavourably, and he therefore remained to brave the storm. He was soon placed under arrest, and, after being most scrutinizingly examined, nothing could be brought against him which would warrant his detention. Again and again, as each fresh fabrication was prepared by his enemies, he was brought before the council, but still nothing could be proved. His truthful transparent answers carried conviction to the minds of all who were not influenced by bitter party spirit. "His manly avowal," says Janney, "of his continued friendship for the exiled King, who had been his own and his father's friend, was in accordance with his candid and noble character, but in striking contrast with the conduct of some who then frequented the court of the reigning monarch."

As the year 1689 waned, there seemed nothing to prevent the Governor of Pennsylvania from returning to his province in the ensuing autumn. He had always kept up a regular correspondence with his provincial council as a body, and with several of the chief officers of the State, in order to maintain good feeling and a sense of his authority among them. One of his letters written about this time to the council, which was composed of Quakers, concludes thus:—

"And now, Friends, I have a word more to you. It is this; that faith, hope, and charity, are the great helps and marks of true Christians; but, above all, charity, divine love. Blessed are they that are come to it, and hold the Truth in it, and work and act in it. Poor indeed they are in their own spirit, but rich in God's. Oh! come into this love more and more; it will preserve peace in the Church, peace in the state, peace in families, aye, and peace in particular bosoms. God Almighty draw, I beseech him, all your hearts into this heavenly love more and more, that the work of it may shine out to God's glory and your comfort.

"For matters here, as to myself, I am well and free, and for the church of God liberty continues. But in the nations of Europe great wars and rumours of wars.

"I am, in the Truth which makes us near to God and one to another, your faithful friend and brother,
"WILLIAM PENN."

The letter which follows has the date of 1690, as an endorsement; and there is reason to infer that it was written in the spring of that year. With the exception of one in the preceding chapter it is the only letter from Gulielma Maria Penn that I have ever seen.

To Margaret Fox.

"Dear and honourable friend, M. F.

"With salutations of true, constant, faithful love is my heart filled to thee. I feel it in that which is beyond words—in the unity of the spirit of Truth.

"It rises in my mind, as I am writing, something that I saw concerning thee in my sleep long ago—about the time of the beginning of these bad spirits. I thought I saw thee and dear George and many Friends in a meeting, where the power of the Lord was greatly manifested; and methought there came in dark wicked spirits, and they strove exceedingly against the [Divine] life that was in the meeting. Their chief aim was at thee and George, but mostly at thee. They strove to hurt thee, but, methought, thou gottest so over them that they could not touch thee, but only tore some little part of thy clothes, and thou escaped unhurt. Then a sweet rejoicing and triumph spread throughout the meeting. That dream was long ago, and the Lord has so brought it to pass that thy life now reigns over them all. It was thee they began with, but the Lord has given and will [further] give thee the victory, to the joy and comfort of thy people.

"Dear Margaret, I received thy acceptable letter long since, but have delayed writing to thee, in the hope to give a fuller account of my husband and of our going. But the winter and spring have been so severe that letters have been hindered; and now that many are come, none of them of late dates are for me, because my husband has been in daily expectation of seeing us there, and I am sorry for his disappointment. I should have been truly glad to have seen him before going, as thou sayest, but am contented, and desire not his coming merely to fetch us, as I know he has a great deal of business to attend to; and also know it is not for want of true love or the desire to see us that keeps him, but it is that he must first mind the duties of the place in which he now stands, and do that which is right, and in which he has peace. If the Lord gives clearness and drawings to come, I would be glad, but see no likelihood at present.

"We have been much hindered, and are still, by reason of the Friend who does our business here being under some trouble; having many years ago been bound for a man who is lately dead, and whose creditors are now coming on him; so that I cannot depend on his remaining here, and know not where to get another that is fit to leave things to at present, which is a great strait to my mind; my husband writing every letter for us.

"I am truly refreshed in the remembrance of thee, and thy lines are very dear to me. I desire thy prayers to the Lord on our behalf, that He may attend us with his sweet and heavenly presence in our undertaking, and then it will be well with us, whether staying or going.

"Dear Margaret, in a sense of this, and in true love I bid thee farewell, and am thy affectionate friend in my measure of the blessed Truth,

"GULI PENN."

"P.S.—My very dear love salutes thy daughter Lower, whose sufferings I have a sense of. My love also to thy daughter and son Abraham, and to Isabel if with you."[*]

---

[*] From Sylvanus Thompson's collection of MSS.

The duties of the place in which William Penn then stood required much wisdom, as his devoted wife well knew. But doing " that which was right, and in which he had peace," brought with it a happiness which the world could not take away.

Autumn came and went, but Gulielma and the children were still unable to visit their transatlantic home. Their cherished plans as to the time for leaving had been overruled, but that prospect was still before them, when, on the 13th of Eleventh-month, 1690, William Penn was summoned to the deathbead of his honoured friend George Fox. In a letter of that night, addressed to the absent widow of the deceased, he says:—" Thy dear husband and my beloved friend finished his glorious testimony this night. Oh! he is gone and has left us with a storm over our heads; surely in great mercy to him, but an evidence to us of sorrows coming."

A storm was indeed gathering over their heads, and it soon burst. A man named Fuller, who hoped to be rewarded by those who were Penn's enemies, had under oath accused him of conspiring with some others to invite the return of the deposed king. It is possible that, even while writing to Margaret Fox, he may have heard that some accusation had been got up against him. His words seem like it, and we are told that the guards sent to arrest him intended to have taken him prisoner while attending his friend's funeral; but, having mistaken the hour, they arrived too late. However, they apprehended him afterwards, and he was brought for examination before the privy council. He begged to be taken before King William and questioned in his presence. This request was complied with, and during the investigation which followed he admitted he had loved King James for the uniform kindness he had met with from him, and, having loved him in his prosperity, he could not dislike him in his adversity. He was willing, he said, to meet his former kindness by any private service in his power, but in no wise nor under any circumstances had he allowed or could he ever allow those feelings to influence him to violate his duty to the state.

After the most searching examination, the King, having heard his manly and straightforward avowal, wished to discharge him; but some of the council objected, and he was retained a prisoner in his own hired lodgings in the city. He was not permitted to go abroad, but was allowed to see any friends who might wish to visit him there. He was thus treated as a suspected person, whom it was necessary to watch.

He again had recourse to his pen, and the three succeeding years of seclusion gave rise to several valuable works. His "fruits of solitude," as he termed them, were numerous and important. One of these publications, which was of great use in that day, and very highly valued by Friends, is entitled, *A Key opening the way to every capacity, how to* distinguish the Religion professed by the People called Quakers from the Perversions and Misrepresentations of their Adversaries. This work went through twelve editions during the lifetime of its author. Another was entitled *An Essay toward the Present and Future Peace of Europe.* It proposes that Europe should recognize a General Diet or Congress of Nations, in which every nation should be represented by deputies, and in which national differences might be settled on just principles without recourse to war. A third is entitled *Some Fruits of Solitude, in Reflections and Maxims relating to the Conduct of Human Life.* The reflections and maxims which it embodies exhibit the experience of a wise and practical Christian, expressed in brief and pithy aphorisms. A fourth was *The Fruits of a Father's Love,* with others of more temporary interest. Here again we may recognize the overruling hand of our Heavenly Father, whose servant, whilst condemned to solitude by unreasonable men, was enabled therein to bring forth much fruit.

Meantime Fuller, on whose accusation William Penn had been imprisoned, was proved through another train of circumstances to be a perjured impostor. By direction of the House of Commons he was brought to trial, and being found guilty was condemned to severe punishment. Notwithstanding this, there were other circumstances unfavourable to the liberation of Penn. The King had been urged to confiscate his estates, and to this he had so far yielded as to include his Irish property among the confiscated lands in that country. But King William himself desired to get possession of Pennsylvania. He did not like the precedent of a government established on a basis of peace, without any military provision, and early in 1692 an order in council was issued depriving William Penn of his government, and annexing it to that of New York. This was a dreadful blow, for in his settlement he had sunk all he could spare from the income he derived from his estates, in addition to what had originally been paid for it. But it was not from pecuniary considerations that his greatest trouble arose; his vested property might still to a certain extent be respected; it was the impending danger to all his plans for a just, free, and peaceful government which pained him most deeply. Yet, through all, hope never forsook him; he believed that his government would yet be restored, and his freedom also. But he would not suffer any of his friends to ask, as a favour from the King, for either the one or the other. They must be given him as his right, or not at all.

Towards the close of 1693 his personal liberty was restored by the King's order, the intelligence being conveyed through the Secretary of State. In writing to Thomas Lloyd, to inform him and his other Pennsylvania friends of the happy change, he says, "From the Secretary I went to our meeting at the Bull and Mouth; thence to visit the sanctuary of my solitude; and, after that, to see my poor wife and children, the eldest being with me all this while. My wife is yet weakly; but I am not without hopes of her recovery, who is one of the best of wives and women."

It was a happiness and a blessing to the gentle invalid to have her husband and her son again by her side; but disease had made too deep an inroad on her delicate constitution to be removed. She lived for three months after their return, and then departed for her heavenly home on the 23rd of the Twelfth-month, 1693, in the fiftieth year of her age. She died at Hoddesden, and was buried at Jordans, near the remains of her four children and her mother. Her husband writes concerning her:—

"She would not suffer me, after I recovered my liberty, to neglect any public meeting upon her account, saying often, 'Oh! go, my dearest; do not hinder any good for me. I desire thee go; I have cast my care upon the Lord; I shall see thee again.' About three hours before her end, on a relation taking leave of her, she said, 'My dear love to all Friends,' and, lifting up her dying hands and eyes, prayed to the Lord to preserve and bless them. About an hour after, causing all to withdraw, we were half an hour together, in which we took our last leave. At her departure our children and most of our family were present. She gently expired in my arms, her head upon my bosom, with a sensible and devout resignation of her soul to Almighty God.

"I hope I may say she was a public as well as a private loss; for she was not only an excellent wife and mother, but an entire and constant friend, of a more than common capacity, and great modesty and humility; yet most equal and undaunted in danger; religious as well as ingenious; without affectation; an easy mistress, and good neighbour, especially to the poor: neither lavish nor penurious; but an example of industry as well as of other virtues: therefore our great loss, though her own eternal gain."

CHAPTER XIV.

1694.

William Penn's testimony respecting George Fox.—Penn applies successfully to Queen Mary for a restoration of his chartered rights in Pennsylvania.—Springett Penn's illness.—His death and character.—Removal of the Penn family to Bristol.—William Penn and his son visit Ireland.—He removes with his family to Pennsylvania.—Is cordially welcomed.—Pennsbury past and present.—Slaves employed there.—Efforts in England to break Penn's charter.—Is obliged to return to defend it.—William Penn jun. in Pennsylvania.—His conduct and character.—Philip Ford's fraudulent claims.—Logan's opinion of him.—Penn in the Fleet prison.—Efforts which led to his release.—The Provincial Assembly of Pennsylvania.—Prosperity of the settlement.—William Penn is attacked by paralysis.—Its effect on his mind during succeeding years.—Thomas Story at Ruscombe.—Death of William Penn.—His will.—Death of William Penn, jun.—His descendants.—Death of Hannah Penn.—Her descendants.—Descendants of the Peningtons.—Death of Thomas and Mary Ellwood.

AFTER the death of George Fox his journal was placed in the hands of Thomas Ellwood to copy, and see it through the press. When, in 1694, it was ready for publication, William Penn wrote a preface detailing the rise, progress, and principles " of the people called Quakers." His testimony to the character of his departed friend gives the following picture of that extraordinary man :—

"Truly I must say, though God had visibly clothed him with a Divine preference and authority, and indeed his very presence expressed a religious majesty, yet he never abused it; but held his place in the church of God with great meekness, and a most engaging humility and moderation. For, upon all occasions, like his blessed Master, he was servant to all; holding and exercising his eldership in the invisible power that had gathered them, with reverence to the Head, and care over the body. He was received only in that spirit and power of Christ, as the first and chief elder in this age; therefore worthy of double honour, which was for that reason given by the faithful of this day; because his authority was inward, not outward, and that he got it and kept it by the love of God. I write by knowledge and not report, and my witness is true, having been with him for weeks and months together on divers occasions, and those of the nearest and most exercising nature, and that by night and by day, by sea and by land, in this and in foreign countries: and I can say I never saw him out of his place, or not a match for every service or occasion. For in all things he acquitted himself like a man, yea, a strong man, a new and heavenly minded man; a divine and a naturalist, and all of God Almighty's making.

"I have been surprised by his questions and answers in natural things; that whilst he was ignorant of useless and sophistical science, he had in him the foundation of useful and commendable knowledge, and cherished it everywhere. Civil beyond all forms of breeding, in his behaviour; very temperate, eating little, and sleeping less, though a bulky person.

"Thus he lived and sojourned amongst us, and as he lived so he died; feeling in his last moments the same eternal power that had raised and preserved him. So full of assurance was he, that he triumphed over death; and so even to the last, as if death were hardly worth notice or mention; recommending to some with him the dispatch and dispersion of an epistle, just before written to the churches of Christ throughout the world, and his own books, but, above all Friends and of all Friends, those in Ireland and America, twice over saying, 'Mind poor Friends in Ireland and America.'"

After William Penn's release, when the state of his affairs came in all their details before him, it seemed hard fully to account for the statements of his confidential agent, Philip Ford. It was true his Irish estates had latterly yielded nothing; the farms of his tenants had been ravaged during the war, and a state of general disorder was produced by the proposed confiscation. His title to the property had been restored, but rents did not soon follow. His English property had been managed by Philip Ford and his son, who, though professedly Quakers, were under that guise cunning, avaricious men. In his difficulty Penn appealed to America for his quit-rents, but little or no rents were sent him. To Colonel Fletcher, the Marshal Governor of New York, under whom Pennsylvania had been placed, the Provincial Assembly had on demand voted such supplies for maintaining the expenses of government, such as they had never granted to their own paternal ruler. Penn felt this deeply; but he also thought it likely that, having found out what others required of them, they would probably do better were he in his rightful position again. He therefore made an application to Queen Mary, the King being absent in Flanders, to reinstate him in the government of Pennsylvania. A close inquiry was instituted, his charter re-examined, the government of the province investigated, and it appearing evident that he had done nothing to invalidate his original chartered rights, they were restored to him.

This was cheering so far as it went. But a source of anxious feeling arose in another direction. He was deeply concerned on noticing the health of his eldest son. Gulielma had left three children, Springett, William, and Letitia. Another daughter, Gulielma Maria, died in 1689; and now Springett, his father's most attached and devoted companion, seemed to be declining. Letitia was still but a child. William was generous, but was too much devoted to amusement and gay company. It was probably from these circumstances in his family that William Penn felt the necessity of choosing another wife. His second choice was Hannah, daughter of Thomas Callowhill, and granddaughter of Dennis Hollister, both eminent merchants of Bristol, and members of the Society of Friends. They were married in the spring of 1696.

Springett's health did not improve with the returning summer. He gradually grew worse, and died about five weeks after the second marriage of his father, who wrote the touching account of his death and character entitled, *Sorrow and Joy in the Loss and End of Springett Penn*, from which the following extracts are taken:—

"One day he said to us, 'I am resigned to what God pleaseth. He knows what is best. I would live if it pleased Him, that I might serve Him; but oh! Lord, not my will but Thine be done!' When he told me he had rested well, and I said it was a mercy, he quickly replied, with a serious yet sweet look, 'All is mercy, dear father.' Another time, when I went to meeting, he said, 'Remember me, my dear father, before the Lord. Though I cannot go to meetings, yet I have here many good meetings. The Lord comes in upon my spirit. I have heavenly meetings with Him by myself.'

"Not many days before he died, the Lord appearing by His holy power upon his spirit, on asking him at my return how he did, he told me, 'Oh! I have had a sweet time, a blessed time! great enjoyments! The power of the Lord overcame my soul!' Telling him how some of the gentry who had been to visit him were gone to their games and sports and pleasures, he said, in reference to the idea of such things bringing happiness, 'It is all stuff, my dear father—sad stuff! Oh that I might live to tell them so!' 'Well, my dear child,' I replied, 'let this be the time of thy entering into secret covenant with God, that if He raise thee thou wilt dedicate thy youth, strength, and life to Him, and His people and service.' He replied, 'Father, that is not now to do,' repeating, with great tenderness of spirit, 'It is not now to do.'

"Being almost ever near him, and doing for him anything he wanted, he broke out with much love, 'My dear father, if I live I will make thee amends.' Speaking to him of divine enjoyments that the eye of man saw not, but which the soul made alive by the spirit of Christ plainly felt, in lively remembrance he cried out, 'Oh! I had a sweet time yesterday by myself! That the Lord hath preserved me to this day, blessed be His name! my soul praises Him for His mercy.' Fixing his eyes upon his sister, he took her by the hand, saying, 'Poor Tishe, look to good things! Poor child, there is no comfort without it! One drop of the love of God is worth more than all the world. I know it; I have tasted it. I have felt as much, or more of the love of God in this weakness, than in all my life before.' At another time, as I stood by him he said, 'Dear father, sit by me! I love thy company, and I know thou lovest mine; if it be the Lord's will that we must part, be not troubled, for that will trouble me.'

"Taking something one night in bed, just before going to rest, he sat up and fervently prayed thus, 'O! Lord God, Thou, whose Son said to His disciples, whatsoever ye ask in my name ye shall receive, I pray thee in His name bless this to me this night, and give me rest, if it be thy blessed will.' And accordingly he had a very comfortable night, of which he took thankful notice before us the next day.

"When at one time more than ordinarily he expressed a desire to live, and entreated me to pray for him, he added, 'And, dear father, if the Lord should raise me, and enable me to serve Him and His people, then I might travel with thee sometimes [meaning in the ministry] and we might ease one another.' He spoke this with great modesty; upon which I said to him, 'My dear child, if it please the Lord to raise thee, I am satisfied it will be so; and if not, then, inasmuch as it is thy fervent desire in the Lord, He will look upon thee just as if thou didst live to serve Him, and thy comfort will be the same. So either way it will be well; for if thou shouldst not live, I verily believe thou wilt have the recompense of thy good desires, without the temptations and troubles that would attend if long life were granted thee.'

"Feeling himself decline apace, somebody fetched

the doctor, but as soon as he came in he said, 'Let my father speak to the doctor, and I'll go asleep,' which he did, and waked no more, breathing his last on my breast, the tenth day of the Second month, between the hours of nine and ten, 1696, in his twenty-first year."

In the year 1697, William Penn removed with his family to Bristol, his wife's native place. The following spring he visited Ireland, taking with him his son William. They arrived in Dublin in due time to attend the half year's meeting. Thomas Story, who was also there on this occasion, speaks of it thus, "Great was the resort of people of all ranks and professions to our meetings; chiefly on account of our friend William Penn, who was ever furnished by the Truth with matter fully to answer their expectations. Many of the clergy were there, and the people with one voice spoke well of what they heard. Of the clergy the Dean of Derry was one, who being there several times, was asked by his bishop whether he heard any thing but blasphemy and nonsense, and whether he took off his hat in time of prayer. He answered that he heard no blasphemy nor nonsense, but the everlasting Truth, and did not only take off his hat at prayer, but his heart said Amen to what he heard." The language of these two dignitaries gives a fair idea of the variety of treatment and opinion which William Penn met with in Ireland as well as in England from the Episcopal church party.

He spent over three months in the island on that occasion, most of which time was occupied in gospel labour from place to place. A few weeks were devoted to the examination of his estates in the county of Cork; first those in the barony of Imokelly, in which was situated Shangarry castle, the scene of some memorable associations of his early days. What reminiscences that region must have awakened! The father and son afterwards proceeded to "the Barony of Ibanne and Barryroe, to view the rest of his estates in those parts."

At Cork and Bandon they had good meetings, attended by large numbers of all ranks and professions. Here they were informed, by letters from England, that during William Penn's absence a base attack had been made upon his character, even in the Yearly Meeting of London. "But this," says Thomas Story, "was done by a shameless and implacable party, being moved by envy at the honour and dignity which the Most High had been pleased to confer on him." He adds that, "soon after receiving those tidings, they had another large and crowded meeting at Cork, where all who had heard of the evil suggestions made at London might be assured that they sprang from a false and evil root, for the Lord was pleased to clothe William that day with majesty, holy zeal, and divine wisdom, to the great satisfaction of Friends, and the admiration and applause of the people."

The "implacable party," to which Thomas Story alludes, were probably those to whom Gulielma Penn referred in her last letter to Margaret Fox, as "bad spirits," who had been disturbing the harmony of their meetings.

Soon after William Penn's return from Ireland, he began preparations for removing with his family to America. With this prospect his arrangements went forward during the early months of 1699. Of Gulielma's children only Letitia went with him. William was married, and he and his young wife chose to remain in England. The documents with which, in his capacity of a minister of the Society of Friends, he was furnished on this occasion, abundantly show (as his American biographer, Samuel Janney, remarks) that he was in full unity with, and greatly beloved by his own fellow-professors. The certificate from the monthly meeting in Essex to which he had belonged for the greater part of his membership in the society, was copied by Janney from the records of Friends in Philadelphia.

From our Monthly Meeting held at Horsham, Old England, 14th 7th Mo. 1699.

To the churches of Christ in Pennsylvania and to all the faithful Friends and brethren unto whom this may come. In the covenant of life, and fellowship of the gospel of our Lord Jesus Christ, and in the unity of the one eternal Spirit of our God, we dearly salute you, most earnestly desiring your everlasting prosperity in the blessed truth.

Now, dear friends and brethren, whereas our worthy friend and elder, William Penn, did acquaint our Monthly Men's Meeting with his intended voyage into his province of Pennsylvania, and although we are right sensible that he needeth no letter of recommendation from us, yet at his request, and for the good order sake that God hath established in His Church and among His people, and for the sincere love we bear to our well-beloved friend, we could do no less than give this small token of our unity and communion with him, as a testimony for him and his service in the Church of Christ, wherein he hath been a blessed instrument in the hand of the Lord, both in his ministry and conversation, and hath always sought the prosperity of the blessed truth, and of peace and concord in the Church. He hath walked among us in all humility, godly sincerity, and true brotherly love, to our great refreshment and comfort: and hath with much labour and great travail on all occasions endeavoured the defence of Truth against its opposers, and the preservation of true unity and good order in the Church of Christ. So, in the unity of the one Eternal Spirit, which is the bond of true peace, we take our leave of him, with earnest breathings and supplications to the great God whom the winds and seas obey, that He would mercifully be pleased to go along with him, and conduct him by the angel of His divine presence to his desired port, and preserve him to the end of his days; and in the end, that he may receive an immortal crown, and be bound up in the bundle of life amongst them that have turned many to righteousness, who shine as the sun in the firmament of God's eternal power, for ever and ever. Amen.

After a voyage of more than three months, the Governor of Pennsylvania, his wife, daughter, and retinue, arrived in their American home, and were most heartily welcomed. Penn brought over with him as his secretary James Logan, who was by birth an Irishman; his parents were both Quakers. On being deprived of an estate in Scotland, they had settled in Lurgan, where James received his early education. Ultimately the family removed to Bristol, which led to his acquaintance with the Penns. In writing to William Penn, jun. announcing their safe arrival, Logan says of their reception on this occasion:—" The highest terms I could use would hardly give an idea of the welcome that thy father received from most of the honester party here. Friends generally concluded that, after all their troubles and disappointments, this province now scarcely wanted anything more to render it completely happy. The faction that had long continued to overthrow the settled constitution received an universal damp" . . . " Friends' love to the Governor was great and sincere; they had long mourned his absence, and passionately desired his return. He, they firmly believed, would compose all their difficulties and repair all that was amiss."

The Governor and his family, after a little time spent in the city, took up their abode at Pennsbury Manor. Before they removed, Hannah Penn's first son was born; he was named John, and used to be spoken of as " the American." The house and grounds of Pennsbury, which was their summer residence, is thus described by Janney:—" This beautiful estate was situated in Bucks county, four miles above Bristol, on the river Delaware. It comprised upwards of six thousand acres of fertile alluvial soil, mostly covered with majestic forests, and, while in possession of an Indian king, had borne the name of Sepassin. It extended about two miles along the river Delaware, lying between Governor's Creek and Welcome Creek, the latter of which, making a bend, nearly enclosed it in the rear, at high water converting it into an island."

The mansion, which was built in 1682 and 1683, with subsequent improvements cost £5,000, a large sum in those days.

That beautiful spot on the banks of the Delaware, which is associated with some of the happiest days of the great Christian philanthropist, exhibits to the view of the traveller, as he sails up the river, scarcely any remains of Pennsbury Manor. The mansion is gone, and a comfortable farmhouse occupies its site. A leaky reservoir on the top of the house is said to have been the cause of the premature ruin of the building, which extended about sixty feet in front, looking down on the river from a moderate eminence. It was surrounded by tastefully arranged gardens and terraces, with vistas which opened into views of the distant woods, and again up the river to the falls of the Delaware. The Governor, after his first return to England, continued to send out European shrubs and trees, to be intermixed with the native varieties in the ornamental grounds around the house. He afterwards sent directions to the gardener about their disposal, and about collecting and cultivating the beautiful native flowers which grew in the surrounding woods.

The furniture and draperies of Pennsbury, as we learn from an inventory which still exists, seem to have been handsome and tasteful, suitable to the station and habits of its occupants. The family at the manor used vehicles of various kinds, among which a coach, a calash, and a sedan-chair are specified, but we are told they generally preferred riding on horseback when in the country. The Governor's usual mode of transit between the city and his country-house was a large barge, with one mast and six oars, for which he seems to have had a decided preference. Writing to James Harrison, his steward, and commending the plants to his watchful care, he says "but, above all dear things, my barge. I hope nobody uses it on any account, and that she is kept in dock, covered from the weather."

We are told that when passing in his barge between Philadelphia and Pennsbury, he frequently stopped at Burlington, to see Governor Jennings of New Jersey, who was also an eminent minister among the Friends. "On one occasion Jennings and some of his friends were enjoying their pipes, a practice which Penn disliked. On hearing that Penn's barge was in sight, they put away their pipes, that their friend might not be annoyed, and endeavoured to conceal from him what they were about. He came upon them, however, somewhat suddenly, and pleasantly remarked that he was glad they had sufficient sense of propriety to be ashamed of the practice. Jennings, who was rarely at a loss for an answer, rejoined that they were not ashamed, but desisted to avoid hurting a weak brother."

Among the recreations of the Governor and his family was the occasional attendance at an Indian fair, or *cantico*—in reference to which his cashbook, kept by James Logan, contains the following entries:—

	£	s.	d.
By my mistress at the fair	2	0	8
By expenses, given to Hannah Carpenter, for a fairing	0	8	0
By do. to two children, for comfits, per order	0	1	6
By the Governor, going to cantico	1	18	4

When visiting the Indians, William Penn, in the overflowing sympathy of his heart, always endeavoured to make them feel as innocently happy as possible, and he found that nothing succeeded better than entering into whatever was going forward among them, such as partaking in hearty good will of their venison, their hominy, or their roasted acorns—whichever happened to be at hand. And when they stood up to try their strength and skill, in the athletic games to which they were accustomed, he used to join them, and in his earlier days is said to have been a full match for any of them, and to have entered into these exercises with great zest and pleasantry.

Isaac Norris, a man of wealth and influence in the colony, remarks in a family letter:—" The Governor's wife and daughter are well; their little son is a lovely babe; his wife is extremely well beloved here, exemplary in her station, and of an excellent spirit, which adds lustre to her character, and she has a great place in the hearts of good people. The Governor is our *pater patriæ*, and his worth is no new thing to us. We value him highly, and hope his life will be preserved till things (now on the wheel) are settled to his peace and comfort, and the people's ease and quiet."

In the early time of the settlement some negroes had been purchased as labourers at Pennsbury, and they continued to be employed prior to William Penn's last visit; but, before he returned to England again, he arranged for them all to have their liberty. In a will left on that occasion with James Logan, in order to make their liberation perfectly secure he says, " I give to my blacks their freedom, as is under my hand already, and to old Sam one hundred acres of land, to be his children's after he and his wife are dead, forever." He was greatly concerned for the general instruction and religious care of the negroes who were occupied or owned by the colonists. While he was in Pennsylvania he endeavoured by legal enactment to secure to them such rightful privileges as he saw were not extended to them by their owners, and he brought a measure for that purpose before the provincial representatives; but his attempts were defeated in the House of Assembly. With his own religious society he had more success, as is proved by the minutes of Philadelphia monthly meeting. Many Friends about that time and shortly afterwards liberated their slaves long before it became an imperative rule of the society to do so.

There were yet "other works on the wheel," much on every side, for the influence and presence of the Governor to realize in Pennsylvania, when he received a most pressing call from his friends in England to return. Nothing else, they said, could prevent the annexation to the Crown of his province, and that of the others in America, at the next session of parliament. A bill with this object was then under discussion in the House of Lords, and would almost certainly be enacted, probably not then, but the very next term, if he were not ready most strenuously to meet the false statements which had been put forth. There was no alternative left but to go. His wife and daughter protested against being left behind; but Hannah Penn assured her husband she would be most willing to return as soon as he was ready to do so. Writing to James Logan he says, "I cannot prevail on my wife to stay, still less Tishe. I know not what to do." And accordingly he took them with him.

In Watson's *Annals of Pennsylvania* we find this certificate of removal, which will be interesting and very intelligible to Friends. It is dated 27th of Seventh-month, 1701.

These may certify that Letitia Penn has for good order sake desired a certificate from us, and we freely certify to all whom it may concern that she hath well behaved herself here, very soberly, and according to the good instructions which she hath received in the way of Truth, being well inclined, courteously carriaged, and sweetly tempered in her conversation among us, and also a diligent comer to meetings. We hope she hath plentifully received of the dew which hath fallen upon God's people, to her settlement and establishment in the same.

It also set forth that, to the best of their knowledge and belief, "she was not under any marriage engagement."

The Penn family arrived in England towards the close of 1701, after an absence of a little more than two years. These years had not added to the steadiness and wisdom of William Penn's son, whom he left in possession of Worminghurst. He had also given up to him the income from his Irish estates, having resolved to rely thenceforward on the returns from the property sunk in America, for the maintenance of himself and his other children. But this young man and his inexperienced wife having been introduced to high society and its expensive surroundings, were not much influenced by simple Quaker habits, although they still professed to be Quakers. It was a source of very great trouble to William Penn to observe all this on his return. He was therefore most anxious that his son should sever himself from the extravagant associates with whom he had become acquainted, and accordingly he urged his going to Pennsylvania to supply his place. The son said he must see the country before he would take his family. His father therefore wrote to James Logan soon after his return, as follows :—

"My son shall hasten. Go with him to Pennsbury. Advise him. Recommend his acquaintance. No rambling to New York. He has promised fair. I know he will regard thee. He has wit, kept the top company, and must be handled with much love and wisdom. Urging the weakness and folly of some behaviour, and the necessity of another conduct, from interest and for reputation, will go far. And get Samuel Carpenter, Edward Shippen, Isaac Norris, Phineas Pemberton, Thomas Masters, and such persons to be soft and kind in teaching. That will do wonders with him. He is conquered in that way, pretends much to humour, and is over generous by half; yet sharp enough to get to spend."

Thus the anxious father spoke to one who was not very much older than William himself. But the Governor knew that James Logan was an honourable and high principled Christian. However, William did not hasten, as his father had hoped he would. After the lapse of another year he informs the same trusty friend:—

"My son (having life) resolves to be with you per first opportunity. His wife this day week was delivered of a fine boy, which he calls William. So that now we are *major*, *minor*, and *minimus*. I bless the Lord, mine are pretty well—Johnny lively, Tommy a lovely large child, and my grandson Springett, a mere Saracen; his sister a beauty. If my son sends hounds, as he has provided two or three couple of choice ones, for deer, foxes and wolves, pray let great care be taken of them."

Meantime no supplies reached the Governor, to enable him to conduct the expensive suit which resulted from the threatened annexation of the province. He says, writing to Logan, "12th mo. 1702. I strictly charge thee to represent to Friends that I am forced to borrow money, adding debts to debts, for conferences, counsel's opinions, hearings, etc., with the charges for these. Guineas melting away, four, five, six a week, and sometimes as many a day." The annexation would have been of all things dreaded by the colonists, as in that case their colonial laws must have been endangered; yet they could not be roused to send their Governor suitable supplies to withstand it.

Eight months later he writes again, "I never was so reduced; for Ireland, my old principal verb, has hardly any money. England severe to her.

No trade but hither (save butter and meat to Flanders and the West Indies) and at England's mercy for prices, so that we must go and eat out half our rents, or we cannot enjoy them."

William Penn, jun. arrived in Pennsylvania the last month of 1703, and the father wrote to his secretary:—"Take him away to Pennsbury, and there give him the true state of things. Weigh down his levities, as well as temper his resentments and inform his understanding. Watch him. Outwit him honestly for his good. Fishings,—little journeys to see the Indians, etc. will divert him; and interest Friends to bear with him all they can, and melt towards him, at least civilly, if not religiously. He will confide in thee. If S. Carpenter, Richard Hill, and Isaac Norris could gain his confidence (and strive to tender Griffith Owen—not the least likely, for he sees and feels) I should rejoice. Pennsylvania has cost me dearer in my poor child than all other considerations. The Lord pity and spare in His great mercy. I yet hope."

At first young Penn, by his open courteous manners, interested and pleased his father's friends in the colony. The Indians, having heard of his arrival, sent a deputation of one hundred, among whom were nine of their kings, with Ohewousiumhook, the chief, who came to Pennsbury to tender their welcome and congratulations, and presented him with some belts of wampum in proof of their goodwill. These he received very graciously. But the young man's expensive habits soon outran all the provision his father had made for him; and as James Logan in a little time lost his influence, he associated with companions of a very different type, the principal among whom was the Deputy-governor Evans, who had come out with him by his father's special appointment. In Evans William Penn had been lamentably mistaken. He had talents, but was wanting in good morals, and all his influence with the young man was to his injury. True to his trust, James Logan let the father know how matters stood. In a letter dated 2nd 8br. 1704, the latter says, after asking him to urge William to send for his wife and family, " I have done when I tell thee to let my poor son know that if he be not a very good husband, I must sell there as well as here, and that all he spends is disabling me so far to clear myself of debt, and that he will pay for it at the long run. Do it in the friendliest manner; that he may co-operate with me to clear our encumbered estates."

At length there was an affray one night in the street, in which both Evans and young Penn were concerned, and both were extremely indignant at being treated like ordinary rioters. The Friends dealt with young Penn as their member, and he, resenting their advice and admonition, resigned his membership, and declared he would forthwith return home.

William Penn, in his next letter to James Logan,

says, "I am sorry to have such a prospect of charges; two houses and the Governors's salary, my son's voyage, stay, and return; and no revenue nor Susquehanna money paid, on which account I ventured my poor child so far away from his wife and pretty children, and my own oversight. Oh! Pennsylvania, what hast thou not cost me? Above £30,000 more than I ever got; two hazardous and fatiguing voyages; my straits and slavery here; and my child's soul, almost."

William returned home, but did not bring any comfort to his father's anxious heart. He had entirely withdrawn from Friends, and declared that if nothing better turned up for him, he would enter the army or navy. However, instead of doing so, he endeavoured to get into Parliament, as his father mentions in the following extract from a letter to Logan, dated 30, 2nd mo. 1705:—"With a load of debt hardly to be answered, from the difficulty of getting in what I have a right to— twice its value—which is like starving in the midst of bread, my head and heart are filled sufficiently with trouble. Yet the Lord holds up my head, and Job's over-righteous and mistaken friends have not sunk my soul from its confidence in God.". . ."My son has lost his election, as also the Lord Keeper's son-in-law, but both hope to recover it by proving bribery upon the two that have it, Lord Windsor and Squire Argill. I wish it might turn his face to privacy and good husbandry." But William's face had been too determinedly turned in other directions to be thus brought round.

In addition to the trials which arose from the conduct of his son, and from his not having sufficiently secured his own pecuniary interest whilst providing for that of his province, the Governor of Pennsylvania met with another great trouble in the evening of his life, through the duplicity of his agents, the Fords. He trusted Philip Ford to the utmost, passing his accounts without scrutiny. For the space of twenty years he suspected nothing, till the final catastrophe. On Ford's death, his widow and his son Philip Ford, jun. presented an account against William Penn, showing him to be £14,000 in their debt. William Penn impugned the statement, and all those concerned being Quakers, he at once prepared to submit the whole to arbitrators for examination and decision. This the Fords spurned, well knowing it could not stand any such test. But, from the cunning way in which the affair had been managed, they expected the law would serve their purpose better.

At one period of the difficulties occasioned by his expenditure on Pennsylvania, William Penn, without the knowledge of any of his friends, had borrowed £2,800 from Philip Ford, for which he gave him security on the province. When, of the income from the English and Irish estates, enough was afterwards left in Ford's hands to pay off the debt, Penn, feeling no doubt of its faithful application, did not look after his bond. Meantime Ford calculated enormous interest and compound interest on the debt, with exorbitant charges for every movement in connection with it, whilst none of the money which had been left in his hands was taken any notice of, till the debt was represented on his death as having amounted to £14,000. A close examination, with such documentary evidence as William Penn could bring forward in Ford's own writing, proved clearly that instead of owing this sum to Ford, Ford owed him £1659. Notwithstanding all this, the bond stood legally against him, with enormous accumulations, and nothing short of the utmost farthing would satisfy the Fords. However, it was found that was only about one half what was claimed.

On non-payment of one of the smaller items of their demands, they took out a warrant against William Penn, which the bailiffs were ordered to execute one day when he should be seated in Gracechurch-meeting. They would have acted up to these instructions but for the interference of Henry Goldney and Herbert Springett, who engaged that he should be ready for them in a few hours. Penn's friends advised him not to pay the claim, but rather go to prison, and he was accordingly lodged in the Fleet. His case called forth the utmost sympathy of his own fellow-professors, which they manifested in every way in their power. Many of his most valued friends repeatedly visited him in the

Fleet prison, and often held their religious meetings with him there. James Logan, in writing to Thomas Callowhill, Hannah Penn's father, under date 13th of Sixth-month, 1706, thus speaks of the circumstances which led to his son-in-law's imprisonment:—" Never was any one more barbarously treated, or baited with undeserved enemies. He has been able to foil all attacks from public adversaries, but it has been his fortune to meet the greatest severities from those that owe most to him. It must be confessed that some of it is owing to his easiness and want of caution. As far as I can gather, Philip Ford's designs were base and barbarous from the beginning; and what might not an old, cunning, self-interested man, with such intentions, be capable of doing, when he had so much goodness, openheartedness, and confidence in his honesty to deal with, is not difficult to imagine."

In Thomas Callowhill's reply he says, " I have seen their accounts stated under both their hands (W. P. and P. F.'s) in which by his easiness and want of caution, as thou observes, he gave the wretch opportunities for his base, barbarous, and wicked extortions; and which, had they been corrected timely, would not have amounted to the tenth part of what they are now. The little knowledge I have of it troubles me; yet I have comfort in this, that though their concern seems so great and exercising, neither he nor my daughter sinks under it, but from divine power have support to their spirits. I pray

God it may turn to their good, and be instruction for their posterity."

On that occasion William Penn remained for nine months a prisoner in the Fleet. His friends had exerted themselves, and by that time raised the sum of £7,500 to pay off the mother, daughter, and son of Philip Ford, rather than allow their friend to remain any longer incarcerated. Those who advanced the money were given due securities on Pennsylvania for its repayment. Penn's excellent and faithful American biographer speaks of that period in the following terms:—" Throughout the whole of this vexatious and humiliating business he evinced the patience and fortitude of the true Christian, whose affections are fixed not on earthly but on heavenly things, and the beautiful remark of Isaac Norris seemed applicable to him, that "God darkens this world to us, that our eyes may behold the greater brightness of His kingdom." It is indeed true that the world did not now seem bright to William Penn. Yet his letters amply manifest that ever and anon he rose above its clouds into a region of divine love and peace.

But Penn still laboured under great pecuniary difficulties, and was likely to feel them so long as he had debts unpaid; and the stinted returns from his American property prevented him from soon discharging them. In his son-in-law William Aubrey, he had a keen, harsh man to deal with, whose temper did not tend to lessen what his father-in-law had to bear in feeling that he owed him anything. Through the publication of the Logan correspondence these trials and difficulties have all been laid open, and they show us very plainly that in his career up to the last there were many things to contend with; but that through all a sustaining sense of divine support was with him.

In Pennsylvania he had many devoted friends, who felt how much the province owed to its founder. Such, with two or three singular exceptions,* was the feeling that existed among the members of his own society. But, from the first, the Quakers wished to avoid everything that might appear to the other colonists to be done in a partizan spirit, or as assuming too much the management of public affairs. The inhabitants of the province were about one half Quakers, yet it had not been their desire that they should be represented in that proportion in the House of Assembly. But the representatives on the other side to a large extent were prompt to battle for all they could obtain for themselves, and against the Governor's necessary subsidies. This was what led to his perplexities and embarrassments. At length the sensible portion of

---

* The exceptions above alluded to were George Keith and David Lloyd. The former eventually renounced Quaker doctrines and withdrew from the Society; the latter was a man of ability, but he was unreasonably prone to fault-finding. He joined the opposition for many years in the Provincial Assembly, and by his letters to England did great mischief for a time to the Pennsylvania Government.

the colonists became annoyed and ashamed of the existing state of things, and determined to return those who would act differently towards the proprietor. The consequence was, as Janney tells us, that in the election of 1710 not a single member was returned but those who were friends of the founder of the province. He says, "By the election of the new assembly, harmony was restored to the government, and all its branches were distinguished by sedulous successful application to business. The expenses of the state were cheerfully supplied; the voice of complaint was hushed, while the manifold blessings enjoyed by the inhabitants were frankly acknowledged. In the year 1712, the ascendency of the Friends in the assembly is indicated by the passage of an act to prevent the importation of negroes into the province. It is pleasing to reflect that, during the last three years of William Penn's participation in colonial affairs, harmony prevailed in the government of his province, and that an act so consonant with his feelings and principles was then passed, though subsequently vetoed by the British crown. It thus entitles Pennsylvania to the honorable distinction of having led the way to a more humane system of legislation on the subject of slavery."

On the 24th of Fifth-month, 1712, William Penn commenced a letter to James Logan, in which, after feelingly alluding to the death of his wife's father and mother, his pen suddenly stopped under the pressure of a paralytic seizure. It was the third time he had been assailed by paralysis, but on the present occasion far more severely than ever; and his intellect never recovered from the effects of this attack. His sweet temper and happy spirit remained, and a heart overflowing with love to God and man was as visible as in his brighter days. In fact, the memory of all recent things, and with it mental anxiety and intellectual power, had vanished, whilst the spirit remained the same. He continued to attend Friends' meetings, and sometimes spoke a few sentences exhorting Friends to love one another; whilst, with a countenance beaming with sympathy and kindness, he used to meet with and part from them. In this condition, life wore away with little variation for five years.

The family, which included the wife and three children of William Penn, jun., continued to reside at Ruscombe in Berkshire; but the young man was seldom seen there. Two years after his father's malady commenced, Hannah Penn remarked in a letter to a friend, "I have not seen him this half-year, nor has he seen his father these eighteen months." After the lapse of another year she mentions him in terms which show that he had become the victim of intemperance; and at a still later date she says, " I left my two daughters, Aubrey and Penn, to take care of their father and the family until my return. The latter is to be pitied, for, poor woman, her husband continues the same."

Under date "Ruscombe, 2nd First-month, 1717," Hannah Penn writes of her husband, "My poor dearest's life is yet continued to us; but I know not how long it may be, for he is very weakly. I have for these last three or four years continued this large house, only to keep him as comfortable as I can; for he has all along delighted in walking and taking the air here, and does so still when the weather allows; and at other times diverts himself from room to room. The satisfaction he takes therein is the greatest pleasure I have in so large a house, which I have long found too much for me, with our shrunk income."

It should be mentioned that Thomas Story and Henry Gouldney of London were not only Hannah Penn's personal friends, but her chief advisers in matters connected with Pennsylvania as well as her own pecuniary affairs. On the 27th of Fifth-month, 1718, Thomas Story, when on his way to Bristol, called at Ruscombe to see his friends, and Hannah Penn appears to have taken him in her carriage to London, and to have returned home immediately, for on the next day she wrote him the following letter:—

"Ruscombe, 28th 5th Mo. 1718.

"Dear Friend,
"I am ready to wish thou had delayed a day longer with us; for though I found my poor husband last night near as I left him, yet this

morning he altered much, was taken with shivering and lowness of spirits, and divers symptoms like a sudden change; on which the desolateness of my circumstances staring me in the face, and no friend with me capable of advising in such a juncture, I then regretted the opportunity I had lost of begging thy advice; which indeed I thought to have done in the coach, but was willing to put the evil day yet further off. But, fearing it is drawing nigh, I would gladly have thy advice both with respect to my own and my children's safety, and for the quiet of Pennsylvania. May I have strength and wisdom to go through this trying day as I ought; for which let me have thy earnest supplications at the Throne of Grace for thy affectionate but afflicted friend,

"H. PENN."

As the letter was not in time for that day's post, Hannah Penn added this postscript on the evening of the same day:—

"28th.—My poor husband is this day so much worse that I cannot expect his continuance till this time to-morrow. Hence I speed this messenger on purpose with my son's horse, to let thee know how it is, desiring thee to break the first notice thereof to him, and get leave of his master to let him come to me. But what induces me yet more is to get thy best advice how to act; for should not Henry Gouldney be able to come down, I should be most desolate and forsaken. I am ready to say, 'Woe is me that I have lived to see this day of stripping—this most desolate day!' My dear love salutes thee and my cousin Webbs. I am your afflicted friend,

"H. P."

On the following morning she added:—

"30th, My poor dearest's last breath was fetched this morning between two and three o'clock. Pray give the enclosed to John."*

Thomas Story says in his Journal, "On the 1st of Sixth-month we arrived at Ruscombe late in the evening, where we found the widow and most of the family together. Our coming occasioned fresh remembrance, and a renewed flood of many tears from all eyes. A solid time (of worship) we had together; but few words among us for some time; it was a deep baptizing season, and the Lord was near."

The interment took place on the 7th of Sixth-month, 1718, at Jordans, where the earthly remains of William Penn were laid beside those of his beloved wife Gulielma.

There were various testimonies issued, expressive of the estimation in which the deceased was held by the Friends of the meetings with which he was

---

* From Hannah Penn's original letter in possession of Silvanus Thompson, York.

associated, and various notices of his character were left on record by those who knew him, all of which agree in their general tenor. But I have seen nothing which, within the same compass, more fully and more comprehensively combines his prominent characteristics than the document issued by the Monthly Meeting of Reading, to which he belonged from the time he settled at Ruscombe. After speaking of his death and burial, and his residence in earlier times within the compass of other meetings, it concludes as follows:—

> He was a man of great abilities, of an excellent sweetness of disposition, quick of thought and ready utterance, full of the qualification of true discipleship, even love without dissimulation; as extensive in charity as comprehensive in knowledge, and to whom malice or ingratitude were utter strangers; so ready to forgive enemies that the ungrateful were not excepted.
>
> Had not the management of his temporal affairs been attended with some difficulties, envy itself would be to seek for matter of accusation; and yet in charity even that part of his conduct may be ascribed to a peculiar sublimity of mind. Notwithstanding which he may, without straining his character, be ranked among the learned, good, and great, whose abilities are sufficiently manifested throughout his elaborate writings, which are so many lasting monuments of his admired qualifications, and are the esteem of learned and judicious men among all persuasions.
>
> And though in old age, by reason of some shocks of a violent distemper, his intellects were much impaired, yet his sweetness and loving disposition surmounted its utmost efforts, and remained when reason almost failed.

In fine, he was learned without vanity, facetious in conversation, yet weighty and serious; apt without forwardness; of an extraordinary greatness of mind, yet void of the stain of ambition; as free from rigid gravity as he was clear of unseemly levity; a man, a scholar, a friend, a minister surpassing in superlative endowments; whose memorial will be valued by the wise, and blessed with the just.

Signed by order of the Monthly Meeting, held at Reading aforesaid, by
WILLIAM LOMBOLL, JUN.

7th of 2nd Mo. 1719.

Numerous addresses and letters of sympathy came from the Friends of Pennsylvania to the bereaved widow. The Indians, hearing of the death of their honoured brother Onas, sent her a message in their own figurative style, expressive of their sense of her great loss; and also a present composed of the skins of wild animals wherewith to form a cloak. This, they said, was to protect her whilst passing through the thorny wilderness without her guide. She alludes to it in the following letter to James Logan:—

"Ruscombe, 12th 1st mo., 1719.

"Dear Friend,

"I take very kindly the sympathy of all those that truly lament mine and that country's loss; which loss has brought a vast load of care, toil of mind, and sorrow upon me.... For my own part I expect a wilderness of care—of briars and thorns transplanted here from thence. Whether I shall be able to explore my way, even with the help of my friends, I have great reason to question, nothwithstanding the Indians' present, which I now want to put on—having the woods and wilderness to travel through indeed!"

Hannah Penn displayed great executive ability and judgment in the dispatch of the business which devolved on her, after her husband's malady incapacitated him for the management of his affairs. She also possessed that true womanly feeling and tenderness, which fitted her to be the sympathizing nurse and companion of him who had chosen so well and wisely when he asked her to be his second wife. About four years after the death of William Penn she had an attack of paralysis, from which she partially recovered, and lived till the year 1726. By her desire her remains were laid in the same grave with those of her husband.

William Penn's Personal Appearance.

Of the personal appearance of the founder of Pennsylvania we are told that "he was tall in stature, and of an athletic make. When a young man he was handsome in person and graceful in his manners; later in life he was inclined to corpulence, but, using much exercise, he retained his activity, and his appearance was then that of a fine, portly man."

Clarkson says, "William Penn was very neat though plain in his dress. He walked generally with a cane. This cane he was accustomed to take with him in the latter part of his life into his study, where, when he dictated to his amanuensis, he would take it in his hand, and walking up and down the room, would mark, by striking it against the floor, the emphasis on points particularly to be noticed." Although he adhered to the simplicity of address peculiar to Friends, his manners were polished and courteous; for, as he said in one of his letters, "I know of no religion which destroys courtesy, civility, and kindness."

William Penn's Will.

The first paragraph in William Penn's will, after the declaration of its being his last will and testament, stands thus:—

"My eldest son being well provided for, by the settlement of his mother's and my father's estates, I give and dispose of the rest of my estates in the manner as followeth."

Letitia Aubrey's husband having got a portion in money with her, and a promise of land in Pennsylvania, ten thousand acres were bequeathed to her, also ten thousand to each of William's children, Gulielma Maria, Springett, and William. All the residue of his property, after the payment of his debts, was to go to his wife Hannah Penn and her five children, in such proportions as she thought fit. They were John, Thomas, Margaret, Richard, and Dennis, all minors.

The prosperity of Pennsylvania eventually rose to such a height, that the wealth of those sons of the founder to whom it was bequeathed became what in that day appeared enormous. They all forsook the habits and principles of the religious society in which they had been educated, though continuing to profess great respect for the Quakers of the province.

William Penn's posterity.

William Penn's eldest son William survived his father about two years. He died in the north of France in 1720, of consumption, deeply regretting his evil courses, and it is said thoroughly penitent. It has not been stated whether any of his family were with him at the time of his death. He had sold Worminghurst, his mother's estate, and had probably squandered the proceeds. The Irish estates descended to his sons. Springett, the elder, dying unmarried, the property reverted to William, the younger brother, who in 1732 married Christiana Forbes, daughter of Alexander Forbes, a London merchant. She died before the expiration of that year, leaving an infant daughter who was named Christiana Gulielma. William Penn was afterwards married to Anne

Vaux. At what period he removed to reside in the county of Cork does not appear, but in the records of the Society of Friends in Cork we find the two following entries*—one respecting his eldest son, who was born there; the other recording his own death :—

"Springett Penn, son of William Penn and Anne his wife, was born at their dwelling-house in Ballyphehane, in the South Liberties of the County of this City, between the hours of 8 and 9 in the evening, the first day of the First-month (March), 1738.

"N. B.—The above memorial was delivered me by the hand of William, the father of the above Springett, and desired it may be registered in this book.

"JOSHUA WIGHT."

"William Penn died at his house at Shangarry, about 15 miles from Cork, of a dropsy, 12th month 6th. 1746."

Springett Penn, whose birth is registered above, died unmarried in 1762, when his mother became his sole heir. He had not at the time of his death paid his sister's fortune. She had been married in the previous year to Peter Gaskill of Bath. Anne, the widow of William Penn, was subsequently married to Alexander Durden in 1767, and, dying soon after, left him her sole heir. Christiana

---

* These particulars have been procured for me from the provincial register at Cork meeting house, by Joshua (John) Strangman of Shangarry, to whom I have been much indebted for many inquiries he has made on my behalf in connection with the present subject.

Gulielma's fortune was never paid, and Durden resisted the claims made upon him to obtain it. The result was a long suit in chancery, which did not terminate till the year 1800, when the Shangarry estate was divided between the heirs-at-law of Peter Gaskill and Alexander Durden.

Gulielma Maria, only daughter of William Penn's eldest son William—she whom her grandfather called the little beauty—was married early in life, and her husband dying soon after, she was married a second time to Charles Fell, great grandson to Judge Fell and his wife Margaret of Swarthmoor Hall. Of their descendants but few traces have been found, and these only through searches made in the Court of Canterbury, which have brought to light the will of their son Robert Edward Fell, who does not appear to have been a married man. His will was proved on the 28th of February, 1787, by Thomas Brookholding, his sole executor, and the husband of his niece Philadelphia. In it he leaves his sword and pistols to his nephew William Hawkins Newcombe.

William Penn's daughter, Letitia Aubrey, was childless. She was interred at Jordans, but there is no record of the time of her death.

John Penn, the eldest of William Penn's children by his second marriage, died unmarried in 1746. His brother *Thomas* married Lady Juliana Fermor, daughter of the Earl of Pomfret; he died in 1775, whilst she lived to 1801. The Penns of Stoke

Pogis, near London, and also those of Pennsylvania Castle, Isle of Portland near Weymouth, are descendants of Thomas Penn. His daughter, Sophia Margaret, was married to Dr. William Stuart, the youngest son of the Earl of Bute, whose wife was Mary, only daughter of Edward Wortley Montague. In the year 1800 Dr. Stuart became Archbishop of Armagh, and died in 1822. His remains were laid in the family vault at Luton, where, on one of the walls of the Old Church, is a marble tablet bearing the following inscription :—

> In the same vault with
> THE HONOURABLE WILLIAM STUART, D.D.
> Primate of all Ireland,
> are deposited the remains of his widow,
> THE HONOURABLE SOPHIA MARGARET,
> the last surviving grand-daughter of
> WILLIAM PENN,
> the celebrated Founder of Pennsylvania;
> Born 25th December, 1764.
> Died 29th April, 1847.
> Also LOUISA, their youngest daughter,
> who departed this life, 20th September, 1823.
> Aged 22 years.

Hannah Penn's only daughter, *Margaret*, was married to Thomas Freame. They had a son who was named Thomas, also a daughter Philadelphia Hannah. This daughter was married to an Irish gentleman named Dawson, who in 1796 was created Lord Cremorne. Philadelphia, who became Lady Cremorne, died in 1826, aged 86 years.

Hannah Penn's son *Richard* had several children, some of whom were married in America, and probably their descendants may still be traced in Pennsylvania.

Dennis Penn died young.

William Penn's British Residences.

Shangarry castle, William Penn's early Irish home, is now an ivy-covered ruin; but its tall tower, rising above the bright green foliage, gives a commanding and picturesque air to the remains.

The house at Rickmansworth, (in Hertfordshire, three miles from Watford,) to which he took his Guli as a bride, is more perfect than any other of his residences. The front has evidently been modernized, perhaps early in the present century; the rear, opening on the garden, appears not to have been altered; but the lawn, with its avenue of fine trees, no longer exists.

Worminghurst House was situated on an eminence overlooking the beautiful south downs of Sussex, and within a few miles of the sea. It was razed to the ground long since, and the Worminghurst estate absorbed in the domains of the Duke of Norfolk. Only the stables now remain to mark the spot where stood that sweet home so long brightened by Guli's presiding presence.

Ruscombe, where William Penn lived during the

latter years of his life, and where he died, is about six miles from Reading in Berkshire. The house, which was a fine one, was pulled down a few years ago to make way for a railway.

The Ellwoods.

Shortly after their marriage, in the year 1669, Thomas and Mary Ellwood removed to Hunger Hill,* a country-house near Larkin's Green, in a part of Hertfordshire enclosed by Buckinghamshire. Here they resided for the rest of their lives. For upwards of forty years the monthly meeting for Buckinghamshire was held at their house, which is beautifully situated, but in a very dilapi-

---

* The following lines are taken from the autograph collection of Thomas Ellwood's Poems so often referred to:—

    Direction to my friend inquiring the way to my house.
  Two miles from Beaconsfield, upon the road
  To Amersham, just where the way grows broad,
  A little spot there is called Larkin's Green,
  Where on a bank some fruit-trees may be seen;
  In midst of which, on the sinister hand,
  A little cottage covertly doth stand.
  "Soho!" the people out, and then inquire
  For Hunger-hill; it lies a little higher.
  But if the people should from home be gone,
  Ride up the bank some twenty paces on,
  And at the orchard's end thou may'st perceive
  Two gates together hung. The nearest leave,
  The furthest take, and straight the hill ascend.
  That path leads to the house where dwells thy friend,
                              T. E.

dated condition. Yet it cannot fail to be an object of interest whilst it holds together, as the chosen home of a good man, who was the familiar friend and pupil of Milton, a most attractive historian of his own life, and unwavering supporter of civil and religious liberty.

Mary Ellwood died in 1708, and was buried at Jordans, five years before her husband. He testifies of her that before their marriage he thought he saw in her "those fair prints of truth and solid virtue" which he "afterwards found in a sublime degree." Except that "she was a solid weighty woman, who had a public testimony for the Lord and his Truth in meetings," nothing has reached us respecting her which has not been already noted in the present volume.

It was after her death that Thomas Ellwood wrote the "History" of his own life, which comes no further down than 1683, when he was in his forty-fourth year; and it is said to have been a cause of regret to him during his last illness that he had not completed it. Joseph Wyeth, the editor, has appended a supplement of more than a hundred pages, which with very slight exception, are devoted to an account of Ellwood's controversial writings; but these no longer have much interest except to the Quaker bibliographer. The personal traits with which he has favoured us are few, but they bring Thomas Ellwood vividly before us. "He had a peculiar gift for government in the Church, and used to come up constantly to the Yearly Meeting in London, and was very serviceable therein by his grave counsel and advice, especially in difficult matters. . . . He lived a private retired life, not concerning himself with much business in the world, but gave himself to reading and writing, and lived in good repute among Friends and all sorts of people to a pretty good age. He bore his age very well, being of a regular life and healthy constitution. . . . In his latter years he was somewhat troubled with an asthma, and at last was taken ill of a palsy. On the eighth day of his sickness, which was the 1st of the Third-month, 1713, he departed this life in the seventy-fourth year of his age, and was buried on the 4th of the same month at Jordans." Joseph Wyeth says " he was a man of comely aspect, of a free and generous disposition, of a courteous and affable temper, and pleasant conversation; a gentleman born and bred, a scholar, a true Christian, an eminent author, a good neighbour, and a kind friend, who is much lamented and will be much missed at home and abroad."

Of his last illness another account informs us that " his sickness was sudden, which soon deprived him of the use of his limbs; yet he retained the faculties of his inward and outward senses clear all along; and notwithstanding at times his pains were great, his exemplary patience and composed resignation were remarkably apparent to those that visited and attended him, so that their sorrow in parting with so dear a friend was intermixed with comfort in beholding the heavenly frame of mind wherewith he was adorned."

I shall conclude this notice with a few passages from the numerous religious testimonies respecting Thomas Ellwood which were issued after his death, as they portray with antique racy quaintness and evident faithfulness his admirable and attractive character:—" He was greatly respected by his neighbours for his services amongst them; his heart and doors were open to the poor; both sick and lame, who wanted help, had it freely; taking care to provide useful things for such occasions—blest also with good success; often saying 'he mattered not what cost he was at to do good.'"

... " He was of a tender spirit, and had dominion over passion, over pride, and over covetousness, so he was comfortable to, and in his family. He was amiable in the Church of Christ, and a doer of good amongst his neighbours." ... " He was a man of a very acceptable and agreeable conversation, as well as sober and religious, both in the church and in the world, being of a free and affable temper and disposition, far from affectation, but of a courteous behaviour and graceful carriage to all, and very serviceable to and amongst his neighbours. He was very near and dear to many of us, who were most intimately acquainted with him, and his memorial is sweet to us." Such are some of the characteristic features which Thomas Ellwood's intimate friends ascribed to him. How much they embraced of all which renders domestic and social life happy may be seen at a glance.

Jordans Meeting House and Burial Ground.

THE Meeting House, which is in the immediate vicinity of the Burial Ground, is a plain brick building, with tiled roof and lattice window. "It stands upon rather high ground; but its site is in a dell, surrounded by meadows and beechwoods. There is one rather large dwelling-house within sight, called Stone Deane, which in former times was a residence of Friends; with this exception the visitor may ramble for some distance without passing any sort of habitation but an occasional homestead. It is a thoroughly agricultural district, and is both primitive and peaceful in its character, as well as peculiarly picturesque and sequestered."* It is situated in a beautiful part of Buckinghamshire, almost exactly midway between Beaconsfield and Chalfont St. Giles, being about two and a quarter miles from each of these places. It is two miles from the village of Chalfont St. Peter,†

---

* See *A Visit to the Grave of William Penn*, London, W. and F. Cash, 1853, for many additional interesting particulars.

† The Grange, the former residence of Isaac Penington, is in the parish of Chalfont, St. Peter; Milton's house is in the parish of Chalfont

six from Amersham, and twenty-three from London. The most convenient means of reaching Jordans from London is by the Great Western Railway to West Drayton station, thence by a short branch to Uxbridge, from whence it is seven miles distant by the high road.

Tombstones have latterly been introduced into this interesting burial-place, which direct the visitor to the graves wherein rest the remains of so many of the Penns and Peningtons, and of Thomas and Mary Ellwood. It is between twenty and thirty years since a question was raised amongst Friends, as to the propriety of reversing a rule against the admission of tombstones into their burial-grounds, which was originally adopted in consequence of some of the relatives of the earlier members of the Society having gone beyond the practice of simply inscribing name and date upon the stone. Indeed it may not be generally known that the grave of George Fox himself was furnished not only with a headstone, but his coffin was provided with a plate engraved with his name and age. Those who are curious in such matters are referred for further information to the *Fells of Swarthmoor Hall and their Friends*, page 369. It was ultimately decided in the Yearly Meeting that any who desired

---

St. Giles, about a mile from the Grange; and Woodside, the last home of the Peningtons, is very near Amersham.

to have small memorial stones, simply inscribed with names and dates, to mark the graves of their friends, should be left at liberty to do so, under the supervision of their respective monthly meetings. Shortly afterwards, the Friends of the meeting to which Jordans belongs had tombstones erected to mark such graves as could be identified from the registry.

Of these the only graves belonging to the Penington family are those of Isaac and Mary Penington, and of their eldest son John, who died in 1710. It is presumed that he left no family behind him. The interment of Hannah Penington, daughter of William and Elizabeth Penington, is recorded under the date of 1696. As no other member of William Penington's family is mentioned, we may infer that they removed from that neighbourhood.

Mary, the only daughter of Isaac and Mary Penington, was married to Daniel Wharley, but I have found no trace of her life or family.

Edward, the youngest of the Penington family, settled in Pennsylvania. He was surveyor-general of the province, and was married in 1699 to Sarah, daughter of Samuel Jennings, the Quaker Governor of New Jersey. He died in Philadelphia two years after his marriage, leaving one son named Isaac, from whom the Peningtons of Philadelphia are descended.

THE END.

www.ingramcontent.com/pod-product-compliance
Lightning Source LLC
Chambersburg PA
CBHW020528300426
44111CB00008B/585